A Propensity to Self-Subversion

A Propensity to

Self - Subversion

Albert O. Hirschman

Harvard University Press
Cambridge, Massachusetts, and London, England   1995

Library of Congress Cataloging-in-Publication Data

Hirschman, Albert O.
    A propensity to self-subversion / Albert O. Hirschman.
        p.   cm.
    Includes index.
    ISBN 0-674-71557-8 — ISBN 0-674-71558-6 (pbk.)
    1. Economic development.   2. Economic history—1990–
3. Hirschman, Albert O.   I. Title.
HD82.H489   1995
338.9—dc20   94-46737
CIP

For Wolf and Annette Lepenies

Contents

III   *New Forays*

A Propensity to Self-Subversion

Introduction

The twenty essays here assembled were all written since 1986, when I published a previous collection.[1] A good part of that earlier volume had been given over to retrospective papers and restatements. I realized that another, quite different book was in the making when my more recent writings came to concentrate rather on questioning, modifying, qualifying, and in general complicating some of my earlier propositions about social change and development. When this tendency became particularly pronounced, I found a term for it: I was, and enjoyed, being "self-subversive" (Chapter 2). Then, once I had named it, I went on to survey and examine it systematically in an essay whose title, "A Propensity to Self-Subversion" (Chapter 5), I later adopted as overall title for the present collection. A more common term might have been "self-criticism," but it has been spoiled, at least for a while, by its constant and corrupt usage in Communist phraseology. Moreover, "self-subversion" has something in common with the titles and intents of two of my previous essay volumes, *A Bias for Hope* (1971) and *Essays in Trespassing* (1981). There the uses of "bias" and "trespassing" also constituted attempts at rehabilitating terms that normally have derogatory connotations. The implicit tension between the conventional and

---

1. *Rival Views of Market Society and Other Recent Essays* (New York: Viking, 1986); paperback edition with a new preface by the author (Cambridge, Mass.: Harvard University Press, 1992).

the newly intended meanings had been effective in arousing attention. Given recent world events, it may be timely to perform a similar operation on that Cold War bugaboo, "subversion."

Besides self-subversion, the other major area in which I wrote repeatedly over the past years deals—symmetrically enough—with self-affirmation. The second group of essays, "On Self," consists of a series of autobiographical fragments. The occasion for many of these pieces was the awarding of honorary degrees. In Europe, this ceremony involves a short acceptance speech by the honoree. When I was asked to give such speeches in various European universities close to places where I had once lived before coming to the United States (in 1941, at the age of twenty-five), I decided to talk about the connections between those sites and my own life experience. But the longest essay of the second part, "Four Reencounters" (Chapter 6), had a different origin: the arresting experience of meeting, within the space of one week, four persons from my diverse German and French pasts, persons whom I had not seen for some fifty years. To relate the story of my past contacts with them became a way of retelling a stretch of my own life while avoiding the boring—and essentially mendacious—linear account. The development of my thinking is similarly explored by indirect approaches: writing a new preface to an old book of mine, as in "A Hidden Ambition" (Chapter 12), and relating intellectual encounters with an old colleague, as in "Convergences with Michel Crozier" (Chapter 13).

The third and final group of essays, entitled "New Forays," serves to demonstrate that I have not gone wholly solipsistic; that besides "self-subversion" and "self" there are quite a few other topics that have captured my attention and interest. In these essays I often return to older themes of mine—industrialization (Chapter 17), Latin American development (Chapter 15), appraisal of market society (Chapter 18)—but also deal with a number of new puzzles. Unsurprisingly, some of the essays are inspired by the enormous political and economic changes brought about by the Eastern European revolutions of 1989. Examples are Chapter 16 where I argue against the common opinion that the end of the Cold War was yet another calamity for the Third World, and Chapter 17, which looks at the contrasting laments over industrialization in the former Soviet zone of influence and in Latin America. Another major essay dealing with the 1989 events centers on the fall of the German Democratic Republic (Chapter 1), but it is to be found in the first rather than the third part of the book, a choice made for a simple reason. To be sure, this essay was a new foray for me—it was the first time since I left Germany in 1933 that I returned to a subject pertaining to that country. But the latest momentous twist of German history also threw an entirely new light on my old concepts of exit and voice, so it became a prime instance of the self-subversion theme.

Similar problems of classification arose in connection with other essays. A considerable amount of autobiography is contained in my account of the Keynesian revolution and its export from the United States after World War II (Chapter 14): I could never have written it without my own first-hand experience with, and somewhat ambivalent attitude toward, the group of U.S. Keynesians during my Marshall Plan years at the Federal Reserve Board in Washington, from 1946 to 1952. I should also note a substantial overlap between "self" and "self-subversion": in the new preface to *Development Projects Observed* (Chapter 12) I call attention to the way that book engaged in self-subversion—*avant la lettre*—by questioning a major thesis of my then recently issued *Strategy of Economic Development*. These multiple interconnections among the three parts of the book—and there are more than the ones just specifically noted—testify perhaps to an underlying unity.

Three points, drawn largely from the last group of essays, seem to me to merit further attention and exploration.

1. I have long had an interest in understanding the dynamic of *sequences* in economic and social change. My early work on linkages "up and down the input-output matrix," and in particular from one industrial branch to another (backward and forward), attempted to appraise the comparative strength that is typically brought to bear on various intersectoral and interregional investment decisions. My special interest went to those sequences that could be shown to be compelling rather than purely facilitating. Lately, in line with my self-subversive proclivities, I realized that the intended sequences in social and economic

change will not simply go forward with greater or smaller energy: an advance in one direction may itself make for conditions that hold back or abort the next advance. Rather than searching for and being fascinated with situations where "one thing *leads* to another," I came to collect cases where "one thing *forestalls* another." Chapter 2 presents some of them in a section entitled "Mapping the Getting-Stuck Syndrome," and further explorations along these lines are in Chapters 3, 15, and 17.

This turns out to be a matter of some current relevance. Ever since the collapse of Communism and the consequent need to recast and reinvent political, social, economic, and cultural structures in the former Communist countries, there has been a great deal of discussion about the sequences with which these multiple tasks, from democratization to privatization (to name just two), are best undertaken. In such investigations it should be helpful to know about the widest possible range of sequences and of failures to achieve sequences—something that has taken me decades to become aware of, although I had long proclaimed my belief in "possibilism."

2. A related point about the multiplicity of social processes results from observations made during my last extended trip through Latin America in 1986. During the eighties certain social indicators continued showing improvement in several countries, while the economy stagnated or went into a decline (Chapter 15). This "uncoupling" or "unhinging" of social from economic processes came as a quite unexpected event to those who are used to thinking of society and of the evolution of its various aspects as an integrated whole. Later, on considering the even more complex relation between economic and political progress (Chapter 19), I found these observations helpful in envisaging how democratic institutions can acquire "a life of their own" and how the urge to sustain this life can become "second nature" to a society.

These concepts, together with those of "uncoupling" and "disjunction," seem to me to offer a way of enriching our understanding of social change and learning.

3. The last chapter of this collection, "Social Conflicts as Pillars of Democratic Market Societies," is perhaps its most ambitious. It was

written in response to the question "How much community spirit does liberal society require?" which had been chosen as theme for a conference organized by a German foundation. The question had an underlying, widely shared assumption: for democratic market societies to be progressive and reasonably stable it is not enough to guarantee basic democratic rights to citizens who then pursue their interests within an appropriate market structure. But agreement stops when the question is asked: what else is required? What is the nature of the trust, moral cohesion, or common purpose whose overriding need is sometimes plausibly asserted? Or, putting it differently, how can society avoid the ever present dangers stemming from what Machiavelli called *corruzione?* Contemporary analysts have rediscovered these dangers and attempted to discuss them under more neutral or technical labels, such as "slack" (Richard Cyert and James March), "X-inefficiency" (Harvey Leibenstein), the "soft state" (Gunnar Myrdal), and "rent-seeking" (Anne Krueger).

In the past I have sometimes nibbled at this fundamental problem and do so again here and there in this book. "Nibbling" is actually a good term for the activity that is indicated: it would be futile to look for a generally valid solution. Historical experience provides us with occasional hints and discoveries, but they are different for different societies and for the same society at different times. Even for a given group at one point in time, we are dealing with one of those vexing problems where the ideal solution is often uncomfortably close to disaster and perdition.

An example of my nibbling approach occurs in Chapter 14, where I suggest that the most important political effect of Keynesianism in the United States was to have raised public-spiritedness in a crucial period of its recent history—the transition to superpower status. On occasion, to be sure, ideology can thus supply an otherwise missing common purpose. But we all know that this injection of ideology can be a dubious and dangerous course. In Chapter 20 I discuss a less synthetic and seemingly more general solution. It has not been widely realized that pluralist market societies are particularly good at drawing strength from the kind of conflicts they typically generate. Along with new wealth they also keep producing new aspects of inequality—personal, sectoral, and regional. Hence demands for reform and justice contin-uously arise, must be dealt with, and, once they are found subject to compromise, leave behind a positive residue: the experience of living in a society that learns to cope with its conflicts.

To view societal cohesion as a by-product of its conflicts is remarkably parsimonious, somewhat paradoxical, and generally attractive. As I also point out in the last chapter, however, this insight sheds light primarily on the past—much like Minerva's owl, spreading its wings in the gath-ering dusk.

I
part

On Self-Subversion

1

chapter

Exit, Voice, and the Fate of the
German Democratic Republic

Es gibt wenig Menschen, die sich mit dem Nächstvergangenen zu beschäftigen
wissen. Entweder das Gegenwärtige hält uns mit Gewalt an sich, oder wir verlieren
uns in die Vergangenheit und suchen das völlig Verlorene . . . wieder hervorzur-
ufen.

(The immediate past is but rarely the object of our interest. Either the present takes
hold of us forcefully or we lose ourselves in the remote past and attempt . . . to re-
create what has been wholly lost.)

—*Goethe, Die Wahlverwandtschaften* (The Elective Affinities)

Introduction

The year 1989 was greeted with something of a yawn. Its first half
would be marked by the elaborate, far-flung, and infinitely wordy bi-
centenary commemoration of the French Revolution. Everything was
laid out well in advance, and the schedule of events was strictly followed
up to the appointed climax, the celebrations of the Fourteenth of July
in Paris. Thereafter, with the bulk of festivities, conferences, and
speeches over, people would return to their usual pursuits. But then,
as though the spirit of revolution, once invoked, assumed a life of its

Published in *World Politics,* 45 (January 1993), pp. 173–202. The German version of this
essay, "Abwanderung, Widerspruch und das Schicksal der Deutschen Demokratischen Republik," was published in *Leviathan,* 20 (September 1992), pp. 330–358, and was awarded
the 1992 Thyssen Foundation prize for the best article published by social science journals
in the German language. In this essay and those that follow, all translations from German
and other texts are mine.

own, came the surprise, the "divine surprise" of that year: a series of totally unexpected political and popular movements broke out in rapid succession in Eastern Europe—from Poland, Hungary, East Germany, and Czechoslovakia to Bulgaria and Romania—overturning the hitherto uncontested power of the Communist parties and thereby altering fundamentally the seemingly stable bipolar world order of the preceding forty-five years.

The most radical of these changes took place in the German Democratic Republic, where the internal convulsion led in short order to the extinction of the political entity in which it occurred. The East German state was unable to survive the collapse of Communist power and was absorbed (*geschluckt,* or "swallowed," is the expressive term often used) by its outsize twin, the Federal Republic of Germany, within a year of the opening of the Berlin Wall.

Despite a considerable outpouring of articles and books—including some autobiographical accounts by key actors—a great deal about the events of 1989 remains poorly understood. The very fact that they came as a total surprise to both spectators and actors suggests that our capacity to comprehend large-scale political and social change remains utterly underdeveloped. Under the circumstances, any conceptual tool that holds out the promise of providing a handle on the enigmatic events is likely to be eagerly seized. This is what happened in Germany to the concepts of "exit" and "voice," which I had proposed in a book published in 1970.[1]

The German translation of that book was published in 1974, under a title that means, literally, "outmigration and contradicting." This was a daringly free, though apt, translation of the terms exit and voice, and it may have been chosen by the translator because even then migration and would-be migration were characteristic alternatives to actual resistance in the German Democratic Republic. So the title, with its accent

1. I refer herewith to Hirschman, *Exit, Voice, and Loyalty: Responses to Decline in Firms, Organizations, and States* (Cambridge, Mass.: Harvard University Press, 1970). In German, the book was published as *Abwanderung und Widerspruch,* trans. Leonhard Walentik (Tübingen: J. C. B. Mohr, 1974). Subsequent essays on it include Hirschman, "Exit and Voice: An Expanding Sphere of Influence," in my collection *Rival Views of Market Society and Other Recent Essays* (New York: Viking, 1986). To avoid frequent self-quotation, I will indicate the source in the text as book or essay, and put the page numbers in parentheses as needed.

on migration as a primary form of exit, may have contributed to making the book appear particularly relevant to the commotion of 1989. In any event, only six days after the spectacular opening of the Berlin Wall on November 9, 1989, the *Frankfurter Allgemeine Zeitung*, Germany's most respected daily newspaper, published an article by Henning Ritter, director of the social science and humanities section, with the title "Abwandern, Widersprechen: Zur aktuellen Bedeutung einer Theorie von A. O. Hirschman" (To exit, to voice: On the current relevance of a theory of A. O. Hirschman). According to Ritter, my 1970 thesis was being tested "experimentally on a large scale" by the upheaval in East Germany. Since then, several political scientists and sociologists have made extensive, if on occasion conflicting, uses of the concepts of exit, voice, and loyalty in interpreting the events of 1989, now generally called *die Wende* (the turn).[2] Eventually the topic even received a degree of official sanction as the Deutsche Forschungsgemeinschaft (German Research Association), an agency of the Federal Republic, listed the exit-voice approach to the analysis of the *Wende* among the research projects eligible for its grants.[3]

I became aware of this interest in my twenty-year-old book when I

2. The most stimulating contributions were by Detlef Pollack, a sociologist of religion at the University of Leipzig. See especially Pollack, "Das Ende einer Organisationsgesellschaft" in *Zeitschrift für Soziologie,* 19 (August 1990). Pollack gives an insightful account of the events in Leipzig during the fall of 1989, which he obviously witnessed at very close range. He points out that the events contradict my model to the extent it asserts a predominantly rival, rather than complementary, relation between exit and voice in social processes. See also Pollack, "Religion und gesellschaftlicher Wandel" (Religion and social change), *Übergänge* (June 1990); "Aussenseiter oder Repräsentanten?" (Outsiders or representatives?), *Deutschland-Archiv,* 23 (1990), pp. 1217–1223; and Pollack and Christiane Heinze, "Zur Funktion der politisch alternativen Gruppen im Prozess des gesellschaftlichen Umbruchs in der DDR" (About the function of politically alienated groups in the social upheaval in the GDR), in Wolf-Jürgen Grabner et al., *Leipzig im Oktober* (Berlin: Wichern, 1990). Other uses of the exit-voice distinction are found in Claus Offe, "Wohlstand, Nation, Republik: Aspekte des deutschen Sonderweges von Sozialismus zum Kapitalismus" (Welfare, nation, republic: Aspects of the unique German path from socialism to capitalism) (Manuscript, Sept. 1990); and Wolfgang Zapf, "Der Zusammenbruch einer Sozialstruktur" (The collapse of a social structure; unpublished, Feb. 1991). Visiting graduate students from the United States also contributed to the discussion. See Rogers Brubaker, "Frontier Theses: Exit, Voice, and Loyalty in East Germany," *Migration World* 18, no. 3–4, (1990), 12–17, and John Torpey, "Exit, Voice, and Loyalty in the 'Peaceful Revolution' in the GDR" (Paper for the 17th Symposium on the German Democratic Republic, University of New Hampshire, June 1991).
   3. Deutsche Forschungsgemeinschaft, press release no. 3, Jan. 29, 1991.

spent the academic year 1990–91 at the Wissenschaftskolleg (Institute for Advanced Study) in Berlin. At that time, I was also able, through reading and interviewing, to become more closely acquainted with the history of the GDR and, in particular, with the remarkable story of its demise. Perhaps not surprisingly, I came to feel that the exit-voice perspective could indeed be of help in seeing some of the events in a new light and that it could itself be enriched by its encounter with a complex historical testing ground. Moreover, to conclude this introduction on a personal note, the topic provided me with a point of reentry into German politics and history after an absence of over half a century from the country where I had spent my first eighteen years.

The Interplay of Exit and Voice: A Reformulation

To set the stage for my inquiry it is useful to present and reformulate as briefly as possible the concepts of exit and voice as they will be used here. They are two contrasting responses of consumers or members of organizations to what they sense as deterioration in the quality of the goods they buy or the services and benefits they receive. Exit is the act of simply leaving, generally because a better good or service or benefit is believed to be provided by another firm or organization. Indirectly and unintentionally exit can cause the deteriorating organization to improve its performance. Voice is the act of complaining or of organizing to complain or to protest, with the intention of achieving directly a recuperation of the quality that has been impaired. Much of my book and of my subsequent writings on this subject dealt with the conditions under which exit or voice or both are activated.

A recurring theme in my book was the assertion that there is no preestablished harmony between exit and voice, that, to the contrary, they often work at cross-purposes and tend to undermine each other, in particular with exit undermining voice. Easy availability of exit was shown to be inimical to voice, for in comparison to exit, voice is costly in terms of effort and time. Moreover, to be effective, voice often requires group action and is thus subject to all the well-known difficulties of organization, representation, and free riding. By contrast, exit, when available, does not require any coordination with others. Hence one of my principal points: "The presence of the exit alternative can . . . *atrophy the development of the art of voice*" (book, 43; emphasis in the original).

This inverse relationship between exit and voice was confirmed by numerous examples from economic and social life. Thus the fact that shares can be readily sold in the stock market makes it difficult for shareholders to have any real influence on management through voice; when exit from a marriage by divorce is easy, less effort will be made at repairing the relationship through voice, that is, through communication and efforts at reconciliation; and, as was affirmed by the influential "Turner thesis," the absence of a strong workers' movement in the United States can be explained in part by the possibility, real or imagined, of "going West"—in the United States mobility was greater, or was widely believed to be greater, than in Europe during the period of rapid industrialization.

In many situations, exit thus tends to undermine voice, particularly, so I argued, when exit deprives the potential carriers of voice of their most articulate and influential members, as is often the case. In the 1986 essay I came to speak of the basic seesaw pattern of exit and voice. This pattern could also be characterized as a simple "hydraulic" model: deterioration generates the pressure of discontent, which will be channeled into voice or exit; the more pressure escapes through exit, the less is available to foment voice.

It is remarkable that so primitive a model was able to account for as many diverse situations and experiences as have been marshaled by myself and others. But it could not be expected to be universally valid, and indeed the events of 1989 in the GDR traced out a very different relationship. As was pointed out by an East German sociologist,[4] here exit (outmigration) and voice (protest demonstrations against the regime) worked in tandem and reinforced each other, achieving jointly the collapse of the regime.

Even before this spectacular case of collaboration of exit and voice, I had become aware of some complications affecting the seesaw or hydraulic model. For example, I noted that since exit and voice are

4. See the articles by Pollack cited in n. 2.

"two basic, complementary ingredients of democratic freedom, [they] have on the whole been enlarged or restricted jointly" (essay, 79). Also, in reconsidering the question of school vouchers, I speculated that the opening up of previously unavailable opportunities of choice or exit may generate feelings of empowerment in parents, who as a result may be more ready than before to participate in school affairs and to speak out.[5] Such a positive relationship between increased availability of exit and increased willingness to voice rests on a structure that is more complex than the one underlying the seesaw pattern. What happens here is that the newly won right to exit actually *changes* the human agents involved. Being allowed more choice, they become more aware of and more willing to explore the whole range of choices at their disposal. Once men and women have won the right to move about as they please, they may well start behaving in general as adult and hence as *vocal* members of their community.

Here, then, is a quite general rationale for thinking that enlarging the opportunity for exit can on occasion make for *more* rather than less participation and voice. This is indeed close to how things worked out in the German Democratic Republic in 1989. But the course of events over the forty-year-long life of that state comprised a large variety of exit-voice relationships. Some correspond faithfully to my original script; others depart from it more or less in the way that has just been sketched but will invite yet new interpretations. Time has come to plunge into "the facts."

Exit as Antagonist of Voice: 1949–1988

From the very day of its founding, the stability of the German Democratic Republic was undermined by its coexistence with the Federal

---

5. Essay, p. 89. In describing the process of slave emancipation in Cuba in the late 19th century, Rebecca Scott has shown how slaves adopted at times a mixed, exit-*cum*-voice strategy; she calls it "voice in pursuit of exit." After 1880, when a new statute had imposed certain obligations on slave owners with regard to treatment and payment of slave labor, a substantial number of slaves, in alliance with abolitionists, brought charges against their masters for violations of this statute. They obtained their freedom in this manner rather than by simply running away. See Scott, "Dismantling Repressive Systems: The Abolition of Slavery in Cuba as a Case Study" in Alejandro Foxley et al., eds., *Development, Democracy, and the Art of Trespassing: Essays in Honor of Albert O. Hirschman* (Notre Dame, Ind.: University of Notre Dame Press, 1986), p. 274.

Republic. The possibility of improving one's lot by just getting out—by moving to the other, bigger, freer, and soon to be more prosperous Germany—fundamentally distinguished the East German postwar experience from that of the Poles, Czechoslovaks, and Hungarians, who had no such alternatives or prospects and who by and large were confined to their countries.

This basic existential difference between the German Democratic Republic and the other three comparatively advanced Soviet satellites in Eastern Europe explains much about their divergent political history. In Poland, Czechoslovakia, and Hungary epic battles were fought against Communist domination, from the 1956 Revolution in Budapest to the Prague Spring of 1968 and the emergence of Solidarity in Poland in 1980. After these movements were forcibly suppressed, new forms of resistance or dissidence promptly reemerged and created new spaces for "civil society," or, as Václav Havel called it, the "independent life of society."[6] In the German Democratic Republic, by contrast, the only important manifestation of discontent was the early and promptly crushed workers' uprising of Berlin on June 16–17, 1953. Thereafter, resistance (other than attempts to exit) and dissidence were minimal—until the powerful movement of autumn 1989, of course.

One may put in a claim right here, then, for a resounding confirmation of the simple hydraulic exit-voice model: the presence, real or imagined, of the exit option did undermine the development of the art of voice in the German Democratic Republic. For many years the GDR was the most reliably tranquil as well as the most supine of the Soviet satellites. In Poland, Hungary, and Czechoslovakia resistance and dissidence were also up against enormous odds, but at least these movements did not have to contend with the lure and sabotage of exit.

Once stated, this very general first finding must be qualified by a more detailed look at exit and voice as they operated in the German Democratic Republic. For the purpose of the history of exit, Table 1 shows yearly data on migration from East to West from 1949 to 1989. Migration was substantial throughout the first twelve years of existence of the new state. Significantly, it reached its high point, close to the record of 1989, in 1953, year of the brief and ill-fated June 17 uprising

6. Václav Havel, "The Power of the Powerless," trans. P. Wilson, in Havel, *Living in Truth*, ed. Jan Vladislav (London: Faber and Faber, 1986), pp. 85ff.

Table 1. Migrants and Refugees from the German Democratic Republic (including East Berlin) to the Federal Republic of Germany (including West Berlin), 1949–1989

Year	Refugees	Authorized migrants	Authorized migrants: ransomed political prisoners	Total
1949	129,245	—	—	129,245
1950	197,788	—	—	197,788
1951	165,648	—	—	165,648
1952	182,393	—	—	182,393
1953	331,396	—	—	331,396
1954	184,198	—	—	184,198
1955	252,870	—	—	252,870
1956	279,189	—	—	279,189
1957	261,622	—	—	261,622
1958	204,092	—	—	204,092
1959	143,917	—	—	143,917
1960	199,188	—	—	199,188
1961	207,026	—	—	207,026
1962	16,741	4,624	—	21,365
1963	12,967	29,665	8	42,632
1964	11,864	30,012	880	41,876
1965	11,886	17,666	1,160	29,552
1966	8,456	15,675	400	24,131
1967	6,385	13,188	550	19,573
1968	4,902	11,134	700	16,036
1969	5,273	11,702	850	16,975
1970	5,047	12,472	900	17,519
1971	5,843	11,565	1,400	17,408
1972	5,537	11,627	730	17,164
1973	6,522	8,667	630	15,189

Table 1.   (continued)

Year	Refugees	Authorized migrants	Authorized migrants: ransomed political prisoners	Total
1974	5,324	7,928	1,100	13,252
1975	6,011	10,274	1,150	16,285
1976	5,110	10,058	1,490	15,168
1977	4,037	8,041	1,470	12,078
1978	3,846	8,271	1,480	12,117
1979	3,512	9,003	900	12,515
1980	3,988	8,775	1,010	12,763
1981	4,340	11,093	1,584	15,433
1982	4,095	9,113	1,491	13,208
1983	3,614	7,729	1,105	11,343
1984	3,651	37,323	2,236	40,974
1985	3,484	21,428	2,676	24,912
1986	4,660	21,518	1,536	26,178
1987	6,252	12,706	1,247	18,958
1988	9,718	27,939	1,083	39,832
1989	—	—	—	343,854

Sources: Thomas Ammer, "Stichwort: Flucht aus der DDR," *Deutschland Archiv,* 22 (1989), p. 1207, and Hartmut Wendt, "Die deutsch-deutschen Wanderungen," *Deutschland Archiv,* 24 (1991), p. 390.

in Berlin. It is not difficult to understand how the failure of this attempt at voice should have led to an exceptionally large exit. But even during the other years of that early period, emigration was high in relation to the total population of about seventeen million.

The existence side-by-side of the two German states was a remarkable historical experiment in migration. Here were contiguous territories inhabited by people speaking the same language and sharing a common history and culture. The ease and attraction of moving from East to West were further increased by the Grundgesetz (basic law or constitution) of the Federal Republic of Germany, which stipulated that GDR citizens settling in the West would be automatically eligible to become FRG citizens. As such, they would then be eligible for the considerable range and substantial level of social welfare benefits available in the Federal Republic.

These structural characteristics would normally make for a considerable flow of emigration in response to even small differences in economic and political conditions. In fact, of course, such differences were large, as the two countries were organized according to wholly opposite economic and political principles. Moreover, in the 1950s and 1960s West Germany achieved a rapid and remarkably steady economic expansion, known as the *Wirtchaftswunder* (economic miracle), whereas the East German economy, burdened by reparations to the Soviet Union (rather than benefiting from that association, as West Germany did from the Marshall Plan) and subjected to central planning on the Stalinist model, experienced only a modest recovery from the large-scale destruction of World War II.

The outflow of its people was large enough to cause concern in the German Democratic Republic. Initially the East German authorities may have shrugged off the "voting with their feet" of many of their citizens and may even have welcomed it. As Fidel Castro felt later with respect to Cubans leaving for Miami, the GDR powerholders probably thought it advantageous to be rid of disgruntled and irreconcilable "class enemies": expropriated landowners, shopkeepers, and other "bourgeois" elements. But soon such complacency would give way to concern and then to alarm: it became clear that in this instance mass emigration was not a safety valve, a metaphor that had often been rather aptly used to describe earlier emigration experiences. Rather, as it continued, the exodus of East Germans to the West—among them many highly skilled members of the labor force—came to be likened to a life-threatening hemorrhage that had to be stopped. The building of the Berlin Wall in 1961 was intended to achieve this objective.

The Wall did succeed in substantially reducing the outflow. After 1961 the statistics distinguish between two flows: first, emigrants who moved to West Germany with the permission of the East German authorities *(Übersiedler)*—often older people allowed to rejoin younger family members who had preceded them; second, there were those, less numerous but still in the thousands, who managed to flee to the West in spite of the Wall and other strict border controls.

Table 1 documents the precipitous drop in the number of total emigrants, from around 200,000 per year to an average of 32,000 during the first five years following the building of the Wall. Thereafter total emigration declined further, reaching its lowest level in the 1970s, when the yearly average was 15,000. In the 1980s the flow swelled again, particularly in 1984, when large numbers of longtime applicants suddenly received permission to leave. Thereafter, the door was shut once again.

The pressure to leave clearly increased in 1988 and forced the authorities to be less restrictive, while the number of unauthorized departures also rose ominously. Then, in 1989, the gates were simply forced wide open and the outflow of people soon exceeded the exodus or hemorrhage levels of the pre-Wall period, until, eventually, the Wall came down.

What is actually surprising about the statistics from 1961 up to 1988–89 is the extent to which the Berlin Wall and the assorted draconian border controls were *unable* to stop the emigration. Though much reduced, outmigration remained throughout in the five-digit range—small in relation to total population, but definitely more than a trickle. As a result, the hope for escape to the West was kept alive year after year by the *actual life experiences* of thousands of exiting people. Both the real emigration of large numbers in the early postwar years and the continuing hope for exit (including the illusion about its possibility) in later years help explain the comparatively low levels of voice.

Moreover, in addition to the actual exits to the West, modern communications technology made possible a vicarious, if temporary, mass escape—via West German television. The East German writer Christoph Hein makes this point in a 1990 interview precisely in order to explain the weakness of the dissident movement in the GDR:

> [In the GDR we had a difficult task because] the whole people could leave the country and move to the West as a man [*geschlossen*] every day at 8 P.M.—via television. That lifted the pressure. Here is the difference with Poland, Czechoslovakia, and the Soviet Union. There the pressure

continued to bear down *and generated counter-pressure* . . . that's why I always envied the Russians and the Poles. . . . In general, the proximity of the Federal Republic was not helpful to our own development. . . . Here we had no samizdat, as long as we had access to the publishing houses of West Germany.[7]

So much for an exit-centered account of the considerable differences in resistance to the Communist regime in the GDR and its neighbors in the Soviet bloc. But I do not wish to claim that differences in the ease of exit are the whole explanation. In looking backward, we hardly ever escape the presence of multiple (hence inconclusive) causation. It is certainly true in the present case that exit was infinitely more available, promising, and beckoning in East Germany than elsewhere in Soviet-dominated Eastern Europe. At the same time, however, the chances for the emergence of voice in some shape or form were also much smaller there, for three principal reasons.

First, unlike the Poles, Czechs, or Hungarians, the citizens of the East German rump state could not look back on a sheltering history or national tradition of their own, nor did they have any established, more or less independent institutions (like the Catholic church of Poland) that would sustain them in a struggle for some autonomy from the all-powerful Communist Party and state. Only at a fairly late stage did the Protestant church in East Germany take on that function to some extent.[8]

Second, it is likely that many East Germans initially embraced the ideology of the new state for reasons intimately connected with the catastrophic historical episode they had just lived through. In addition to the Communist Party cadres and militants who had survived the Nazi regime and the war, there were those who, having been first seduced and later disenchanted and perhaps appalled by national socialism, eagerly embraced the ersatz ideology or *Weltanschauung* that was now

7. Christoph Hein, *Texte, Daten, Bilder,* ed. Lothar Baier (Frankfurt: Luchterhand, 1990), p. 42.

8. Full documentation is in Gerhard Rein, *Die protestantische Revolution, 1982–1990* (Berlin: Wichern, 1990); see also Ehrhart Neubert, "Eine protestantische Revolution," *Deutschland-Archiv,* 23 (May 1990).

tendered to them in the guise of antifascism and true socialism.[9] To accept this new creed meant that they could almost providentially forget the past or even atone for it. During the early postwar period this reaction fulfilled a cleansing function in East Germany that was the equivalent of the unremitting pursuit of work and prosperity in the West. In the other countries of Eastern Europe, with their very different histories, the newly installed Communist regimes never held that sort of initial ideological advantage.

Third, and probably most important, East Germany was different from the other Communist-dominated countries of Eastern Europe in that it was the front line of the extended Soviet empire in its contest with the West. It was in East Germany that the highest concentration of Russian troops and tanks was to be found, and it was there that the Soviet short- and medium-range atomic missiles were later located. It therefore seemed unthinkable that the Soviets would ever permit any loosening of the leash that tied the East German regime to their own. "The more the day of reunification approached, the greater became the agreement among the theorists [of politics] about the impossibility, the dangers, and the uselessness of reunification."[10] No one in his or her wildest dreams ever imagined that the Soviet empire would disintegrate from within, the way it did in 1989 (and then again in 1991). Hence, the only conceivable scenario for East Germany recovering some freedom of movement was the defeat of the Soviet Union after a nuclear exchange between the two superpowers—a prospect too awful to behold and generally excluded from one's field of vision or discourse. The chances for successful voice were accordingly seen as being extremely low in East Germany, far more so than in less strategically situated areas where some relaxation of imperial controls was conceivable.

In sum, the direct obstacles to voice, that is, to any political move-

9. Christa Wolf, who was sixteen years old when the Nazi regime collapsed in 1945, speaks of this experience in an interview in 1987/88: "My generation has early on exchanged one ideology for another." See Wolf, *Christa Wolf im Dialog* (Frankfurt: Luchterhand, 1990), p. 26. In another interview she amplifies this theme: "Today we see—some of us, anyway— that we were in danger of exchanging one salvation doctrine for another; for it is much more difficult to develop new forms of feeling and thinking than to exchange simply (though that was not so 'simple' either) old articles of faith for new ones" (p. 74). This experience is also recreated in two of her finest novels, *Nachdenken über Christa T.* and *Kindheitsmuster*.

10. Günter de Bruyn, *Jubelschreie, Trauergesänge* (Frankfurt: S. Fischer, 1991), p. 29.

ments of resistance or dissidence, were enormous. They must be added to the indirect undermining of voice by the real or imagined availability of exit to the West. Jointly these direct and indirect restraints on voice produced an exit-voice balance that was tilted far more against voice and in favor of exit than that prevailing in other Soviet-controlled East European territories, with the already noted result of substantially divergent political behavior in East Germany.

Moreover, throughout the forty-year existence of the GDR, authorities there showed every sign of being fully aware of the basic seesaw pattern of exit and voice. This is apparent from their frequent attempts to manipulate and exploit it. Particularly after they had substantially reduced exit by building the Wall, they realized that they could weaken internal opposition by a selective policy of permitting certain people to leave and of expelling outright those critical voices considered to be dangerous or obnoxious. The best-known instance of such conscious manipulation of the exit-voice seesaw was the withdrawal of citizenship, on November 16, 1976, from the satirical poet and chansonnier Wolf Biermann while he was on tour in West Germany. As a result, he was unable to return home. In this way a critical, ironic voice that was gathering a growing group of enthusiastic admirers was in effect removed. The banning of Biermann gave rise to a rare voice event: twelve of the GDR's most prominent writers, artists, and intellectuals signed a declaration protesting the official action and asking for reconsideration, and in the following days the document was endorsed by another hundred signatories.

The episode marked the end of any hope that Erich Honecker, who had succeeded the hard-line regime of Walter Ulbricht in 1971, would be more tolerant of criticism and dissent. In the following years the authorities systematically used forced exit to reduce voice. The special verb *abschieben* (to push out or to push over the border) came into use to denote the decision to get rid of certain critics by allowing, encouraging, or obliging them to leave for the Federal Republic. In the caustic formulation of Günter de Bruyn:

> The most creative, most critical or simply most adventurous people moved, often at the risk of their lives, across the German-German border and thereby contributed to the consolidation of stagnation and medioc-

rity [in the East]. Only when groups of dissidents started to advocate change in the GDR instead of simply leaving it, did the leaders of the country, who had long been aware of the damaging impact of the exodus on the economy, understand that it did contribute to political stability, with the result that they now resorted to *Abschiebung* as a sedative. In this way they also revealed that the mediocrity of the country matched their own to a fault.[11]

Among the prominent people who were thus pushed out were many well-known writers (for example, Jurek Becker, Erich Loest, Sarah Kirsch, and Monika Maron), as well as actors (Manfred Krug) and composers (Thilo Medek).[12]

In this manner the GDR authorities continuously beheaded oppositional groups in their early stages and eliminated dissenting voices *without* having to resort to overt acts of heightened domestic repression at a time of increasing international monitoring of human rights violations. They also found a way to get rid of many political opponents who did land in prison: soon after the Wall was built, the GDR systematically "sold" such people to the Federal Republic, which was willing to pay good ransom money for them. With the price per head often said to be as much as DM 40,000, this trade of voice for exit became a valuable source of hard currency for the GDR. As Table 1 shows, this unsavory trade peaked in the mid-1980s.

These various forms of manipulating the exit-voice seesaw were attractive to the GDR for yet another reason. The people who were ransomed, expelled, "let go," or cajoled into leaving did not constitute compact, plotting, and therefore threatening exile communities on the model of nineteenth-century Italian or Russian exiles in Paris or London. Those writers and intellectuals who left settled easily in a variety of locations in the Federal Republic; they tended to blend into their new environments and did not maintain much cohesion as an

11. Bruyn (n. 10), pp. 36–37.
12. Hermann Weber, *DDR: Grundriss der Geschichte, 1945–1990* (Hannover: Fackelträger, 1991), p. 170. This is a good general guide to the history of the GDR; other principal sources of information are the journal *Deutschland-Archiv* and Bundesministerium für innerdeutsche Beziehungen, *Texte zur Deutschlandpolitik;* Christoph Links, Hannes Bahrmann, *Wir sind das Volk: Die DDR im Aufbruch* (We are the people: The GDR is breaking up) (Berlin: Aufbau, 1990).

émigré group. In the short term, the East German powerholders could justifiably feel that their policy of selective pushing out was both riskless and effective in reducing unwanted voice.

In the longer run, of course, the policy was to prove disastrous for the survival of the GDR. The comparison with Poland, Czechoslovakia, and Hungary—where there was no exit alternative to speak of—is again instructive. Here dissenters stayed put. Even when, as was often the case, they started out as "deviationists" (that is, as Communists unhappy with the party line), they eventually came to occupy a wide political spectrum from nationalism to liberalism to various social democratic tendencies. Hence, a pluralistic political discourse could evolve in these countries after the breakup of the Communist regimes in 1989. Not so in the GDR; here the most vocal opponents of the regime had been pushed out to the Federal Republic, where they had joined the existing political groups and had little interest in returning to the GDR. What dissident voices were to be heard in the GDR in 1988–89 came largely from a narrow band of reform-minded Communists that had remained inside the party (SED) and criticized the "really existing socialism" exclusively in the name of some "true" Marxism or socialism. As the well-known dissident Bärbel Bohley said as late as mid-1989, in comparing the GDR and Czech situations: "Here change from below is out of the question. . . . Too many of those who would be in a position to take on political responsibility have left."[13] The resulting exit-induced vacuum of leadership and of political life explains a good deal about the eventual collapse of the GDR as an independent entity and its easy absorption by the Federal Republic.

Exit and Voice as Confederates: The Collapse of the Communist Regime in 1989

The exit-voice seesaw was a sturdy reality with multiple aspects and extensive consequences throughout the first thirty-nine years of the short life of the GDR. So what happened in the final climactic year of

13. Bärbel Bohley in an interview with Katja Havemann, in Bohley et al., *40 Jahre DDR* (Frankfurt: Büchergilde Gutenberg, 1989), p. 184.

1989 when the seesaw of exit and voice suddenly turned into a joint grave-digging act?

Before addressing this critical question, I must go back to an earlier puzzle. I have argued that, in contrast to the situation in the three neighboring Soviet-controlled countries, exit in the GDR remained a live option throughout the postwar years, whether such exit was a realistic project, a matter of hope and fantasy, or a crude stratagem for the authorities. From the point of view of the citizens, nevertheless, the building of the Wall in 1961 represented a considerable shift from exit as a feasible project to exit as hope and fantasy. Would one not expect such a shift to reinforce voice in line with the seesaw or hydraulic exit-voice model?

Some such response can actually be noted. A few critical voices arose, particularly in the late 1960s and the 1970s. The best-known case, already mentioned, was that of chansonnier Wolf Biermann, followed by the protest of leading GDR intellectuals after his banishment in 1976. But viewed against the sustained oppositional movements in Poland and Czechoslovakia, the absence of a crescendo in criticism or dissent in the years following 1961 was striking. It rather looks as if the brutal repression of exit signaled by the erection of the Wall were also understood as a further repression of voice. Formulated in these terms, the absence of the seesaw in this instance has a certain plausibility. The decision to tear the city of Berlin asunder with a 165-kilometer-long wall, turning it into two noncommunicating halves, was an extraordinary affirmation of state power that signaled the GDR's general readiness to be more aggressive against "state enemies." In other words, not only did the building of the Wall restrain exit, but it also projected an enhanced willingness to rein in voice. Under the conditions, the increase in voice that might normally be expected when exit alone is curtailed did not and could not occur.

The simultaneous repression of exit and voice in 1961 was to have its counterpart twenty-eight years later, when exit and voice exploded jointly and brought down the whole edifice of the GDR. In a first cut, the events of 1989 look like the exact inverse of what happened, or failed to happen, after August 1961. The inability of the GDR, starting in the spring 1989, to prevent a large-scale flight of its citizens to West

Germany, via Hungary, Poland, or Czechoslovakia, signaled a novel, serious, and *general* decline in state authority. It was thus taken to imply a similar decline in the ability and readiness to repress voice—with the result that citizens started to demonstrate against the regime for the first time since June 1953. Precisely because the East German regime had made the repression of exit into the touchstone of its authority, its sudden incapacity to enforce its writ in this area meant a huge loss of face that emboldened people to other kinds of transgression.

This account of the collaboration of voice and exit in 1989 follows the lines of reasoning that have already been laid out in the introductory section. There I suggested that when previously unavailable opportunities to exit are forced open, people may experience new feelings of empowerment. They might then consider or reconsider other options, including that of reacting to an odious state of affairs by a direct attempt at change—through voice—instead of flight. This sort of *conjunction* of exit and voice turned out to be exceptionally powerful in the German case and took some striking forms. It will now be traced in some detail.[14]

Initially, exit played the lead part in the drama. Already in 1988 the pressure to leave the GDR is clearly on the increase, as a record 39,000 people manage to leave as compared with an average 22,000 for the three preceding years (see Table 1). As is shown in the monthly figures of Table 2, the coming of spring heightens exit activity in 1989, particularly after Hungary decides on May 2 to take down the barbed wire fence on its frontier with Austria. This means that East Germans coming to Hungary as "tourists" can now slip into Austria and then reach West Germany with a much smaller risk of being stopped than before. Numerous GDR citizens soon take advantage of this opening, and on August 19, on the occasion of a meeting of the Pan-European Union in Hungary, over 600 East Germans make it to Austria. At the same

14. The following account is in part based on the sources cited in n. 12, in part on publications cited here. See in particular Gerhard Rein, ed., *Die Opposition in der DDR* (Berlin: Wichern, 1989) and the *Chronik der Ereignisse in der DDR* (August 1989-May 1990), *Edition Deutschland Archiv,* 1990. Interviews with Gerhard and Gudrun Rein and with Detlev Pollack in Berlin in early 1991 were most helpful. In May 1992 I spent several days in Leipzig and Dresden and talked with a number of participants in the 1989 events. I am greatly indebted to all of them.

Table 2. Migration from East to West Germany, 1989

January	4,627
February	5,008
March	5,671
April	5,887
May	10,642
June	12,428
July	11,707
August	20,955
September	33,255
October	57,024
November	133,429
December	43,221
Total for year	343,854

Source: Wendt, "Die deutsch-deutschen Wanderungen," p. 393.

time, the West German embassies in Budapest, Prague, Warsaw, and East Berlin are filling up with hundreds of East Germans looking for asylum and hoping somehow to be allowed to move to the West.

International and media attention is focused on the human drama and mass flight that is shaping up just as the East German regime is preparing for a Gorbachev visit and the celebration of the fortieth anniversary of its founding. On September 10 the Hungarian government further facilitates exit by officially authorizing all East Germans on its territory to pass into Austria. By the end of September over 25,000 *Ausreiser* (outward-bound travelers) will have taken advantage of this escape route. In the meantime the situation in the embassies becomes increasingly unmanageable, as thousands of refugees keep crowding into them. As a result of high-level talks between the foreign ministers of the two German states, an agreement is reached to transport them by train to West Germany. The one face-saving concession obtained by the East Germans is that the trains are routed through its territory, so that the East German state is seen itself to expel its alienated citizens—

a move that, as will be noted shortly, was to have remarkable unintended consequences. Special sealed trains thus bring some 14,000 Ausreiser from Poland and Czechoslovakia to West Germany on October 1, 4, and 5, giving a grotesque cast to the fortieth anniversary celebrations on October 6 and 7. In one more month, marked now primarily by ever more massive demonstrations, the Berlin Wall would come down.

Such, in briefest outline, is the chronicle of exit from the GDR in 1989. Let me now try a similarly concise review of the course of voice. As in the case of exit, premonitory signs of future explosions of voice stand out in retrospect. From the early 1980s on, the Nikolaikirche, a church in the center of Leipzig, served on Monday afternoons as a meeting point for "peace prayers."[15] In 1988 these occasions become a rallying point for Ausreiser or *Ausreisewillige*—people who wish to leave and are waiting for the official permit. On January 15, 1989, an unauthorized silent march *(Schweigemarsch)* takes place in Leipzig on the occasion of the seventieth anniversary of the assassination of Karl Liebknecht and Rosa Luxemburg (who had become something of a hero to the counterculture, largely because she had said "Freedom always means freedom for those who think differently"); 150 participants are taken into custody by the police. On May 7 municipal elections are held; when a 98 percent victory for the ruling party is announced, unprecedented, widely scattered protests break out against irregularities and forgeries, and 120 arrests are made in East Berlin alone. In May-June the regular Monday meetings at the Nikolaikirche in Leipzig increasingly turn into protest meetings, with ever larger groups of Ausreiser participating. Even in the presence of a considerable police force they often chant their slogan: "Wir wollen raus" (we want out).

In June, after the Tiananmen Square massacre in Beijing, the Honecker government vows not to give an inch, by declaring its unconditional solidarity with the Chinese Communist regime. But at the same time, the mass exodus via Hungary becomes widely known. This leads to a loss of authority for the GDR, which comes to be referred to derisively as *Der Dumme Rest* (= DDR), or "the dumb remainder."

15. For the events in Leipzig, see in particular Grabner (n. 2) and Neues Forum Leipzig, *Jetzt oder nie—Demokratie* (München: Bertelsmann, 1990).

After a brief summer recess the Monday church meetings resume in Leipzig, and on September 4 a single shout of "Ich bleibe hier" (I'm staying here) is heard for the first time, in response to the chant (we want out) of the Ausreiser.[16] This turns into the collective "Wir bleiben hier" (we're staying here) on September 11 *and becomes a rival rallying cry.* According to participant observers, a number of meanings were implied: "We're staying so as to make sure that things will not stay as they are"; or "We're staying even though we don't like things here"; or "You won't be able to get rid of *us.*"[17] Despite the pervasive tension and fear, the back and forth of the two slogans—"we want out" and "we're staying here"—introduces an element of entertaining street theater into the demonstration, which now emerges from the church and spills over into the adjoining streets. There it is met and dissolved by massed police units, which use force and make numerous arrests.

For a while the Ausreiser, the partisans of exit, and the *Bleiber,* the partisans of voice, form separate, even somewhat antagonistic, groups.[18] Eventually they merge under the slogan "*Wir* sind das Volk" (*we* are the people), which, particularly when the first word is accented, trenchantly denies the basic tenet of the Communist state's structure and ideology: that there is a complete identity of views and interests between the ruling Party and the population. This arresting slogan also seems to echo Bertolt Brecht's poem on the insurrection of June 17, 1953, with its final caustic suggestion that the government may wish to dissolve the people and elect another.[19]

16. Albrecht Dönert, Paulus Rummel, "Die Leipziger Montagsdemonstrationen," in Grabner (n. 2), p. 149.

17. The first meaning is noted in Peter Schütt, "Bleiben, damit es nicht so bleibt, wie es ist," *Deutschland-Archiv,* 22 (1989), pp. 1209–1213. The other interpretations ("Wir bleiben, obwohl's uns nicht gefällt" and "*Uns* werdet Ihr nicht los") were reported by activists in interviews held in May 1992 in Leipzig.

18. Petra Bornhöft, "Ausreiser und Bleiber marschieren getrennt: Auf der Demonstration in Leipzig trennten sich die Wege: abwandern oder reformieren?" ("'Ausreiser' and 'Bleiber' march separately: during the demonstration in Leipzig the roads parted—to exit or to reform?), *Tageszeitung* (Berlin), September 9, 1989, reprinted in the *Tageszeitung* brochure, *DDR: Journal zur November-Revolution* (Berlin: s.d.), p. 8.

19. At the end of his poem "Die Lösung" (The Solution), Brecht asks: Would it in that case / Not be simpler if the Government / Dissolved the People / And elected another? [Wäre es da / Nicht doch einfacher, die Regierung / Löste das Volk auf und / Wählte ein anderes?] See Bertolt Brecht, *Werke,* Werner Hecht et al., eds. (Berlin: Aufbau, 1988; and Frankfurt: Suhrkamp, 1988), 12:310.

Another important center of voice is the city of Dresden,[20] where the number of would-be Ausreiser is especially large. According to one (paradoxical) explanation this is so *because* West German television did *not* reach the low-lying Dresden area, which was therefore called the *Tal der Ahnungslosen* (valley of those who are out of it). The local people are thus unaware of some of the unpleasant realities of life in the West—unemployment, hard work, and so forth—while they routinely *dis*believe the propaganda emanating from the radio and television programs of the GDR! But another aspect of Dresden's geographical position is more important in explaining the presence of many would-be emigrants. The city was the GDR's major rail and road gateway to Czechoslovakia, and from there to Hungary and the West. In September it fills up with many people from points west and north in the GDR—people who are planning to leave the country. Then, two major events occur in rapid succession. On October 3, the official East German news agency announces that the frontier with Czechoslovakia is being closed "temporarily," except to GDR citizens with passports and valid visas. (Up to then, GDR citizens could travel freely to Czechoslovakia, which, with its hard-line regime, was considered to be the most "fraternal" of all socialist countries.) As a result, many people are stuck in Dresden as well as intensely frustrated over being shut in *(eingesperrt)*. The next day, October 4, the news circulates that sealed trains with East German Ausreiser from the Federal Republic embassies in Prague and Warsaw are about to pass through the city on their way to West Germany. As a result, large groups of would-be Ausreiser congregate in and around the main railroad station in hopes of somehow boarding these trains. The police are alerted and brutally clear the station area. This, in turn, leads to resistance, rioting, considerable damage to the station, and further demonstrations during which, once again, there are shouts of both "Wir wollen raus" and "Wir bleiben hier."

There is a second and curious story about the origin of the rallying cry "Wir bleiben hier" during those days. Before the police intervened, a railway official—a woman—apparently attempted to get the crowd of Ausreiser to leave the Dresden station by telling them: "Citizens, go

20. The events in Dresden are chronicled in Eckhard Bahr, *Sieben Tage im Oktober: Aufbruch in Dresden* (Seven days in October: Upheaval in Dresden) (Leipzig: Forum, 1990).

home—we promise you that all of you will be permitted to emigrate [*ausreisen*]." Whereupon a good many in the crowd, disbelieving such promises and unwilling to vacate the station, shouted back: "Wir bleiben hier"—we're staying right here![21] Only later, according to this account, did the meaning of the slogan change to the more sophisticated concept, "we want to change things by staying." Hence, voice may have arisen out of intended exit—not as a result of opposition to exit as such, but through linguistic ambiguity and slippage.[22]

Whatever the case, the riots at the Dresden station are followed by daily protest demonstrations that draw up to 10,000 people. They take place in the midst of the fortieth anniversary celebrations of October 7; perhaps not to mar that occasion too badly, police violence remains sporadic. Then, on October 8, a large group of protesters stages a sit-in in a square near the station, and a young priest manages to obtain approval from a police official for the crowd to appoint representatives who will negotiate its demands with the authorities. Delegates are somehow selected, and as they stand up, they are applauded by the seated crowd by way of investiture. Thus is born the Dresden "group of twenty," which actually convenes with the mayor of Dresden the next day and works out concessions that lead to a relaxation of tensions. In the short span of five days, the Dresden crowd will have traveled all the way from a desperate push for exit to organized voice, complete with representation and delegation.

At this stage, Berlin's voice is lagging behind those of Dresden and Leipzig, but on October 7, after the official celebrations, several hundred young people gather on Alexanderplatz and, for the first time the slogan "Wir bleiben hier" is heard there in response to the initial "Wir

21. Kurt Nowak, *Jenseits des mehrheitlichen Schweigens: Texte vom Juni bis Dezember des Jahres 1989* (Beyond human silence: Texts from June to December, 1989) (Berlin: Union, 1990), pp. 20–21.

22. A correspondingly literal use of the opposite slogan "Wir wollen raus" was reported to me in Leipzig in 1992. In October, when groups of demonstrators found themselves cut off on all sides by mobile police forces, they would shout "Wir wollen raus" simply to indicate their demand to break out of the police trap. But in this case the wider meaning, "we want to be free to leave the GDR," certainly antedated the narrower one. Well known by then, the wider meaning probably inspired the demonstrators to use the slogan in the narrow sense. By contrast, in the case of "we're staying here," it is possible that, at least in Dresden, the narrow meaning preceded the wider one.

wollen raus." The whole group then marches in the direction of the nearby Palace of the Republic, where Gorbachev and other high-ranking special guests from the "fraternal" Communist countries are being entertained. Another widely heard, significant cry is "Gorbi hilf uns" (Gorbi help us) as well as, more simply, "Gorbi, Gorbi."

The watershed event is the next Monday demonstration in Leipzig, on October 9, frequently referred to since as *Schicksalstag*—the fateful day. During the preceding days there are ominous rumors—no doubt officially inspired—of an imminent "Chinese solution." The most widely read daily newspaper, the *Leipziger Volkszeitung*, publishes a virulent declaration by a group of militant Communists; the group attacks the "counterrevolutionary actions" and urges they be "stopped once and for all, if need be with weapons in hand."[23] Stories circulate about hospital floors being emptied of their occupants in anticipation of a flood of new arrivals, and about supplies of frozen blood being readied. So great is the apprehension that six prominent citizens, including three high functionaries of the SED and the symphony director Kurt Masur, issue an urgent appeal for moderation and dialogue among all parties.[24] Then, issuing not only, as on previous Mondays, from the Nikolai-kirche, but converging by advance arrangements from three other inner-city churches as well, the biggest demonstration ever takes place on the afternoon of October 9. Some 70,000 participate in a peaceful march, shouting "Wir sind das Volk" and "Keine Gewalt" (no violence). Another slogan expressing the hope for avoidance of violence is "Widerrede ist nicht Widerstand," which can be translated as "to voice does not mean to resist." For all the tension of the situation on that Monday afternoon, the police do not intervene, no blood is shed—and the authority of the GDR is shattered forever. As one eyewitness put it later: "In the late evening of October 9, the GDR had become something different. This was obvious to all participants."[25]

Thereafter, while thousands continue to flee to the West (the restriction on travel to Czechoslovakia that was imposed in early October is

---

23. Links, Bahrmann (n. 12), p. 16.
24. Neues Forum Leipzig (n. 15), p. 82.
25. Christoph Wielepp, "Montags abends in Leipzig," in Thomas Blanke and Rainer Erd, eds., *DDR-Ein Staat vergeht* (Frankfurt: Fischer, 1990), p. 72.

lifted in the middle of the month), events accelerate and the center of the stage moves to East Berlin. By October 18, the Central Committee of the SED has become sufficiently concerned about the future of the regime and the immobility of the Party leadership to force Erich Honecker to resign as secretary and all-powerful government leader. On November 4 the largest voice event on record, a huge protest demonstration of over half a million people, takes place in East Berlin. It is followed in short order by the most spectacular exit event: with the opening of the Berlin Wall on November 9, millions of Easterners cross into West Berlin to enjoy their newly won *Freizügigkeit* (freedom to move).

As in many other demonstrations throughout East Germany, the two principal demands of the November demonstration in Berlin were free elections (more voice) and freedom to travel (free exit). The latter is achieved directly with the opening of the Wall and the subsequent abolition of other border controls. It takes a little longer to organize free elections; they are held on March 18, 1990, with shattering results for the SED.

In the year following the opening of the Wall, the state structure of the GDR disintegrates rapidly. As one East German commentator wryly noted, the famous "final stage of communism" in which the state is supposed to "wither away" is virtually reached in those months during which the GDR, along with its once formidable police, slowly expires.[26] The GDR ceases to exist on October 3, 1990, when its territory is incorporated as five new provinces *(Länder)* into the Federal Republic.

Interpretation

The foregoing account, with its close intertwining and mutual stimulation of exit and voice, may not strike the reader as particularly problematic. It becomes more so, however, when the year 1989 is contrasted with the previous thirty-nine years. During those years, as shown earlier, exit took place by and large at the expense of voice and was

---

26. Friedrich Dieckmann, *Glockenläuten und offene Fragen* (Frankfurt: Suhrkamp, 1991), p. 205.

often engineered from above for that very purpose. That classical hydraulic pattern still put in a fleeting, if influential, appearance during the 1989 events, when the closing of the Czech border on October 3—the *prohibition* of exit—contributed a great deal to the powerful development of voice in and about the Dresden railway station. But on the whole it was the confluence of the two forces that characterized their interaction in 1989. To appreciate the peculiarity of this situation it is helpful, first of all, to recall a few distinguishing conceptual properties of exit and voice.

Exit—be it the decision to look for and go over to a more satisfactory supplier of goods and services or the decision to emigrate, to leave for a more satisfactory country—is essentially a *private* and also typically a silent decision and activity. One can do it alone: there is no need to talk it over with anyone. Exit is therefore a minimalist way of expressing dissent—one does not act in concert with others and leaves without noise, under the cover of night. Nobody can exit for you, however: the fact that others exit may influence one's decision to do likewise, but it can never substitute for that decision. Thus exit is not only a private decision; it is also a private good in that it cannot be had through the exertions of others, as a result of some sort of free ride.

The characteristics of voice could not be more different. Voice is typically a *public* activity. Though it does not indispensably require organization, action in concert with others, delegation, and all the other features of collective action, voice thrives on it. Voice activities such as petitions and demonstrations are therefore subject to the well-known liabilities of free riding—even though, as I have amply argued elsewhere, these liabilities can on occasion turn into assets.

According to this brief recapitulation, exit and voice have very different impulses and are likely to arise in very different circumstances—they would seem to inhabit quite different worlds. How then did the two come to be so intimately bound up together during the events of 1989?

Now it must be pointed out that exit—experienced in East Germany as departure for the West—initially ran true to the form just described. For example, during the exit wave of 1984, when unusually large numbers of requests for emigration, mostly of young people, were granted by GDR authorities, Heinrich Rathke, the Protestant bishop for the province of Mecklenburg, declared: "Precisely in these weeks large numbers of people are leaving us *secretly, softly, and silently" (heimlich, still und leise)*. At the same time, another pastor lamented the "loss of speech" of the young.[27] This loss of speech (*Verlust der Sprache*, or *Sprachlosigkeit*, "speechlessness") is also a much noted characteristic of those who left via Hungary or Czechoslovakia in the spring of 1989. Robert Darnton witnessed a silent exit scene near the West German embassy in Prague:

> I was especially struck by a young couple who arrived with a baby in a taxi. The mother stepped out. She lifted a pram from the taxi's trunk, unfolded it, and placed the baby inside. Then she pushed the pram ahead of her, while her husband carried two large suitcases, looking grimly at the embassy door. When they stopped in front of it, she suddenly burst into tears. I nearly did, too.[28]

Others were similarly shaken. Fearing, Cassandra-like, that events might take a disastrous turn, Christa Wolf, the prominent writer, managed to slip into West Berlin for a radio interview with Gerhard Rein on the eve of the October 9 demonstration in Leipzig. It was a last-minute attempt to help avert another Tiananmen Square. She began by speaking at length about the deep distress *(Erschütterung)* she and her friends had experienced during the preceding weeks over the spectacle of so many young people leaving the GDR:

> These last days, in conversing with people, I have always come up against questions that are also my own: Do we really know these young people? Why do they leave so easily? Why are they in part so speechless [*sprachlos*]? Why do they find it so difficult to articulate what they dislike here and what they look for elsewhere? . . . During the last four or five weeks we in the GDR were all dominated by these images, couldn't sleep, were in despair.

Later on in the interview, she lodged an impassioned protest against the official reaction of the SED leadership to the mass exodus:

27. Wolfgang Büscher, "Warum bleibe ich eigentlich? Reaktionen der evangelischen Kirchen in der DDR auf die Ausreisewelle" (Why do I stay? Reactions of the evangelical church in the GDR to the emigration wave) *Deutschland-Archiv,* 17 (1984), pp. 684–685.

28. Darnton, *Berlin Journal, 1989–1990* (New York: Norton, 1991), p. 73.

There should not be any mockery. No one has the right to come out with this sentence that has been tremendously upsetting for many people, including myself: "We do not shed a single tear over those who leave." [Wir weinen denjenigen, die weggehen, keine Träne nach]. That is awful [*schrecklich*]. It is absolutely awful to say such a thing while 40,000 young people leave our country.[29]

Christoph Hein, another major writer of the GDR, spoke in similar terms as early as mid-September. He too was indignant at the "not a single tear" statement and affirmed, to the contrary, that to live in a country that is constantly being abandoned by its citizens made him "physically and emotionally sick."[30] Jens Reich, a principal founder of the citizens' movement "New Forum" in September 1989, put it this way: "This outmigration torments [*quält*] us already for many years . . . for various reasons we have lost many friends . . . that was so bitter, this feeling of sitting in the waiting room of a railroad station and everything around you is breaking loose. In the end it was unbearable."[31]

There was something particularly devastating about these *silent, private* exits—they drove some of the more conscientious remaining citizens, such as Wolf, Reich, and Hein, to a passionate voicing of their concern and despair. It is not too daring a conjecture that we touch here also on the backdrop to a major, still largely unexplained nondecision of these months. Why did the hardest and most rigid Communist regime in the East not follow the Chinese example it had hailed just a few weeks earlier? Why did it fail to defend itself "weapons in hand" *(mit der Waffe in der Hand)* as it had many times boasted it would? Among the explanations that have been offered, the most prominent has been the assumption of a deus ex machina—Gorbachev was thought to have discouraged any such course during his October visit. But I find it plausible that not only Christa Wolf and her friends were devastated by the mass exodus of the summer: the Communist rulers themselves may well have suffered self-doubt and a loss of nerve and were in the end unable or unwilling to perpetrate yet another *Schrecklichkeit.*

29. Wolf (n. 9), pp. 77, 83.
30. Irene Charlotte Streul, "Die Kulturszene der DDR im Aufbruch," *Deutschland-Archiv*, 22 (1989), p. 1404.
31. Rein (n. 14), p. 27.

In fact, Günter Schabowski, the member of the Politburo of the SED who was later to give the signal, perhaps unwittingly, for the breaching of the Berlin Wall on November 9, speaks in his recollections about the exodus in terms quite similar to those of Christa Wolf and Jens Reich: he calls the resulting situation "tormenting" *(quälend)* and "most deeply shaming" *(zutiefst beschämend)*.[32] According to his account, moreover, the opposition to Honecker and the other hardliners that arose within the Politburo in September–October and led to the ouster of Honecker on October 18 had really gotten under way when Krenz and Schabowski agreed to circulate a position paper criticizing the "not a single tear" statement. (The statement had appeared in the Party newspaper *Neues Deutschland* of October 2 and was widely attributed to Honecker.) The position paper stressed, to the contrary, that the exodus was a matter of great concern for the GDR and that every departure must be felt as a loss.

This story helps to understand how public voice was stimulated by private exit in the fall of 1989, instead of being undermined by it, as had been the case previously. A closer look reveals the sequence of events to be a variant of the usual way exit is supposed to work in alerting "management" to its failings. The normal pattern is as follows: when customers take their business away from a firm or members desert a political party, the managers of these organizations soon become aware of declining sales or other evidence that something is wrong; they then search for the reasons and take steps to repair whatever lapses are responsible for the customers' or members' evident unhappiness (book, pp. 21–25). In the case of the GDR, this straightforward feedback mechanism worked very poorly, because the managers of the GDR had inured themselves to it—note the "not a single tear" phrase—and were in general an insensitive and inflexible bunch. But the mass exodus did sufficiently impress, depress, and alert some of the more loyal citizens, those who had no thought of exiting, so that they finally decided to speak out. The mobilization and voice of these citizens can thus be seen as a substitute for the failed response of the GDR managers or as a second wake-up call for them. The normal sequence of events that is supposed to be set off by exit has simply become more roundabout.

32. Schabowski, *Das Politbüro* (Hamburg: Rowohlt, 1990), pp. 62, 81.

The collaboration of exit and voice during the events of 1989 can also be explained by an appeal to the concept of loyalty, as discussed in my book. There, loyalty was shown to delay exit (as well as voice) when there was a decline in the performance of an organization to which one belonged. In counterpart, when that decline passed a certain threshold, the voice of the loyal members tended to become particularly vigorous. All along, however, I had made the simplifying assumption that at any one time organizations (families, political parties, nations, and so forth) ordinarily evoke a specific degree of loyalty among their members (or that characteristics such as loyalty have some sort of normal distribution around a specific mean intensity). If we now complicate this assumption and imagine an organization with two very different kinds of members, those with a great deal of loyalty and those with little or none, reactions to deterioration will take two distinct forms: those who are unburdened by feelings of loyalty will be prone to exit, while the loyalists will resort to voice. The former are the Ausreiser, the latter the Bleiber. Although the concurrent emergence of these two distinct groups could thus have been predicted from an elementary complication of my loyalty model, in fact the inventiveness of history was needed to suggest the complication and to reveal its importance.

It may look as though the conjunction of exit and voice during 1989 in the GDR has been adequately explained by the two considerations that have just been put forward. In the process, as expected, the theory has already been enriched by the historical events themselves. Nevertheless, the intimate fusion of exit and voice that was so characteristic of the protest movement in the GDR requires further comment.

The real mystery of the 1989 events is the transformation of what started and was intended as a purely *private* activity—the effort of scattered individuals to move from East to West—into a broad movement of *public* protest. How and when did public elements intrude upon the private sphere? How and when did they overwhelm the original intentions of the actors? The answer is contained in the historical account that has been presented. Originally the 1989 Ausreiser conceived their departure from the GDR as a totally private affair: as in 1984, they were intent on leaving *heimlich, still und leise*—in secret, silently, on tiptoe. But these intentions were frustrated by two circumstances: too many people had the same idea, and, as a result of external events such as the relaxation of frontier controls between Hungary and Austria, their moves were too successful to remain secret and private. Pictures of the exodus soon flooded the TV screens, causing established critics like Christa Wolf and Jens Reich to sharpen their criticism while making activists out of long-passive average citizens. As a Protestant pastor of Leipzig said in November 1989, looking back on the crucial September events in that city:

> [As] the others fled West, the folks here said: . . . We won't go along [*mitmachen*] any longer. People who are forty-five, fifty, fifty-five years old, who previously never raised a finger, who were totally indifferent, who have perhaps been cussing and saw clearly how everything went to the dogs—they now got worried about seeing their own children waving at them on TV the next day from Prague or Budapest. That's what motivated them.[33]

Exit also ignited voice in another, more direct way. As the Ausreiser themselves converged at key points (border crossings, railroad stations, embassies), they realized they were no longer alone, recognized each other as being of similar mind, and *rejoiced in the community they had unwittingly forged.* The most remarkable episode of this sort was the massive occupation of the Dresden railroad station by would-be Ausreiser hoping to board the refugee-laden trains that would pass through. Upon looking at each other and particularly upon being told to clear the station, those erstwhile private Dresden Ausreiser *went public.* The very chant "Wir wollen raus" turned them instantly from private to public citizens with a common cause. At this point those in the crowd who had no thought of leaving felt obliged to manifest their position in turn: their contrary chant, "Wir bleiben hier," became inevitable, irresistible, as one East German writer put it.[34] Thus private exit turned into public exit, which in turn generated public voice and even organized delegation and negotiation with the authorities—all within a matter of days.

At first the chant "Wir bleiben hier" may have been a mere reflex, a

33. Rein (n. 14), p. 180.
34. Dieckmann (n. 26), p. 64

clever linguistic invention, an automatic reply, initially without much content, to the rallying cry of the Ausreiser. Whereas the latter knew exactly what they wanted, namely, "out," those who viscerally disagreed with that solution had no such certainties. Having asserted their will to stay they now had to come up with some good reasons for doing so. Their rallying cry rather slowly and haltingly took on reformist meanings and messages. Perhaps "Wir bleiben hier" was an effective slogan just because of its vagueness and ambiguity—everyone who intoned it could endow it with his or her own content.

This interpretation carries considerable conviction. It is actually intermediate between the two earlier interpretations: (1) that the chant had a definite reformist message from the start, and (2) that it arose totally by happenstance, initially expressing nothing more than the refusal of demonstrators to obey an order to vacate the Dresden railroad station, and was later misunderstood or reinterpreted to assume a broader political meaning.

Seeing "Wir bleiben hier" as a purely verbal reply-reflex to the "Wir wollen raus" of the Ausreiser gains plausibility from the slogan "*Wir* sind das Volk" (*we* are the people) that eventually supplanted the two warring pro-exit and pro-voice slogans. "*Wir* sind das Volk" inherited the ambiguity of "Wir bleiben hier" and was similarly enigmatic and vaguely threatening. So much ambiguity could not be sustained for long, however. In the end, as is well known, a slight variation in wording endowed the Volk motto with a quite concrete and down-to-earth meaning. Just as "Wir wollen raus" led to "Wir bleiben hier," so did "*Wir* sind das Volk" turn into "Wir sind *ein* Volk" (we are *one* people)—a slogan that asked for the merger of the two Germanies and, implicitly, for the obliteration of the GDR.

This outcome is yet another aspect of the 1989 events that must confront my original script and in particular its happy-end scenario. My book had been written with the constructive purpose of exploring how exit and voice could help restore or nurture a faltering organization back to tolerable performance and health. Both exit and voice were seen primarily as mechanisms that would alert management to its failings after a "repairable lapse." Yet the possibility that an organization might actually fail to recover and instead succumb to the blows inflicted on it by exit and voice (as well as by its own weaknesses) was not entirely ruled out. I had argued that exit and voice would yield the desired constructive results only if they came forth *with moderation,* thereby not only alerting management but also giving it the time needed to mend its ways.

For the survival and recuperation of both business firms and political organizations, a mixture of "alert and inert" citizens or customers would be far better, so I argued, than either total, permanent activism or total apathy (book, pp. 24, 32). This consideration points to one of several reasons why the combination of massive exit and tumultuous voice in 1989 led to the death of the GDR rather than to its rebirth: that twofold critique, so long repressed, was simply too devastating to allow for any recuperation mechanism to work. Attempts to stay the course were made: notably the famous November 26 appeal, *Für unser Land* (for our country), drafted by Christa Wolf and signed by a group of GDR writers and professionals that included several well-known dissidents.[35] It argued for a reformed but socialist and "humanist" GDR as an autonomous entity—and proved totally ineffectual. The headlong rush to reunification was not to be halted. Indeed, the extinction of the German Democratic Republic can be seen as the ultimate penalty for the long suppression of both exit and voice.

Conclusion

In this "essay in conceptual history" I have looked at the GDR and its demise through some special lenses, in hopes of discerning new patterns, significant connections, and improved interpretations. The details of the story are therefore its essence, but two general observations will provide a conclusion.

First, the 1989 upheaval in the GDR represents a reversal of a movement that has been held to be characteristic—disastrously characteristic—of German history. A great deal has been written about the propensity of Germans in various historical circumstances to retreat from the public domain to the strictly private—to the famous (or infamous)

35. Wolf (n. 9), pp. 170–171.

Innerlichkeit. This movement is supposed to have come all too easily to Germans, particularly when they were confronted with distasteful and repugnant events in the public domain. The idea, often traced to Luther, that the inner, private sphere is something infinitely precious, pristine, and inviolable may indeed have undercut the emergence of the public citizen who assumes responsibility for the political life of his or her community. From this point of view, the story that has been told here provides a welcome counterpoint: it essentially chronicles how many East Germans found the road back from exit and apathy to voice, from withdrawal and purely private reaction to public action. However unintended this movement was initially, it became nevertheless a powerful and successful citizen movement. Thus it stands in contrast to the many failed revolutions as well as failures to resist tyranny that have marked German history since the Reformation. It is therefore perhaps to be regretted that language downgraded the movement from "peaceful revolution" to *Wende* (turn) soon after it was over. Strangely, once Germans had finally succeeded in toppling, at considerable risk but without major bloodshed, an oppressive and ruinous regime, they designated the event with a term that almost deliberately understated it. In this they resemble people who, on the basis of past missteps, have a poor self-image—when confronted by success in some new endeavor, they will strain to reinterpret that unfamiliar experience as yet another failure or, at best, as "nothing to write home about." By contrast, Richard von Weizsäcker, Germany's Federal President, showed a better appreciation of the 1989 events when he said in a recent speech: "With their nonviolent actions, the revolutionaries of the year 1989 have given all Germans a new awareness of liberty. The past is not extinguished in consequence. But a decisive new chapter has been added to our history."[36]

My second point reflects on method. I have attempted to give some shape to the story of the short-lived German Democratic Republic by retelling it in terms of the contrasting categories of private exit and public voice. Such an enterprise runs the risk of making too much of a

---

36. *Frankfurter Rundschau*, December 18, 1991, p. 7. Speech on the occasion of the award to Weizsäcker of the Heine prize for 1991.

theoretical construct. In 1909 the French anthropologist Robert Hertz published an article about the extravagant extrapolation of the right hand-left hand dichotomy by language and culture to encompass ever more basic contrasts, such as right-wrong, good-evil, divine-profane, and so forth.[37] For quite some time, then, we have known about the strange proclivity of the human (or Western?) mind to exaggerate differences, to blow up what Hertz called an "almost insignificant asymmetry" into unbridgeable binary oppositions—in short, to make socially constructed mountains out of natural molehills. I, too, may have engaged in this pastime as I collected conclusive evidence for the existence in many realms of a fundamental antagonism between private exit and public voice. Here the German story of 1989 stands as a reminder of Sportin' Life's maxim, "It ain't necessarily so"—a principle in theoretical modesty that social scientists disregard at their peril. In some momentous constellations, so we have learned, exit can cooperate with voice, voice can emerge from exit, and exit can reinforce voice.

I noted a number of specific ways where the role of exit turned around in this fashion. The German language has a peculiar gift for compact verbs, such as *umschlagen* and the famous Hegelian *aufheben,* which endow such turnabouts with seeming reality. I deliberately avoided these terms, as they evoke the famous dialectic, the "negation of the negation," and similar mysterious, if preordained, processes that dissolve all contrasts and reconcile all opposites. The longing for such reconciliation is of course the exact counterpart of the inordinate fondness for building up dichotomies that was noted by Hertz.

The events of 1989 were not experienced as stemming from an enigmatic turnabout in the functioning of social processes. Those who lived through them were not troubled at all by the fact that exit and voice now worked hand in glove after having undermined each other for four decades. A problem arises only for the social scientist who seeks

---

37. Hertz, "La prééminence de la main droite: Étude sur la polarité religieuse," in Hertz, *Mélanges de sociologie religieuse et folklore* (Paris: Alcan, 1928), pp. 99–129. The article was originally published in *Revue Philosophique,* 68 (1909). For an English translation see Hertz, *Death and the Right Hand,* trans. Rodney and Claudia Needham (Glencoe, Ill.: Free Press, 1960).

a deeper understanding and who, in the course of this attempt, fashions a conceptual framework that initially makes it easier, but subsequently can make it more complicated, to understand what is going on. In that case, of course, our analyst may still come out on top by showing how instructive it is that events should have diverged from the original scheme!

The Rhetoric of Reaction—
Two Years Later

Why Revisit So Soon?

There are various reasons why an author may wish to return, not to the "classic" he wrote thirty years ago (this is a widely practiced and accepted form of narcissism), but to a book he has only recently published. One such reason could be that he suffers from an acute case of what the French call *esprit de l'escalier*—thinking of the brilliant remark one might have made during the conversation only as one walks down the stairs after leaving the party. Another possibility is that the book was attacked and that some new ideas occurred to the author as he replied to his detractors. Also, upon reflecting on his book, he may discover some connecting link between it and his earlier writings which he feels he would like to explore. While working on a new book, its author is often providentially protected by the illusion that he is engaged on an entirely novel and original enterprise. We may need this feeling to set out at all. Only after we are finished do we recognize that an argument we have put forth is closely related to points which we have made long ago or which, alternatively, stand in some tension to it.

As will become evident, I hope, I can invoke all of these excuses for

This essay was published in *Government and Opposition*, 28 (Summer 1993), 292–314, as part of a series "Author/Author" in which an author goes back to an earlier work, comments on its reception, and puts forward additional and related thoughts.

returning so soon to my most recent book.[1] In addition, there is a more contingent, but perhaps more commanding reason: my book was largely drafted between 1985 and 1989, that is, before the abrupt collapse of communism in Eastern Europe (even though I managed to refer to the crumbling of the Berlin Wall in the Preface) and, of course, long before the end of the Reagan-Bush era in the United States. I had written the book during that seemingly endless era as a tract—properly learned and scholarly, but still a tract—against the then aggressive and would-be triumphant neoconservative positions on social and economic policy-making. A question might then arise about the utility or function of the book in the new situation. This matter will be dealt with later in the chapter.

Perversity and Futility: Some Major Distinctions

The book contains three long chapters that deal with the perversity, futility, and jeopardy theses. According to some critics, I have given primacy to the perversity thesis. This false impression may have arisen because the chapter on the perversity thesis was the only one to have been published separately both as a Tanner Lecture and, reaching a much larger public, in *The Atlantic Monthly*.[2] The perversity argument is certainly the most striking and, if correct, the most crushing of all objections to what Merton called "purposive social action," the one that comes first to mind as a beckoning rhetorical strategy when one looks for a decisive argument against some proposed reform. Precisely for these reasons, I gave it first place in my treatment, but otherwise did not bestow upon it any sort of primacy. To the contrary, as I wrote the book I became increasingly interested in the futility thesis and in its hitherto little noticed differences from the perversity thesis and eventually even more in the more sophisticated, historically oriented jeopardy thesis. This shift of my interest is reflected by the increasing

1. *The Rhetoric of Reaction: Perversity, Futility, Jeopardy* (Cambridge, Mass: Harvard University Press, 1991).
2. *Two Hundred Years of Reactionary Rhetoric: The Case of the Perverse Effect*, The Tanner Lectures in Human Values, vol. 10 (Salt Lake City: University of Utah Press, 1989), pp. 1–32 and "Reactionary Rhetoric," *The Atlantic Monthly* (May 1989), 63–70.

number of pages I devoted to each of the three arguments—32 to perversity, 39 to futility, and 52 to jeopardy.

As I look back on these chapters, a few major findings stand out in my mind. With the perversity thesis, I returned to a famous topic in the social sciences: the unintended effects of human action. It came as a pleasant surprise that new discoveries can still be made in this well-worked terrain. First of all, I point there to a fairly abrupt, but not widely noticed turn-around in the historical development of the concept. In the writings of Pascal, Nicole, Vico, Mandeville, Adam Smith, and up to Goethe's *Faust,* the principal form taken by the idea was that individual actions, motivated by greed and other sinful or deplorable passions, can have a benign, a positive social outcome. These situations are therefore similar to what is often called "blessings in disguise." It was only with the experience of the French Revolution that the idea of unintended consequences, applied to a very different underlying situation, came to stand for a process in the course of which well-intentioned human actions have an undesirable or disastrous social outcome. The very term "perverse effect" is of course born out of that modern interpretation of the concept of unintended consequences. Perhaps it is not an accident that the term *(effet pervers)* has become particularly popular in the country whose revolutionary history is responsible for the reversal in the concept's earlier meaning of blessings in disguise.

In addition, I attempted to sharpen the distinction between unintended effects and perverse effects—the distinction itself had been made long ago by Robert Merton in his classic 1936 article, "The Unanticipated Consequences of Purposive Social Action."[3] I pointed to the semantic drift which tends to equate "unintended" with "undesirable," and suggested that the perverse effect acts as a magnet for all those who abhor complexity and crave certainty and therefore feel basically uncomfortable with the notion of unintended consequences: "The perverse effect, which appears to be a mere variant of the concept of unintended consequences, is in one important respect its denial and even betrayal. The concept of unintended consequences originally in-

---

3. *American Sociological Review,* 1 (Dec. 1936), 895; as cited in *Rhetoric,* p. 38.

troduced uncertainty and open-endedness into social thought, but in an escape from their new freedom the purveyors of the perverse effect retreat to viewing the social universe as once again wholly predictable" (pp. 36–37).

As I say elsewhere, this observation is not meant to deny that perverse effects do happen. But a useful function is surely served by the exploration and exposure of certain systematic biases toward which our minds may be predisposed.

Amartya Sen's Darwin Lecture of 1992 makes a considerable contribution to this sort of inquiry.[4] He shows how the Darwinian perspective on evolution, with its emphasis on natural selection within a given or slowly changing environment, makes for "concentration on adapting the species rather than adjusting the environment in which the species lead their lives." In Darwin's view, reproduction and progress of the species was assured through the impersonal, decentralized, yet highly reliable forces of natural selection, a view that had much in common with the way in which Adam Smith's Invisible Hand or the competitive market mechanism was expected to work to bring about economic equilibrium and progress.

The discovery of these beneficent processes represented a considerable achievement which made progress emerge happily from ferocious struggle, but it entailed, as Sen shows, not only an understandable fondness for these processes, but a hostility to other conceivable forms of bringing about progressive change. Such alternative forms, consisting, for example, in changing the conditions under which the "struggle for life" is taking place, were decried as "meddling," "tampering," "interfering," and were automatically but unjustifiedly viewed as likely to be ineffective and worse, that is, "perverse."

In my book I showed how the various reactionary arguments—in particular the perversity thesis—draw strength from their affinity to various ancient myths, such as Hubris-Nemesis, the Oedipus story, and to certain images of a vengeful Divine Providence. To these sources of bias in the collective unconscious, the enormous influence of a major contemporary scientific doctrine can now be added.

4. See *The London Review of Books,* vol. 14, no. 21, Nov. 1992.

To recapitulate the two distinctions I made with regard to the concept of unintended consequences of human action: first, in its historical evolution the concept underwent an abrupt change in meaning during the French Revolution, from "blessing in disguise" to being (primarily) understood as "perverse effect." Second, I drew a sharp distinction between a general alertness to various unintended consequences of human actions, an attitude basic to any critical work in the social sciences, and the misguided singleminded search for perverse effects alone, such effects being considered the ultimate triumph of the analyst.

With the futility thesis I then made a third distinction: that between actions having unintended effects that alter the actually intended outcome in various ways, and actions having no effect, no grip whatever on reality. Instead of a more or less predictable and fortunate or unfortunate side-effect, what occurs is a "null" effect—hence my term "futility thesis." Far be it for me to claim that the discovery of this null effect ranks with the famous invention of the zero concept by the Indians and Arabs, but the sharp distinction between the perversity and futility thesis did make it possible to delineate two very different styles of thinking about the resistance of the social order to human action and planning: in the case of the perverse effect, the social world is seen as highly volatile, with every move leading to numerous unpredictable countermoves; in the case of the futility effect, to the contrary, the social world is viewed as remarkably stable and as being structured in accordance with laws that human action is impotent to modify.[5] As a result of their sharp differences the two arguments, while frequently used concurrently, are often logically incompatible; in any event, they have very different polemical postures and bites, with the futility thesis being often more insulting to the advocates of change and reform than the perversity thesis.

The Jeopardy Thesis and Its Offshoots

The longest chapter of the book, on the jeopardy thesis, is the argument that the adoption of a new reform would endanger some existing and

5. Ibid., p. 72.

hard-won accomplishment. Writing this chapter made me explore the fascinating history of the two principal electoral Reform Bills adopted by England in the course of the nineteenth century (in 1832 and 1867)—the two bills that transformed the English political system from an oligarchy to a democracy. In the parliamentary debates around these bills and in particular in the speeches of their opponents, I found remarkable evidence for the prominence of the jeopardy argument. Time and again it was argued that adoption of these bills would gravely jeopardize England's ancient and unique achievement—its Liberty, or the individual liberties of its citizens.

Similarly, when the discussion shifted in this century to social security and other welfare state policies, the opponents of reform would often argue that the proposed measures represented a considerable danger to individual liberties as well as to democratic politics. This line of argument is best presented in the polemical writings of Friedrich Hayek, and can be found in his famous *Road to Serfdom* (1944), as well as in subsequent works, such as *The Constitution of Liberty* (1960). The argument was again used prominently in more recent debates, when it was argued that the expansion of the welfare state undermined the "governability of the democracies," a concern much voiced by various conservatives in the 1970s.

As critics of my book have not failed to remark, the mere finding that reform proposals have indeed been attacked with the help of one (or several) of my typical "rhetorical" arguments by no means constitutes in and of itself a refutation of what is being argued. To be sure, when the identical argument (say the perversity thesis) is used time and again to assault a wide variety of policies or policy proposals, there is reason to suspect that it is brought up as an automatic response or cliché and is unlikely to be equally pertinent in all cases. Moreover, in the case of the jeopardy thesis, an implicit refutation of the argument results from the mere demonstration that the argument has been invoked— whenever history has obviously taken a different path from the one predicted by the original warnings. For example, the invocation of the jeopardy thesis in nineteenth-century England—the warning that the extension of the franchise would spell the death of liberty—looks in retrospect like a piece of silly alarm-mongering.

When One Thing Forestalls Another:
Mapping the Getting-Stuck Syndrome

With its rich historical dimension, the jeopardy thesis opened up several new fields of inquiry, or at least of curiosity. First of all, the frequent use of the jeopardy argument and the influence it often carried in the course of historical processes of change gave me pause, particularly in view of my earlier interest in, and advocacy of, sequential processes in development. Could it be on occasion a disadvantage, rather than a fortunate circumstance, for a country or human group to set out on what is deemed to be a sequential path, because there is danger of *getting stuck* at an early stage of the alleged sequence? Up to this point I had always taken it for granted that the chance of breaking down a complex of interrelated tasks—such as typically, the famous "vicious circle" of poverty or underdevelopment—into a series of sequential steps would be something for which we should cultivate the sharpest possible eye. But sequential or allegedly sequential solutions would obviously lose much of their charm if they were likely to abort.

It seems therefore useful to look more closely into the getting-stuck syndrome and into the conditions under which it appears and perhaps even thrives. At this point, all I can do is to stake out the considerable dimensions of this topic by pointing to a few historical examples or illustrations from different areas of the social world.

I return to the original situation which made me formulate the getting-stuck concept, that is, to the passage from T. H. Marshall's second stage of citizenship, where individual liberties and universal manhood suffrage have both been secured, to the third stage, where the rights of citizens to education, health, minimal well-being, and economic security would also be guaranteed or widely respected. With regard to this particular transition or intended but uncertain sequence, I had written that "a society which has pioneered in securing these [individual] liberties is likely to experience special difficulties in subsequently establishing comprehensive social welfare policies. The very values that serve such a society well in one phase—the belief in the supreme value of individuality, the insistence on individual achievement and individual responsibility—may be something of an embarrassment later on when a communitarian, solidaristic ethos needs to be stressed" (p. 131).

The institutions of a welfare state draw on a solidarity ethos that is likely to stand in considerable tension to the liberal tradition. Hence the more solidly rooted are a country's liberal values, and the prouder it is of this heritage, the more will the jeopardy thesis fall on fertile ground when an effort is made to establish welfare state guarantees or provisions. This does not mean that a consensus on welfare provisions cannot eventually be found or engineered, or that it is better for a country lacking both individual liberties and welfare state provisions to move directly to the welfare state without first establishing individual liberties. There is, nevertheless, value in appreciating the peculiar difficulties some countries are likely to experience in negotiating certain transitions or sequences.

Another area where a sequence, once believed to be normal or even easy and self-propelling, is later recognized to be strewn with obstacles, concerns the industrialization of less-developed countries. I am referring to industrialization via backward linkage, a process of "one thing leading to another," which I had myself adduced—with some fanfare— as an original, sequential path that is characteristic of the "late" industrializers of the twentieth century in my *Strategy of Economic Development* (1958). Actually, even as I described and celebrated this path as an "unbalanced growth" sequence, I did call attention to some of its built-in difficulties. In particular, so I pointed out, there are several reasons why the industrialists who start the sequence with the "last touches" or "final bits of value added" may oppose, rather than favor and promote, the extension of industrialization through the manufacture of intermediate products and machinery they currently import. In summarizing these resistances, I wrote, "Whereas the first steps [of this type of industrialization] are easy to take by themselves, they can make it difficult to take the next ones."[6] As I returned to this topic a decade later, I dwelt further on these resistances and cited them as an argument in favor of a greater-than-usual reliance on public policy in the new industrialization processes.[7] This specific illustration of the getting-

6. *The Strategy of Economic Development,* (New Haven: Yale University Press, 1958), pp. 118–119.

7. "The Political Economy of Import-Substituting Industrialization in Latin America," in *A Bias for Hope* (New Haven: Yale University Press, 1971), pp. 85–123. A particularly insid-

stuck syndrome was not lost on Latin American analysts and intellectuals. After an early and brief wave of enthusiasm, they grew thoroughly disenchanted with an industrialization, which was sharply criticized and decried as "truncated," "fragmented," or "unintegrated."[8]

This particular way of becoming or getting stuck does not look, at first sight, as though it had much to do with the jeopardy thesis. But the connection is not far to seek. The jeopardy thesis argues that an existing reform is likely to be endangered by a proposed new reform. In the case just discussed it is, rather similarly, the profitability of existing firms that might be threatened by domestic production of inputs which are currently imported. It is the self-interest of these firms that makes them lukewarm or outright opposed to new members joining the club.[9]

A more famous chapter in the history of industrialization may serve as a further example of the getting-stuck syndrome, or at least as an example of a well-known variant, the syndrome of getting stuck *comparatively speaking,* that is, the experience of falling behind after having been a leader. The most notorious case is the failure of British industry, historically the undisputed leader in industrialization, to keep up with its increasingly successful competitors in Germany, the United States, and elsewhere, starting in the later decades of the nineteenth century. This topic has called forth a vast literature, but one component of the "penalty of an early start" (Veblen) is widely agreed to have been the unwillingness of British industrialists to adapt or respond to certain new financial and organizational patterns that were proving successful elsewhere.[10] In other words, they were unwilling to risk jeopardizing their existing way of life.

---

ious role among these resistances had been uncovered and given considerable attention at the time by studies of the *effective* (as opposed to nominal) protection rate. (See pp. 107 and 110, n. 28).

8. See Chapter 17, below.

9. Similar difficulties in completing industrialization have been characteristic of the former Soviet Union and its satellites in Eastern Europe, but in the opposite direction. Here the emphasis had long been on the building up of heavy industry and machinery, but somehow the "next" stage, during which preferential attention would be given to satisfying the consumer, was never reached. This contrast between the Latin American and Soviet experiences in getting stuck is discussed in Chapter 17.

10. A general and industry-by-industry survey is in Bernard Elbaum and William Lazonick,

When the getting-stuck syndrome is interpreted in such broad terms, other significant experiences come within its compass even though the connection with the jeopardy argument may become more tenuous. An interesting case is the evolution of the franchise in France. As is well known, France was the first country to institute universal manhood suffrage. The principle was established during the high tide of the Revolution by the Constitution of 1793. No elections were ever held under this document which was soon rewritten. Yet even in 1848 France was still the first country ever to hold elections under a regime of universal suffrage for men, which had now been reinstated by the February Revolution. But that is where voting rights in France got stuck; it was to take almost a century, until 1944, for the franchise to be extended to women. In other countries, where unrestricted voting rights for men were achieved quite a bit later, women had to wait much less long to win the vote. In many countries that achieved independence during the twentieth century, voting rights were extended simultaneously to both men and women.

According to a comprehensive and thoughtful recent study, the decisions of 1793 and 1848, with their discrimination against women, had strong doctrinal or philosophical underpinnings: in spite of the urgings of Condorcet and of a few feminists like Olympe de Gouges, general opinion among the revolutionaries followed Rousseau in seeing only men as making up the *public* realm. Men alone were recognized as individuals and citizens, whereas women were thought to belong, along with children, to the private, domestic, familial, or natural sphere.[11]

Once universal suffrage for men was justified by so elaborate a conceptual distinction between the genders, a significant barrier to the extension of voting rights to women had been erected. In addition, once men had the right to vote, it could be argued on less doctrinal grounds that giving that right to women would have various calamitous

eds., *The Decline of the British Economy* (Oxford: Clarendon, 1986). A review of this book and a general survey of the "decline" literature is in M. W. Kirby, "Institutional Rigidities and Economic Decline: Reflections on the British Experience," *Economic History Review,* 45 (1992), 637–660.

11. Pierre Rosanvallon, *Le Sacre du citoyen: Histoire du suffrage universel en France* (Paris: Gallimard, 1992), pp. 130–145 and pp. 393–412.

results for the newly established democratic order: the family, that foundation of society, might be endangered if the question of how to vote became a matter of dispute between husbands and wives.[12] Moreover, women were more subject than men to the influence of the Church, and their vote would therefore tilt the election results in a clerical, antirepublican direction.[13] These arguments, with their appeals to both Right and Left and their distinct jeopardy flavor, carried enough weight with successive French parliaments to prevent, for many decades, the introduction of voting rights for women.

The foregoing illustrations suggest that the getting-stuck syndrome, being fairly ubiquitous in time and space, deserves close attention by the students of social change. Moreover, watching out for it is especially important at the present time as various reforms and transitions are the order of the day in the many countries that have experienced the collapse of Communist regimes. The multiple tasks usually mentioned there as urgent include democratization, privatization, economic restructuring, macroeconomic stabilization, indemnification of previous owners, and others. A great deal is currently being written on what would be the smoothest and most expeditious order in which to tackle and solve these many problems.

This literature on proper "sequencing" reminds me of my *Strategy of Economic Development,* where I dealt at length with alternative sequential investment paths for developing economies. I distinguished in particular between what I called "permissive" and "compulsive" sequences in development and made a case for the more "compulsive" (that is, compelling) ones that often seemed to put "the cart before the horse." Because of the interrelated structure of economic activities, I thought at the time only in terms of *more or less* strong pressures that might be exerted by one forward step toward the next, for example, from infrastructure to directly productive activities or vice versa. A similar (basically optimistic) assumption about sequences seems to be prevalent today. But my argument in the preceding pages is meant to warn that in considering intended sequences attention must also be paid to

12. Rosanvallon (n. 11), p. 397.
13. Rosanvallon (n. 11), p. 394.

situations where one forward step will forestall the next.[14] Such possibilities certainly exist with regard to the current array of tasks in the former Communist countries; for example, the unremitting pursuit of macro balance and price stability could make it difficult or even impossible for a country to proceed expeditiously with restructuring, privatization, or even democratization. Awareness and systematic exploration of such potentially abortive sequences could draw attention to some of the more insidious dangers that lie in wait for the current experiments in social change.

The getting-stuck syndrome is one large area of inquiry that is opened up by the jeopardy argument. In my book I gave it only a few pages (127–132) within the chapter on the jeopardy thesis, but it obviously deserves more ample treatment. At the same time, reflections on the jeopardy thesis led me to an even larger topic: the world of progressive as opposed to reactionary rhetoric. I decided to sketch it out in the originally quite unplanned Chapter 6, which then also led to the shaping of the concluding chapter. But there is much room for further elaboration. It is worth commenting on the origin of Chapter 6, on its reception, and on its possible uses.

Genesis and Reception of a "Self-Subversive" Chapter

The original impulse behind my book is fairly obvious from its very first sentence, in which I relate how in 1985, not long after the reelection of Ronald Reagan, the Ford Foundation was "concerned over mounting neoconservative critiques of social security and other social

---

14. In an earlier amendment to the "unbalanced" sequences of *The Strategy of Economic Development* and to the distinction between "compulsive" or "permissive" sequences, I called attention to the possible existence of a "sailing-against-the-wind" sequence: here a country or society wishes to move forward in two directions, say growth and equity, but it so happens that, at any one time, it can move forward in one of these directions only at the cost of *retreating* in the other. I showed that it is conceivable that a country can still make progress in both directions by following this pattern. See "A Dissenter's Confession: *The Strategy of Economic Development* Revisited," in Hirschman, *Rival Views of Market Society and Other Recent Essays* (New York: Viking, 1986), pp. 27–32. The "sailing-against-the-wind" sequence is no doubt more troublesome than the various unbalanced-growth sequences which I had envisaged earlier, but it is still superior to the abortive sequences I have passed in review here.

welfare programs" and therefore took the initiative in bringing together a group of citizens to consider the so-called Crisis of the Welfare State. The fact is, of course, that I was similarly concerned. What is more, I was intensely unhappy about the direction my country seemed to be taking. The sense of danger and feeling of anger over the neoconservative offensive probably accounts for the tone of the first five chapters of the book. They were written in a combative mood of a kind I had not experienced for some time. These chapters give the book the character of an anticonservative or, perhaps, anti-neo-conservative manifesto, that was noted by sympathetic critics such as Jean Daniel, as he wrote in his editorial in the *Nouvel Observateur* (25 April 1991) that my book had stilled his "doubts whether left-wing thought still existed."

For the same reason other critics were less pleased: in fact, the stance of the book's first five chapters appears to have the gift of infuriating some of my readers. The best illustration of this reaction is the violent critique of Raymond Boudon in the Paris bi-monthly *Le Débat*.[15] In the United States, *The Public Interest*, a quarterly that, ever since its neoconservative turn in the 1970s, made a career out of demonstrating the perversity of any and all government programs for social welfare, also featured a hostile review.[16]

Given the admittedly strong political emotion behind my book, the question arises how I came to reverse my polemical stance with Chapter 6, "From Reactionary to Progressive Rhetoric." I shall now tell the story of that decision. For about three to four years, while the manuscript was in progress, I had no thought whatever of writing such a chapter. That was probably all to the good: had I planned on it from the beginning I might never have written the book at all, for the combative élan that carried me along during the first phase of writing might have been stunted. Providentially, the possibility of delineating types of progressive arguments that are quite different from the reactionary

15. This magazine published concurrently a reply on my part. See Raymond Boudon, "La rhétorique est-elle réactionnaire?" and Hirschman, "L'argument intransigeant comme idée reçue. En guise de réponse à Raymond Boudon," *Le Débat*, 69 (March-April 1992), 92–109. I have drawn on my reply to Boudon in part of this chapter.

16. Jerry Z. Muller, "Albert Hirschman's Rhetoric of Recrimination," *Public Interest*, 104 (Summer 1991), 81–92.

ones, yet can be shown to be their counterpart, opened up for me only when I had completed the lengthy parading of the perversity, futility, and jeopardy theses through the three historical epochs with which I was concerned in the three major chapters, that is, when I had written the bulk of the book.[17] Only as I drafted the "Reflections on the Jeopardy Thesis" (pp. 121–27) did it strike me that this thesis—a proposed reform is likely to endanger an earlier, more precious accomplishment—can easily be turned around; this would be achieved by arguing, along "mutual support" lines, that a proposed reform is, on the contrary, essential to give "robustness and meaning" (p. 124) to the earlier one. Only then, with my previously built edifice securely in place and with every cell of my three-by-three table (p. 135) nicely filled in, did it occur to me that there may exist a whole array of progressive arguments that would be comparable, item by item, to the reactionary litany. From the progressive "mutual support" argument that is so directly opposed to the reactionary jeopardy thesis, I thus moved on to search for similar, if considerably less obvious, counterparts to the futility and perversity theses.

It was clearly a "self-subversive" enterprise—to adapt a term Nietzsche used when he set out to write his virulent anti-Wagner tract after having long been an ardent admirer and close friend of the composer.[18] I did hesitate a bit as I realized the risks involved—the possible accusations of inconsistency and of weakening the case against reactionary rhetoric which I had made so far. Nevertheless, I proceeded to write that chapter for various reasons I found compelling.

First of all, there was sheer *fun* in pursuing my argument into this originally unexpected direction. As is well known, criticizing one's friends is more demanding and therefore much more interesting than to expose once again the boring errors of one's adversaries. So there was some intellectual exhilaration in my exercise at self-subversion.

17. My argument here is related to the "principle of the hiding hand" which I put forward twenty-five years ago to explain how development projects can sometimes be successful *because* their costs (or difficulties in general) have been underestimated initially. See *Development Projects Observed* (Washington, D.C.: Brookings, 1968), ch. 1. For some comments on this principle, see Chapter 12 below.

18. Nietzsche's term was "Selbstüberwindung" (self-overcoming); see "Nietzsche contra Wagner," in *Werke,* ed. Karl Schlechta (Munich: Hanser, 1960), vol. 2, p. 903.

But I do not wish totally to dismiss the possibility that moral and intellectual values have also been responsible for my decision to proceed with the writing of Chapter 6. Once that idea had crossed my mind, it became a *duty* to go ahead—not to do so would have been equivalent to self-censorship and concealment. Intellectual *tastes* may also have been a factor. Over the years I have collected aphorisms and other pronouncements that I find particularly insightful or congenial. Sometimes they come in contrasting pairs. An outstanding example consists of, on the one hand, the famous proto-Romantic pronouncement of Vauvenargues: "Les grandes idées viennent du coeur" (Great ideas come from the heart) and, on the other, Paul Valéry's striking counteraffirmation: "Nos plus importantes pensées sont celles qui contredisent nos sentiments" (Our most important ideas are those that contradict our feelings). As Niels Bohr once noted, there are two kinds of truth: the truth of "simple and clear" statements whose opposite is obviously wrong, and the "deep truths" whose "opposite also contains deep truth."[19] The Vauvenargues-Valéry pair is a particularly good illustration of such deep truths. In retrospect I might say that writing my book gave me a chance to demonstrate my fondness for both aphorisms: Vauvenargues presides over the first chapters and then gives way to Valéry as patron-saint of the last two.

Finally and more prosaically, I was impelled to write Chapter 6 because doing so promised a substantial *benefit:* that of being able to conclude the book on a broad and positive note. Without the chapter I would probably have finished with the somewhat gratuitous advice to the practitioners of reactionary rhetoric to "plead their cause with greater originality, sophistication, and restraint" which I had proffered at the end of my *Atlantic* article, where I had published a short version of the perversity chapter. The new chapter on progressive rhetoric would permit a more ambitious conclusion: having denounced both reactionary and progressive rhetoric, I would be able to show how dis-

---

19. According to Niels Bohr, by the way, the progress of science consists in moving from the "deep truths" to the others. Niels Bohr, "Discussion with Einstein on Epistemological Problems in Atomic Physics," in P. A. Schilpp, ed., *Albert Einstein: Philosopher-Scientist* (Evanston, Ill.: The Library of Living Philosophers, 1949), p. 240. I owe this reference to Freeman Dyson.

cussions between reactionaries and progressives—each with their own brand of intransigent arguments—are "dialogues of the deaf" and contraptions to avoid that genuine deliberation and communication between contending groups that is supposed to be characteristic of democracy.

With the last two chapters it became clear to me that the nature of my message had changed. My book was no longer exclusively about "The Rhetoric of Reaction" which, together with "Reactionary Rhetoric," had been my working title since 1985. My treatment had become more even-handed and consequently I suggested to my publisher a new title that would reflect this change: *The Rhetoric* (or *Rhetorics*) *of Intransigence,* a phrase that had actually come under my pen in the course of writing the concluding chapter (p. 168). But my publisher objected to having "intransigence" in the title. That term was said to be largely unknown to (and, if known, likely to be mispronounced by) the average American. So I went back to the original title. I can report, however, that "Rhetorics of Intransigence" was adopted, on my urging, by the Italian, Brazilian, and Mexican publishers of the book. In France, where there is a strong demand for books with a historical dimension, my publisher preferred the title "Two Centuries of Reactionary Rhetoric" ("Deux siècles de rhétorique réactionnaire").

What has been the reception of Chapter 6 by the critics? As was perhaps to be expected, the chapter has not done me much good. Conservatives and neoconservatives, on the one hand, did not give me any credit for taking on the progressive rhetoric: they simply took the inclusion of that chapter for a base maneuver. Thus Boudon suggests that in writing the chapter I was merely trying to "establish my impartiality."[20] On the other hand, those who like the message of the early chapters find the inclusion of this chapter a form of excessive intellectual "virtuosity."[21] Many critics seem to be nonplussed by a discussion that confounds their simplistic categories and expectations. An exception must be made for a review (of the German edition of the book) that appeared in the weekly *Die Zeit* (Frankfurt Book Fair Supplement, 2 October 1992). The reviewer, Otto Kallscheuer, declares here that

20. Boudon (n. 15), p. 99.
21. This term is used by René Rémond in his highly favorable review in *Le Monde*, 19 April 1991.

Chapter 6 is the "real point" *(eigentliche Clou)* of the book precisely because it permits me to conclude on a nonpartisan note.

The story of Chapter 6 as I have told it, at perhaps excessive length, allows some further comments. First of all, it raises some doubts about the open-mindedness with which scholars and intellectuals are generally thought to carry forward their inquiries. While they are said to be engaged in the "search for truth wherever it may lead" or to travel "wherever the spirit takes them," there seems to be much frowning when these fine phrases are taken seriously to the point where an author actively pursues a thought that is at variance with a point made previously or that stands in some tension to it.

Social scientists are of course forever (and properly) eager to detect unintended effects of social actions and policies. But are they similarly looking out for *unintended consequences of their own thoughts,* that is, for thoughts they did not initially expect or intend to come up with? Actually, it is not easy to cite examples of such unintended thoughts having been expressly acknowledged and assiduously explored by their authors within one and the same book. In principle, thoughts of this kind should not be too rare. After all, the person who develops a given line of reasoning is best placed to think of objections and counterarguments. But then self-censorship sets in and the imperative of cognitive consistency generally wins out, so that such objections are not fully developed. In my own case, I was able to develop counterpoints to my original position only because of the peculiar time sequence in which they occurred to me. In the absence of such favorable and rather exceptional circumstances, most authors will stick to the conventional unitary thesis. Only the works of the most creative, expansive, and innovative thinkers are allowed to be full of unresolved contradictions. To get on with their work these thinkers seem to agree with Emerson that "consistency is the hobgoblin of little minds"; they leave it to their critics to expose the contradictions and to their interpreters to labor at reconciling them.

Some Uses of My Book for Reformers

As already noted, one reason for writing Chapter 6 was the expectation that it would enable me to end the book on a constructive, rather than purely polemical note. But the chapter's usefulness has turned out to be even greater, largely because of intervening events. In 1992 I was invited to participate in a conference organized by the French Planning Commission, held in Paris in November, on "Social Justice and Inequalities," a topic that was high on the Commission's current agenda. I was specifically asked to base my contribution on Chapter 6. Clearly, the organizers of the conference were interested in hearing from me, in greater detail than I had done in the book, about the kind of "intransigent rhetoric" they should *avoid* if and when they would be ready to present policy proposals arising out of their current work on the theme of the conference. In the meantime, of course, an important political change took place in the United States with the presidential election victory of Bill Clinton in November 1992. Unlike the French planning officials, our new leaders have not so far shown a great deal of interest in possible advice on my part. Nevertheless, I shall transcribe here the thoughts I submitted to my French friends.[22] Their relevance to new programs and policies likely to be proposed in Washington will be obvious, I hope.

In the light of the critique addressed in my book to both reactionary and progressive rhetoric, how should a reform agenda be formulated and presented today? My answer comes in two parts; the first inherent in the first chapters of the book, which spell out the principal categories of "reactionary" rhetoric, the second found in Chapter 6, on progressive rhetoric.

Awareness of the Reactionary Arguments

Obviously, reformers would do well to be prepared for the attacks likely to be leveled against their proposals. They also should look out for the *real* dangers of these proposals, for which their adversaries will of course have a particularly sharp eye. For both reasons reformers should know about the principal reactionary arguments and take them seriously. I believe that my chapters on the perversity, futility, and jeopardy theses will be useful to reformers on both these counts, as they provide them

22. See "La rhétorique progressiste et le réformateur," *Commentaire*, 62 (Summer 1993), 303–309.

with a conceptual guide to the principal counterarguments as well as to the several actual pitfalls any proposed reform may face.

This sort of prospecting for dangers and objections is actually rather common today. Because of experience with recent reforms and their critiques, the watch for conceivable perverse effects is particularly intense. On occasion, in fact, it risks being overdone.

For example, not long ago, various proposals for strengthening child support were made in the United States. In the case of single-parent households, part of that increased support was proposed to be extracted from the absent or "noncustodial" parent (generally the father) by attaching his income through automatic withholding of wage payments. This way of improving the economic status of poor children had been pioneered in the state of Wisconsin and the proposal was to introduce it more widely, through federal legislation.

At that point, an interesting memorandum was circulated to the participants in the discussion.[23] It attempted to list all the conceivable "unintended repercussions" that might flow from the proposed scheme. The list was surprisingly long and diverse. If future fathers who are unmarried face an assured long-term drain on their incomes, how might they react? They may insist that the woman they impregnate have an abortion; or they may be attracted to "off-the-book" jobs whose wages could not be attached; or they might "disappear," move to another state, and assume a new identity and social security number; and so forth. The strategies open to individuals intent on evading the proposed measure are obviously extremely varied. It is no doubt important to think in advance about such strategies and about the likelihood that they will be widely adopted, with the result that the proposed policy would be thwarted and would generate perverse results, such as a widespread increase in crime, abortions, and other ills.

The mere visualization of perverse reactions says of course very little about their likely *incidence*. I have moreover attempted to show in my chapter on the perversity thesis that many *unintended* consequences of public policies are not necessarily *perverse,* and that perverse effects are

---

23. Its author was Robert D. Reischauer, then a senior economist at the Brookings Institution and presently Director, Joint Congressional Economic Committee. I am grateful to him for making his memorandum available to me.

often such that "some positive margin survives [their] onslaught" (p. 41). In evaluating the prospective outcome of public policies, reformers should certainly be attentive to such possibilities as well as to the probable extent of truly perverse effects. Otherwise they would become affected by over-sophisticated skittishness and, in general, be paralyzed by imaginary fears.

The point can be generalized: while the new fashion to look out in advance for dangers that may lurk in reform proposals is to be welcomed, reformers should be aware of the elementary economic principle that a search is not to be pushed beyond the point where the marginal cost of the search begins to exceed its marginal benefit.[24]

Two observations can make this principle a bit less abstract (and less tautological). In the first place, a thorough search for negative repercussions has a psychological cost: overconfidence. The relentless prospecting for perverse effects may itself have a perverse effect; it is apt to make the reformer insufficiently alert to newly emerging dangers. More important, reformers must realize that it is impossible to guard in advance against all possible risks and dangers. The most thorough prospecting will miss out on some negative effects that will appear only as events unfold. This inability to foresee future trouble will strike us as less disturbing once we realize that we are similarly unable to think in advance of the remedial measures that may become available or that we may devise once trouble occurs.[25] As Racine sums up the matter in *Andromaque:*

> . . . tant de prudence entraîne trop de soin
> Je ne sais point prévoir les malheurs de si loin
> (So much prudence requires too much care
> I am unable to foresee misfortunes from so far).

Self-Restraint in the Use of Progressive Rhetoric
I now turn to the intransigent rhetorical arguments often used by reformers. The message of Chapter 6 to reformers is essentially to ask

24. For the locus classicus of this point, see George J. Stigler, "The Economics of Information," *Journal of Political Economy,* 61 (June 1961), 213–225.
25. This point is also related to the "principle of the hiding hand" mentioned in n. 17.

them for self-restraint: I implicitly plead that they should refrain from using—or that they should use with moderation—these arguments in the advocacy of their programs and policies, no matter how effective and persuasive they may be or may seem to be.

(1) We should adopt a certain reform or policy because, as things are, we are caught or will shortly land in a *desperate predicament* that makes immediate action imperative regardless of the consequences— this argument attempts to deflect and neutralize the perversity thesis.

(2) We should adopt a certain reform or policy because such is the "law" or "tide" of history—this argument is the counterpart of the futility thesis, according to which attempts at change will come to naught because of various "iron laws."

(3) We should adopt a certain reform or policy because it will *solidify* earlier accomplishments—this is the progressive's retort to the jeopardy claim that the reform is bound to wreck some earlier progress.

How difficult would it be for reformers to give up these kinds of arguments? I have just listed them, I believe, in decreasing order of dispensability.

The most dispensable of the three arguments is the alarmist claim that disaster is upon us if we fail to take this or that progressive step. This way of arguing might be called "impending-disaster" or "impending-revolution" blackmail. It has been the common fashion in which many Western progressives or reformers presented their programs, particularly since 1917, when the threat of social revolution appeared on the horizon of Western societies. An important variant of this way of arguing became current after World War II in discussions on aid for the low-income countries of the Third World: here the joint disaster to be fought off—by extending generous financial aid—was revolution and the prospect of these countries being "lost" to the Soviet zone of influence.

For some time now these ways of arguing for national or international redistribution of income had gone stale from overuse. Since the events of 1989–91, they have become largely unusable as a result of the collapse of communism and the Soviet Union. As Gunnar Myrdal argued long ago, progressives can and should make a convincing case for the policies they advocate on the ground that they are *right* and *just,* rather than by alleging that they are needed to stave off some imaginary disaster.

What about the argument that a certain progressive policy should be adopted because such is the "tide" of history, the "wave of the future" which it is futile as well as knavish to oppose? This argument also should not be too difficult to discard, in part, I will admit, because, with the latest upheavals and *pace* Francis Fukuyama, the tide of history appears to run quite strongly against the tide-of-history view of things!

The argument that a certain policy should be adopted because it is in line with some inevitable drift of history so that any opposition to this drift will end up in history's "dustbin" is actually close to the view that disaster will inevitably strike unless we adopt a certain progressive program. While I was at pains to point out in my book the considerable differences between the perversity and the futility theses, the progressive counterparts to these two arguments turn out to have much in common. In both cases an appeal is made, not to human reason and judgment, but to anxiety and fear. And both views share the characteristic that, as a result of recent historical experience, they are highly discredited at the present time. Hence there is not much sacrifice involved in following my advice against using them.

Things are rather different in the case of yet another typical progressive argument which I implicitly ask my friends to use sparingly. It is the argument that a proposed reform is not only compatible with previous progressive achievements but will actually strengthen them and will be strengthened by them. Similarly, progressives will often argue that "all good things go together" or that there is no conceivable area of conflict between two desirable objectives (for example, "the choice between environmental protection and economic growth is a false one"). In itself, this is an attractive and seemingly innocuous way of arguing and my advice to reformers cannot be never to use this argument. Given their considerable interest in arguing along mutual support rather than jeopardy lines, reformers may actually come upon, and will obviously then want to invoke, various obvious and not obvious reasons why synergy between two reforms exists or can be expected to come into being.

My point is, rather, that reformers should not leave it to their opponents but should *themselves* make an effort to explore also the opposite possibility: that of some conflict or friction existing or arising between a proposed and a past reform or between two currently proposed programs. If reformers fail to look in this direction and, in general, are not prepared to entertain the notion that any reform is likely to have some costs, then they will be ill-equipped for useful discussions with their conservative opponents.

And there is a worse scenario. The conviction, born from the mutual benefit thesis, that a given reform carries no conceivable cost and that therefore nothing stands in its way can easily shade over into the feeling that nothing *should* stand in its way. In other words, those who have convinced themselves that there cannot possibly be any conflict between a reform they advocate and other worthwhile aspects of their society may resentfully turn against these very aspects if and when, against all expectations, they do turn out to be obstacles to the desired change. The advocates of that change will then be tempted to act in accordance with the maxim "the end justifies the means" and may well *prove the jeopardy thesis right* by their willingness to sacrifice positive accomplishments of their society for the sake of the specific forward step on which they have set their hearts. An extreme version of this sort of dynamic is powerfully portrayed in Kleist's novella *Michael Kohlhaas,* where one man's boundless passion for justice makes him turn into a criminal. There is of course no logical necessity for progressives to go down this path or slippery slope, but the fact that they have been known to do so in the past is a strong argument for moderation and qualification of "mutual benefit," "synergy," or "false choice" claims in the future.

My "practical" advice for the reformer can be summed up in the following three points:

1. Reformers should be aware of the principal objections that are likely to be raised against their proposals and attempt to minimize the vulnerability of these proposals on perversity, futility, or jeopardy grounds. While doing so, reformers should not become unduly timorous; in particular, they need not endlessly search for all conceivable perverse effects.

2. Reformers should refrain from claiming that history is on their side

or that, if a reform they advocate is not adopted, revolution or some other disaster is sure to follow. Since the Communist collapse, these types of arguments are no longer as appealing or persuasive as they once were; there is less need therefore to caution reformers against using or overusing them. Suddenly it has become far more *expedient* than heretofore to argue for reforms on purely moral grounds.

3. This does not mean, of course that there are no longer any intransigent poses available to reformers. An example is the popular synergy thesis which holds that all reforms, past, present, and future, lend each other mutual support and that any conflict among them is inconceivable. Such an attitude disregards the complexity of the societies we live in and is injurious to democratic deliberations whose essence is trade-off and compromise. Moreover, the amiable maxim "all good things go together" can mask a reformer's readiness to push through one good thing *at the cost*, if need be, of the others.

Reformers would actually do well to canvass what damage their proposals might inflict on other values and goals of their society. For example, it would be disingenuous to pretend that stimulating economic growth and correcting or attenuating inequalities that arise in the course of growth require exactly the same policies. The problem rather consists in finding an optimal combination of policies that does as little damage as possible to either objective. We are more likely to find something close to this optimum if we admit from the outset that we are in the presence of two objectives between which there exists normally a good deal of tension and conflict.

Conclusion: Virtue Rewarded?

As originally conceived my book had a simple motive: I wanted to help stem the neoconservative tide of the 1980s. In these pages I have shown how, in a changed political environment, the book may now have a very different use: to suggest a new style and rhetoric around progressive policy-making. Such versatility is unusual; it must be credited to my decision of following up some unintended thoughts that intruded in the course of writing. This decision thus carried a substantial and unexpected reward. The moral: even in intellectual pursuits, honesty can turn out to be the best policy.

3
chapter

The Case against "One Thing at a Time"

It often happens to the dissenter that his or her views become in turn a new orthodoxy. So far this fate has fortunately not befallen *The Strategy of Economic Development,* a book I wrote over thirty years ago as a dissent from prevailing opinions and doctrines. But the occasion for this essay, a conference organized in part to celebrate the old book, may be an ominous cloud on the horizon. I shall therefore use this opportunity to take a precaution: present an argument that contradicts or qualifies a central proposition of the book. To be more specific, I intend to show that the validity of that proposition has limits, that it is more applicable in some situations than in others, and finally, that the course I advocated is not without some problems of its own.

Let me first return to a story I told earlier, in the 1980s, when the World Bank asked me, along with other "pioneers" of development economics, to write about the origins of the ideas on economic development I had put forward in *Strategy* and about my subsequent appraisal of those ideas. In response to that request I recalled something

Originally presented at the University of Buenos Aires in November 1989, when the author was awarded an honorary degree in conjunction with a conference organized by the Inter-American Development Bank and held at the Instituto di Tella in Buenos Aires, on "Hirschman's Work and a New Development Strategy for Latin America." This essay was published in *World Development,* 18 (August 1990), 1119–1122 (copyright © by Elsevier Science Ltd; reprinted by permission), and in the book resulting from the conference: Simon Teitel, ed., *Towards a New Development Strategy for Latin America: Pathways from Hirschman's Thought* (Baltimore: Johns Hopkins University Press, 1992), pp. 13–19.

that happened to me in Argentina around 1968, shortly after the military coup that overthrew the civilian regime of Arturo Illia and brought to power General Ongania. One official or supporter of the new military government suggested to me at the time that

> all our government is really doing is applying *your* ideas of unbalanced growth. In Argentina we cannot achieve all our political, social, and economic objectives at once: therefore we have decided to proceed by stages, as though in an unbalanced growth sequence. First we must straighten out the economic problems, that is, restore economic stability and stimulate growth; thereafter, we will look out for greater social equity; and only then will the country be ready for a restoration of civil liberties and for other political advances.[1]

I was appalled by this suggestion. My writings were invoked to justify the "temporary" suppression or restriction of democratic rights and liberties for the sake of achieving economic objectives such as stability and growth, when all I had argued was that it may be possible and in certain circumstances even desirable to push ahead with, say, industrial development in spite of inadequate infrastructure such as electric power-generating capacity and transportation.

I took a positive view of these *kinds* of disequilibria because they seemed to me to be self-correcting, not necessarily through the forces of the market alone, but because of the predictable corrective reactions on the part of both market forces and public policy responses. But it was far from clear how such corrective forces can be activated when a disequilibrium or disproportionality arises, not between sectors of the economy, but between economic and political progress.

Considerable economic growth and progress and perhaps also an improvement in the distribution of income can take place without any concomitant advance in political openness or decline in repression, just as the inverse development can go on for a considerable period: a strengthening of democracy can go hand in hand with a weakening of the economy. There is no *general* reason why these various good things should necessarily go together except for the fact that we wish it were

1. Hirschman, "A Dissenter's Confession: 'The Strategy of Economic Development' Revisited," in Gerald M. Meier and Dudley Seers, eds., *Pioneers in Development* (New York: Oxford University Press, 1984), p. 104.

so—it would make for a less complicated world. One can obviously think of some reasons why such disequilibria or disproportionalities should bring equilibrating forces into play; but there are others that make for the opposite movement, that is, for an accentuation of the disequilibria. For example, once an authoritarian regime achieves economic progress, the government could very well find itself more popular and more strongly entrenched and therefore under less pressure than before to evolve in the direction of pluralism and human rights. Accordingly, one might suspect the good faith of such a government when it says the "time is not ripe" for moving in this direction, while proclaiming its determination to do so "eventually."

There is much commonsense appeal in the old rule "one thing at a time," but apparently it can be a mixed blessing to be able to order tasks in this manner. I have recently come upon some new thoughts in this field, and shall present them briefly.

In the United States, we are passing through a period during which conservative or neoconservative thinkers are on the offensive. One thing conservatives are traditionally doing is denouncing as harmful or disastrous certain progressive policies of social or political reform that are proposed or may have been carried out. Among the arguments most commonly used in such debates one stereotypical pronouncement is: if you adopt this or that policy or reform, you will greatly endanger an earlier achievement which is among our most precious accomplishments and most cherished possessions. For example, if we go "forward" in the direction of universal suffrage—a view repeatedly argued in England in the course of the nineteenth century—we will lose our Ancient Liberty. Later it was similarly argued that the adoption of some new program of social welfare will inflict a damaging blow on both liberty and democracy, however desirable the program may be in itself.

I call this sort of argument the *jeopardy thesis*.[2] It urges that a step forward will jeopardize an earlier progressive step that is to be valued more highly than the one under discussion. The thesis has been put forward primarily in countries like England, which had a long history

---

2. See Hirschman, *The Rhetoric of Reaction: Perversity, Futility, Jeopardy* (Cambridge, Mass.: Harvard University Press, 1991). In the following paragraphs I am drawing on chapter 4 of that book.

of gradual political and social change. Most of the examples come indeed from that country, from the opposition to the Electoral Reform Acts of the nineteenth century to the anti-welfare state literature, starting with Hayek's famous *Road to Serfdom* written in London during World War II.[3] This book has the concept of jeopardy right in its title.

The jeopardy argument simply cannot be used in countries that do not have that sort of gradual history of political and social reform. It is impossible to endanger previous progress when there has been none! The matter is related to a once much discussed topic in "political development." In Western Europe, as various authors have pointed out, the distinct "tasks" of nation building—achieving territorial identity, securing authority all over that territory, enlisting and managing mass participation—were undertaken one after the other, over a period of centuries, while the new nations of the Third World are faced with all of them at once. Similarly, the progression from civil rights to mass participation in politics through universal suffrage to socioeconomic welfare state entitlements proceeded in a far more leisurely and orderly manner in Great Britain than in most continental countries, not to speak of the others.

In the debate on political development, the distinction between the few countries which were able to solve their problems one by one over a long period, and the (presumably less fortunate) others, for which that period is highly compressed, served an obvious purpose: to demonstrate that latecomers face a daunting task, to appreciate fully the special difficulties of nation building in the twentieth century. Let us accept this argument for the moment. The latecoming countries are then seen to have at least one *advantage* on their side: when they come to adopt, for instance, welfare state institutions, it will not be possible to combat this advance in the name of preserving a tradition of democracy or of individual liberties since that tradition hardly exists. In other words, the jeopardy thesis cannot be invoked in such cases.

The rhetorical advantage making life easier for welfare state advocates in the latecomers may seem a small consolation in comparison to the

3. Friedrich A. Hayek, *The Road to Serfdom* (Chicago: University of Chicago Press, 1943).

disadvantage—the need to solve several problems of state building at once—under which latecoming societies are said to labor. But that disadvantage looks rather less formidable once the underlying argument is called into question. To begin with, it is simply not true that the advanced countries always enjoy the luxury of sequential problem solving, whereas latecomers are uniformly forced into a virtually simultaneous operation. Take the stages of industrialization: it has not been adequately noted, probably because of the lack of communication between economists and political scientists, that here it is the inverse relationship that holds. With intermediate and capital goods being available from abroad, the latecomers, for a change, are the ones able to move leisurely, in accordance with the backward linkage dynamic, from the last stages of production to the earlier ones and on to the production of capital goods (if they ever get that far), while the pioneering industrial countries often had to produce concurrently all needed inputs including their own capital goods, if only by artisan methods. In this case, however, the compulsion for the pioneering industrial countries to occupy all stages of production at once has been considered an *advantage* (from the point of view of the dynamic of industrialization), whereas the sequential nature of the industrialization process among the later industrializers could be looked at correspondingly as a drawback, because of the risks of getting stuck at the finished consumer goods stage. These risks are real: as already explained in *Strategy,* "the industrialist who has worked hitherto with imported materials will often be hostile to the establishment of domestic industries producing these materials" and, more generally, "whereas the first steps [of industrialization] are easy to take by themselves, they can make it difficult to take the next ones."[4]

A comparison of the dynamics of industrialization and of political development seems to yield at first only one rather disconcerting generalization: no matter whether the tasks facing the advanced countries can be tackled sequentially or must be solved all at once, these countries always have the better part of the deal. But that should hardly come as

4. Hirschman, *The Strategy of Economic Development* (New Haven: Yale University Press, 1958), pp. 118–119.

a surprise—it is one of the many interlocking reasons why these countries *are* advanced.

Actually there is a more interesting conclusion to be drawn from the comparison of the two dynamics: leisurely, sequential problem-solving is not necessarily a pure blessing, as has been so plausibly argued in the literature on political development. *Sequential problem-solving brings with it the risk of getting stuck.*[5] This risk may apply not only to the sequence from the production of consumer goods to that of machinery and intermediate goods, but, in a different form, to the complex progression sketched in a famous 1949 lecture by the English sociologist T. H. Marshall: from individual liberties to universal suffrage and on to the welfare state.[6] A society which has pioneered in securing individual liberties is likely to experience special difficulties in subsequently establishing comprehensive social welfare policies. The very values that served such a society well in one phase—the belief in the supreme value of individuality, the insistence on individual achievement and individual responsibility—may be something of an embarrassment later on, when a communitarian ethos of solidarity needs to be stressed.

Perhaps this is the basic explanation why social welfare policies were pioneered by Bismarck's Germany, a country singularly unencumbered by a strong liberal tradition. Similarly, the recent rhetorical assault against the welfare state in the West has not been nearly as vigorous and sustained in Continental Western Europe as in England and the United States. None of this implies that in countries with a strong liberal tradition it is impossible to establish a comprehensive set of social welfare policies. But it is here that their introduction appears to require the concurrence of exceptional circumstances, such as the pressures created by depression or war, as well as special feats of social, political, and ideological engineering. Moreover, once introduced, welfare state provisions will again come under attack at the first opportunity. The tension between the liberal tradition and the new solidarity ethos will re-

---

5. This point is treated more extensively in Chapter 2 above, in the section "When One Thing Forestalls Another: Mapping the Getting-Stuck Syndrome."

6. T. H. Marshall, "Citizenship and Social Class," lectures given at Cambridge University in 1949, published in T. H. Marshall, *Class, Citizenship, and Social Development* (New York: Doubleday, 1965), chap. 4.

main unresolved for a long time, and the jeopardy thesis will be invoked with predictable regularity and will always find a receptive audience.

The argument I have just developed is, in many ways, the exact counterpoint to my argument in favor of unbalanced growth of more than thirty years ago. In *Strategy* I argued against the idea that, because of the interdependence of the economy from either the supply or the demand side, no progress could be achieved unless expansion of investment and output were increased simultaneously in all key sectors by means of "integrated investment planning," or a "big push." Instead, I searched, in theory as well as in actual historical development experiences, for the possibility of sequential solutions to the growth problem.

But now my argument has come full circle as I have met with some real drawbacks of sequential solutions, particularly where interdependence among tasks is weak or nonexistent. The problem may then be the opposite: several tasks need to be undertaken, but far from requiring an "integrated" approach and solution as a result of interdependence, they are all too separable. In such circumstances, it is easy and tempting to move forward in only one of several desirable policy areas, with the idea or pretext that others are going to be tackled later on. But because of the resonance of the jeopardy argument and for related reasons, that first advance may make it more difficult and perhaps impossible to act later in the other areas. It often is the case, of course, that politicians who use the "one thing at a time" or the "time is not ripe" arguments are not really eager to move in those areas of public policy or reform that they say they must "unfortunately" postpone.[7]

7. In a discussion of this essay during a seminar at MIT in 1990, Myron Weiner asked about the relevance of these considerations to the Soviet experience. In writing my paper I had for obvious reasons focused on Latin America, and to some extent on the West, but it struck me immediately that the political and economic history of the Soviet Union provides perhaps the most striking illustration of what I call here the danger of getting stuck at one stage of development, despite long-standing professed intentions to move on from that stage to some "higher" stage or stages. This holds for both politics and economics. Politically the country remained stuck, at least until Gorbachev, in the stage officially known as "dictatorship of the proletariat" (a euphemism, to be sure, for a much more narrowly based dictatorship) when the proclaimed objective was to leave that "transitional" stage behind at some point and to move on to true communism, perfect democracy, and the "withering away of the state." In economics, similarly, the country has been unable, in spite of a few, always frustrated attempts, to move from the stage where commanding priority is given to heavy industry and

In closing, let me plead that the intellectual path I have followed is not altogether bizarre. Repelled by a policy prescription (balanced growth) that seemed to me excessively demanding, dangerous in its policy implications, as well as simply wrong, I elaborated an alternative approach. Later I looked at some situations where events had taken the sequential course and noticed that it in turn harbored some dangers and risks of its own. This is only natural, for there is no riskless action. Recognizing those risks does not mean either that we should not act at all or that the proposition against which I argued originally is rehabilitated.

Rather, the story I have told here has two lessons. First, there is a compensation or, to go back to a favorite concept of mine, a blessing in disguise in store for those societies which come up all at once against a variety of policy tasks other countries were able to solve one after the other over a long period.

Second, looking for uniform solutions to development problems invariably leads us astray; this is so for the imperatives of simultaneity and sequentiality alike, that is, for the insistence on "integrated planning" as well as for the injunction to postpone certain tasks in the name of "one thing at a time."

With this conclusion I can lay claim to at least one element of continuity in my thought: the refusal to define "one best way."

---

capital goods, to the obvious "next" stage where the emphasis would be on satisfying the consumer. It might be instructive to look at that Soviet experience of getting multiply stuck in the light of the dynamic (or rather *lack* of dynamic) that I have outlined here. See Chapters 2, 5, and 17 for further discussion on "getting stuck" and on biases in industrialization.

4
chapter

Opinionated Opinions and Democracy

She thought it could scarcely escape him to feel that a persuadable temper might sometimes be as much in favour of happiness as a very resolute character.
—Jane Austen, *Persuasion*

When economists focus on the quality of life, their minds turn to ingredients of human satisfaction other than the bundles of consumer goods and services that have traditionally been the main subject of economic analysis. In recent decades we have rediscovered that man does not live by bread, nor even by GNP, alone, and have realized that a number of heretofore neglected items must be incorporated into individual utility functions: examples are reasonably clean air, feelings of participation and community, and an atmosphere of security and trust within and among nations. While being nondivisible, difficult to measure, and public, such "goods" have nevertheless been thought to partake of some basic characteristics of the typical consumer good: satis-

Published under the title "Having Opinions—One of the Elements of Well-Being?" in *American Economic Review—Papers and Proceedings,* 19 (May 1989), 75–79. Originally written for the annual meetings of the American Economic Association, this essay was presented in a session on "The Quality of Life." Most of it was incorporated into the talk I gave at the Freie Universität of Berlin, where I was awarded an honorary degree in November 1988. On this occasion I added an autobiographical note, which is reproduced here as Chapter 7. A shortened version of the Berlin talk was published in *Dissent* (Summer 1989), 393–395. The reference to Trollope's *Barchester Towers* (n. 4) has been added here, along with Jane Austen's epigram.

faction increases indefinitely as their availability increases, and does so at a decreasing rate. As a result, traditional and powerful economic concepts and tools, such as "maximization under constraints" and "equalization at the margin," could continue to be applied to the new goods. Under the circumstances, economists have perhaps not learned as much as they might have from the widening of their horizon that no doubt has taken place. I now wish to look at a good that, it seems to me, is not nearly as "well behaved" as those that have previously been selected for study.

The good—or ingredient of the quality of life—I shall examine is that of *having opinions.* Is it a good thing to have opinions? In his short story "The Darling," Chekhov appears to answer this question very much in the positive:

> And what was worst of all, she [Olenka] no longer had any opinions whatever. She saw the objects about her and understood what was going on, but she could not form an opinion about anything and did not know what to talk about. *And how awful it is not to have any opinions!* You see, for instance, a bottle, or the rain, or a peasant driving in his cart, but what the bottle is for, or the rain, or the peasant, and what is the meaning of it, you can't say, and could not even for a thousand rubles. When she had Kukin, or Pustovalov or, later, the veterinary surgeon, Olenka could explain it all and give her opinions about anything you like, but now there was the same emptiness in her head and in her heart as in her yard outside. She was filled with dread and bitterness. . . . (1984, p. 16; emphasis added.)

Here Chekhov seems to be saying that not to have any opinions is tantamount to not having individuality, personhood, identity, character, self. And a person who has no self can hardly have any self-respect.

Not to have opinions is thus symptomatic of a basic lack and of a desperate predicament. It is, in fact, the opposite condition that has been widely commended by social scientists, psychologists, and philosophers: to have opinions very much of one's own. Wilhelm von Humboldt went perhaps farthest in this direction when he proclaimed *individuality (Eigentümlichkeit)* and *originality (Originalität)* as "that on which all the greatness of man rests in the last instance and after which he must ceaselessly strive" (1851, p. 1). Humboldt's views strongly influenced John Stuart Mill, who cited and explicated them at length in his essay *On Liberty* (1859), in a chapter with the demonstrative title "Of Individuality, as One of the Elements of Well-Being."[1] Closer to our time, Erik Erikson stressed the struggle to achieve identity as a crucial formative life experience, and John Rawls, in his *Theory of Justice* (1971), included self-respect (presumably based on identity, character, and the holding of opinions) among the "primary goods" that a well-ordered society must supply to its citizens.

At first blush, it seems therefore that, like other aspects of the quality of life, opinions can be treated like consumer goods: the more the better, as well as, in this case, the stronger the better. Not only in social thought, but in much of Western culture has this position been endorsed, and the value of exhibiting strong opinions and of taking a principled stand celebrated, to the point where there is even some doubt whether the principle of decreasing returns applies to the good under examination. Conversely, indifference and lack of conviction have been denounced in the harshest terms, as illustrated by Dante and his scathing portrayal of the angels who would not take sides in the battle between God and the devil, and of the lukewarm in general. In a powerful passage he singled out these wretches as deprived of the "hope of death" and relegated them to the vestibule of Hell for the reason that, if they were let in, the damned would have someone to look down on (*Inferno* III, 25–50).

A few centuries later, much the same value judgment found another famous poetic expression: "The best lack all conviction, while the worst / Are full of passionate intensity." Yeats explicates here how it is that "things fall apart" (1959, p. 185). To him it is apparent that a well-ordered society requires the inverse arrangement: the best, not the worst, should be full of passionate intensity, that is, of sharply articulated and firmly held opinions.

In short, vacillation, indifference, or weakly held opinions have long met with utmost contempt, while approval and admiration have been bestowed on firmness, fullness, and articulateness of opinion.[2]

1. Originally written in 1792, Humboldt's essay was published in its entirety for the first time in 1851, long after his death. An English translation appeared in 1854, just as John Stuart Mill began drafting *On Liberty*. See J. W. Burrow's introduction to Humboldt, 1969.

2. Recently I have come across a remarkable exception to this rule: the inability (on a *man's* part, moreover) to come forward with a strong opinion about a much debated issue is not only not denounced, but is implied to be outright lovable. This rare moment in the annals

Yet matters are hardly that simple. Indeed, Chekhov's story itself intimates that to have a lot of ready-made opinions can be as ridiculous as to have no opinions is "bitter." For all his Olenka does in her happier moments is to parrot, each time with considerable conviction and aplomb, the opinions of her successive husbands and lovers. When Anthony Downs wrote his *Economic Theory of Democracy* (1956), he thought it was one of the advantages of political parties to offer citizens a full range of ready-made and firm opinions on all the issues of the day. In the meantime, however, we have come to appreciate that this time-saving feature of political parties, particularly of those with an ideological bent (those that in Germany were called *Weltanschauung- sparteien*), and the ensuing "free ride" to a full set of strong opinions, actually come at a considerable cost. We express our doubts about the value of the Downs mechanism by designating those who take advantage of it as "knee-jerk liberals," or "knee-jerk conservatives." Perhaps, to paraphrase a famous Chicago theorem, there ain't no such thing as a free *ride!*

Introducing the knee-jerk concept complicates the appraisal of the benefits that flow from having opinions. Apparently it can be just as much a denial of individuality, personhood, and self—a sort of damaging "escape from freedom"—to be outfitted with a full set of strong opinions on all the issues of the day, as to suffer Olenka's "awful"

---

of Western literature occurs toward the end of Trollope's *Barchester Towers,* in the crucial scene where Eleanor Bold and Francis Arabin are finally united in love after a series of misunderstandings and quarrels that had kept them apart for hundreds of pages. The scene starts with a rather awkward conversation about the comparative merits of "progress" and "old-fashionedness":

"I don't know about that," said Mr. Arabin, gently laughing. "That is an opinion on which very much may be said on either side. It is strange how widely the world is divided on a subject which so nearly concerns us all, and which is so close beneath our eyes. Some think that we are quickly progressing towards perfection, while others imagine that virtue is disappearing from the earth."

"And you, Mr. Arabin, what do you think?" said Eleanor. She felt somewhat surprised at the tone which his conversation was taking, and yet she was relieved at his saying something which enabled herself to speak without showing her own emotion.

"What do I think, Mrs. Bold?" and then he rumbled his money with his hands in his trowsers pockets, and looked and spoke very little like a thriving lover. "It is the bane of my life that on important subjects I acquire no fixed opinion. I think, and think, and go on thinking; and yet my thoughts are running ever in different directions" (vol 2, p. 232).

Barely two pages after this exchange, Eleanor and Francis are in each other's arms!

condition of not having any opinions whatever. While the goods we buy in the market are unambiguously conducive to material welfare, opinions are not necessarily the key to individuality and self-respect; it all seems to depend on some further, complex specifications regarding the more or less autonomous manner in which the opinions have been formed.

Some progress can perhaps be made with our topic if it is viewed from a collective rather than from an individual angle. Thus far I have primarily inquired into the contribution to *individual* satisfaction and happiness that is made by the acquisition and possession of a wide set of strongly formulated opinions. But surely such opinions, widely diffused among the citizenry, also have important effects, positive and negative, on the character of society. An important influence on the quality of life of individual citizens could then be exerted in this indirect way. The desirability of economic progress has often been evaluated in this dual fashion. One looks not only at the impact of, say, economic growth on individual well-being, but also on its contribution to the maintenance and strengthening of a free democratic society. Ecology aside, the consensus has lately been that the social and political effects of economic growth are as beneficent as its direct effect on the individual's welfare. But such harmony between the direct and indirect, or individual and social, effects was not always taken for granted. Up to the eighteenth century, for example, political economists and philosophers frequently worried about the corrupting effect of increases in wealth on the state. In the end, the state's ruin would then affect its citizens adversely, however much they may have prospered for a time.

Old-fashioned as it may seem, this sort of reasoning may well be worth refurbishing in conjunction with the problem at hand. Recent contributions to the theory of democracy have stressed the role of deliberation in the democratic process: for a democracy to function well and to endure, it is essential, so it has been argued, that opinions *not* be fully formed *in advance* of the process of deliberation.[3] The participants in this process—both the public at large and its representatives—should maintain a degree of openness or tentativeness in their opinions

3. See Bernard Manin, 1987, and Amy Gutmann and Dennis Thompson, 1989.

and be ready to modify them, both as a result of the arguments that will be put forward by the contending parties and, more simply, in the light of new information that could be developed in the course of public debates. Without a political process that manifests at least some aspiration toward this admittedly somewhat idyllic picture, democracy loses its legitimacy and will thus be endangered.

If this view has merit, then the traditional strong emphasis of Western culture on the virtue of strong opinions turns out to be curiously wrongheaded. The suspicion arises that this emphasis is rooted in a long aristocratic tradition, and has not been suitably modified by the subsequent, still rather young democratic age. As is well known, ideological relics of this sort have considerable potential for mischief. Social scientists and psychologists who hold forth so volubly on the virtues of individuality, personality, and identity might therefore do well to explore how to combine these desiderata with such democratic qualities as intellectual openness, flexibility, and readiness to appreciate a new argument, perhaps even pleasure in embracing it.

To put the matter in the economist's language: given the basic need for identity in our culture, the forming and acquiring of opinions yields considerable utility to the individual. At the same time, if carried beyond some point, the process has dangerous side-effects—it is hazardous for the functioning and stability of the democratic order. Under present cultural values these noxious side-effects do not enter the individual calculus—they are what economists call external diseconomies. Hence there will be an *overproduction* of opinionated opinion.[4] The most straightforward way of avoiding this overproduction would be for individuals to change the value system under which they operate. Might they learn to value both having opinions and keeping an open mind, to mix the delights of winning an argument with the pleasures of being good listeners and of having Jane Austen's "persuadable temper"?

In conclusion I return to the earlier argument, which evaluated the utility of having opinions from the individual, rather than collective, point of view. There I suggested that holding many strong opinions is

---

4. A formally similar argument is made by Tibor Scitovsky, 1976. He shows how certain socially useful activities, such as careful shopping, are not engaged in by consumers because the ensuing benefits are widely diffused as external economies.

an ambiguous indicator of well-being: it may or may not lastingly fulfill the promise of endowing the holders with true identity and rich personality. I also showed that the possession of opinions will be the less effective in those respects the more the opinions are acquired through the wholesale embrace of an ideology, that is, the more pronounced is their knee-jerk character. Now one way of acquiring opinions in the opposite, personality-enriching manner is to give them definite shape only after they have passed through intense confrontation with other views, that is, through the process of democratic deliberation. It turns out, therefore, that the public interest in democratic decision-making converges nicely with the private interest in forming opinions in such a manner as to enhance one's self-respect.

I have moved far away from economics. In fact, I may as well admit that I have been out of order all along, for my principal motivation in writing this note was to raise a point in the theory of democracy, to reflect on an ancient theme—the micro or personality foundations of a democratic society. But the argument I have developed about opinions may yield some helpful hints for a matter of interest to economics in general, and to the quality of life in particular: the concept of tastes and of changes therein.

Clearly, the traditional concept of the consumer with exogenously given, firm, and *non-est-disputandum* tastes bears a considerable resemblance to that of the citizen with a full array of strong and fully formed opinions. It is in fact likely that the two concepts owe something to, and reinforce, each other. I have argued here that our traditional bias in favor of strong opinions ought to be modified, in part because it might be dangerous to the health of our democracy. The question may therefore be raised whether a similar change is to be recommended for the concept of given tastes. To be sure, tastes are different from opinions: to become effective in the marketplace, they do not have to go through the process of deliberation characteristic of opinions in a democracy. But as a result of newly accumulating medical, environmental, and other research findings, many entrenched tastes (for tobacco, for cholesterol-laden foods, for using the automobile rather than public transportation, and so on) are being questioned ever more frequently, in both the individual and the public interest. As with our opinions, it therefore becomes increasingly desirable also with respect to our tastes that we do not regard them as being etched in granite.

A final suggestion. Those who labor to change some specific taste, say for cigarettes, have generally mounted a head-on assault on the habit, primarily by trying to convince smokers of the baneful consequences that follow from indulging their taste for tobacco. This approach could be usefully complemented, in line with the present discussion, by an indirect strategy. As part of their education for democracy, consumers could be encouraged to look at their tastes in general in a slightly questioning mood: any single consumption habit may be easier to rein in or give up once people no longer consider their tastes as proud possessions that cannot be altered or abandoned without some grievous loss of personality, character, identity, or self.

References

Chekhov, Anton. *The Darling and Other Stories* (*The Tales of Chekhov*, vol. 1), transl. by Constance Garnett. New York: Ecco Press, 1984.

Downs, Anthony. *An Economic Theory of Democracy*. New York: Harper and Row, 1957.

Gutmann, Amy and Thompson, Dennis. "The Place of Philosophy in Public Affairs." in Judith Lichtenberg and Henry Shue, eds., *The Public Turn in Philosophy*. Totowa: Rowman and Allanheld, 1989.

Humboldt, Wilhelm von. *Ideen zu einem Versuch, die Grenzen der Wirksamkeit des Staats zu bestimmen,* Breslau, 1851. Published in English as *The Limits of State Action,* introduction by J. W. Burrow. Cambridge: Cambridge University Press, 1969.

Mill, John Stuart. *On Liberty*. 1859.

Rawls, John. *A Theory of Justice*. Cambridge, Mass.: Harvard University Press, 1971.

Scitovsky, Tibor. *The Joyless Economy*. New York: Oxford University Press, 1976.

Trollope, Anthony. *Barchester Towers,* eds. M. Sadleir and F. Page. London: Oxford University Press, 1953.

Yeats, W. B. "The Second Coming," in *The Collected Poems*. New York: Macmillan, 1959.

5

chapter

A Propensity to Self-Subversion

Probably one of the most hackneyed and certainly one of the best Jewish stories is about a Jewish mother who gives her son two ties for his birthday. The next day, to please his mother, he puts on one of them, whereupon she exclaims reproachfully: "And the other, you didn't like?!" The reason this is such a fine story is, of course, that it makes implicitly a general point about human nature. We authors (of more than one book) are, I submit, similarly touchy and insatiable for praise. When a reader sincerely wishes to show admiration and declares "I liked your book a lot," are we not slightly offended and feel like asking, "Which one?" meaning in effect: "And what about the others?"

Also, and now I may be speaking for myself alone, when a reader praises my critique of the "Search for Paradigms," or of the "Quest for Parsimony" in economics or social science[1] I tend to be once again

Written for a faculty seminar held at M.I.T. about my work during the fall semester of 1992–1993. Published in *Common Knowledge*, 3 (Fall 1994), 10–15, and in the collective volume resulting from the seminar: Lloyd Rodwin and Donald A. Schon, eds., *Rethinking the Development Experience: Essays Provoked by the Work of Albert O. Hirschman,* Washington: Brookings Institution, 1994).

1. See my two articles, "The Search for Paradigms as a Hindrance to Understanding," *World Politics,* 22 (March 1970), 329–343, reprinted in *A Bias for Hope: Essays on Development and Latin America* (New Haven: Yale University Press, 1971), pp. 342–360, and "Against Parsimony: Three Easy Ways of Complicating Some Categories of Economic Discourse," in *Economics and Philosophy,* 1 (April 1985), 7–21, reprinted in *Rival Views of Market Society and Other Recent Essays* (New York: Viking, 1986), paperback ed. (Cambridge, Mass.: Harvard University Press, 1991), pp. 142–162.

ungracious and am liable to rebuff the tribute by exclaiming: "Wait a minute! I am not, you know, all that much set against paradigms or theorizing." For I like to claim that I have come up with quite a few theoretical notions of my own, from the early distinction between the "supply effect" and the "influence effect" of trade in *National Power and the Structure of Foreign Trade,* all the way to my latest book, *The Rhetoric of Reaction,* where I undertake to array all arguments against change or reform into three newly invented categories: perversity, futility, and jeopardy.[2]

For reasons that will become evident, I shall quickly cite some other instances of theory-building on my part. In spite of its title and of its origin in practical advisory work in Colombia, *The Strategy of Economic Development* (1958) was widely regarded as a contribution to development theory.[3] A simple principle—"unbalanced growth" or the idea of maximizing induced decision-making—was here shown to yield suggestions on a wide range of development problems, from investment priorities to industrialization patterns, from inflation and balance-of-payments policies to new attitudes toward population growth, from the choice of technology to the role of the state in development. Among my subsequent writings on development, I might mention my "tunnel effect" paper, which dealt with the effect on political stability of a growth process that brings with it, as is often the case initially in market economies, increased income inequality. I drew a theoretical distinction between an early phase of political tolerance for this inequality and a subsequent phase of impatience. The resulting model helped to explain a variety of political developments in the Third World during the fifties and sixties and lent itself to being translated into quite simple mathematics.[4] Finally, my theoretical bent is perhaps best illustrated by my

---

2. *National Power and the Structure of Foreign Trade* (Berkeley: University of California Press, 1944); and *The Rhetoric of Reaction: Perversity, Futility, Jeopardy* (Cambridge, Mass.: Harvard University Press, 1991).

3. *The Strategy of Economic Development* (New Haven: Yale University Press, 1958).

4. See "The Changing Tolerance for Income Inequality in the Course of Economic Development," *Quarterly Journal of Economics,* 87 (November 1973), 544–565, with a mathematical appendix by Michael Rothschild; reprinted (without the appendix) in my collection *Essays in Trespassing: Economics to Politics and Beyond* (New York: Cambridge University Press, 1981), pp. 39–58.

book *Exit, Voice, and Loyalty.*[5] In that volume and subsequent elaborations, I tried to show that these simple concepts and their interrelations can be used to throw new light on a vast range of seemingly
disparate social, political, and economic situations—surely the hallmark
of useful theory building.

So I bristle a bit when I am pigeonholed as "atheoretical" or "an-
titheoretical" or even as "institutional" and cannot wholly agree when
I am portrayed—as Michael McPherson once did in a generally most
perceptive paper—as someone who is primarily interested in noticing
and underlining what more systematic-minded (theoretical) economists
or social scientists have overlooked.[6] I do admit to having frequently a
reaction, perhaps something approaching a reflex, to other people's
theories, of the "It ain't necessarily so" variety. Skepticism toward *other*
people's claims to spectacular theoretical discoveries is, of course, not
a particularly noteworthy trait. It is, however, more unusual to develop
this sort of reaction to *one's own* generalizations or theoretical con-
structs. And this has become increasingly the characteristic of my writings that I wish to look at here.

In *National Power and the Structure of Foreign Trade* I showed how
relations of influence, dependence, and domination arise directly from
those commercial transactions between sovereign nations that had long
been characterized as "mutually beneficial" by the theory of international trade. Even if one agreed with the classical theory on the economic gains from trade, it could be shown that the *political* effects of
foreign trade were likely to be *asymmetrical* and to favor, at least initially, the larger and richer countries. This basic finding was one reason
my book was "rediscovered" in the sixties, when a number of writers—
such as Fernando Henrique Cardoso, Osvaldo Sunkel, and André
Gunder Frank—developed the so-called *dependencia* thesis. Actually I
never felt comfortable being cast as a "forerunner" of this group, whose
economic and political analysis I often found excessively somber. In

5. *Exit, Voice, and Loyalty: Responses to Decline in Firms, Organizations, and States* (Cambridge, Mass.: Harvard University Press, 1970).

6. Michael S. McPherson, "The Social Scientist as Constructive Skeptic: On Hirschman's
Role," in Alejandro Foxley, Michael S. McPherson, and Guillermo O'Donnell, eds., *Devel-
opment, Democracy, and the Art of Trespassing: Essays in Honor of Albert O. Hirschman* (Notre
Dame, Ind.: University of Notre Dame Press, 1986), pp. 305–316.

1977 an occasion arose to explain my attitude toward the *dependencia* school, and I decided to do so by criticizing my own thesis of a quarter of a century before.[7] I tried to show that the very situation of dependence that a small, poor country may experience initially as a result of trading with a large and rich country can give rise to various counter-tendencies, both economic and political, that in time would reduce this dependence. For example, while trade between a powerful large country and a small country makes initially for subordination of the latter, this situation will lead to a reaction that has some chance of success on account of what I called the "disparity of attention": the large country is unable and unlikely to focus its attention on its relations to a small trading partner with the single-mindedness that is available to, and characteristic of, the latter ("the [dependent] country is likely to pursue its escape from domination more actively and energetically than the dominant country will work on preventing this escape.")[8]

My propensity to self-subversion manifests itself again in *The Strategy of Economic Development*. One of its principal chapters dealt with the characteristic features of the process of industrialization in less developed countries. I pointed out that industrial development in these countries typically proceeds by means of what I called backward linkages—an industry supplying a good proved to be in demand through prior imports will be established first on the basis of imported inputs, such as semi-finished materials and machinery, and domestic manufacture of these inputs will then follow via backward linkage. This sequence is very different from the way in which industry was established in the pioneering industrial countries, where locally made machinery and intermediate materials had to be available from the start. But I celebrated the backward linkage dynamic just because it followed a different road and could qualify as an original discovery of the late industrializers.

Already in *Strategy* I made some cautionary remarks on the conceivable drawbacks of the backward linkage dynamic, particularly on the

7. "Beyond Asymmetry: Critical Notes on Myself as a Young Man and on Some Other Old Friends," *International Organization*, 32 (Winter 1978), 45–50, reprinted in my *Essays in Trespassing*, pp. 27–33.
8. Ibid., p. 30.

possibility that it may turn out not to be all that dynamic, with the interests of the early industrialists often being opposed (for various reasons) to the domestic production of inputs. In an article that was written ten years later I expanded on this theme and have now come to see this industrialization as liable to get stuck, or as an example of what I call the "getting-stuck syndrome" that seems to affect a number of intended but potentially abortive sequences.[9]

A further example of arguing against my own propositions is my recent attempt—see Chapter 1, above—to understand the events that led to the downfall of the German Democratic Republic in 1989 with the help of the concepts of my 1970 book *Exit, Voice, and Loyalty.* In the book I had explained at length how exit undermines voice and how the inability to exit can strengthen voice. What happened in the German Democratic Republic in the course of 1989 seemed to contradict this model: here the massive flight toward the West contributed powerfully to the mass demonstrations against the Communist regime, which was brought down by the combined blows inflicted by exit and voice. It was this unexpected and effective collaboration of exit and voice that excited my interest and made me examine closely the sequence of events. In the process I came upon some complications of the original model that, once being introduced, made it quite easy to understand how exit and voice could work in unison rather than at cross purposes. But, as I wrote above, the inventiveness of history was needed to suggest the complication and to reveal its importance.

Finally, I come to *The Rhetoric of Reaction.* This is perhaps the most pronounced instance of my propensity to ferret, undermine, or stand in some tension to propositions I have put forward, most pronounced because I engage in this propensity *within the same book,* rather than some years or decades later in a separate publication. The book was largely written from 1986 to 1989 and, as I already mentioned, was in effect a tract—properly learned and scholarly, but still a tract—against the then aggressive and would-be triumphant neoconservative positions on social and economic policy making. Its major portion is devoted to three arguments that I show to have been marshaled time and again

9. See Chapter 2 above.

against the principal proposals for change and reform over the past two centuries: the arguments of perversity (the proposed change for the better will actually backfire and make things worse), of futility (the proposed change will be wholly ineffective), and of jeopardy (the proposed change will endanger some earlier advance).

But, as I explain at greater length in Chapter 2, it occurred to me, in the course of considering the last of these arguments, that the jeopardy thesis is easily turned around: countering the view that a new reform will endanger an earlier advance, the partisans of that reform will often assert that the proposed reform will complement and strengthen the earlier one. I then looked for other progressive arguments that would be similarly, if less obviously, related to the perversity and futility theses. As a result, I wrote a chapter I had not planned to write, "From Reactionary to Progressive Rhetoric," that shows in some detail how "reactionaries have no monopoly on simplistic, peremptory, and intransigent rhetoric."[10] I do not believe that this chapter blunted the polemical thrust of my book. Still, the demonstration that progressives can be just as given to arguing along doctrinaire and routine-ridden lines as reactionaries modified my overall message and brought me to conclude the book, originally written in a combative mood, on a quite unintended constructive note.

In the follow-up article (Chapter 2, above) I characterize my "Progressive Rhetoric" chapter as "self-subversive." *Self-subversion* may in fact be apt as a general term for the intellectual wanderings I have been describing here by drawing on various writings of mine. Such self-subversion is probably rather unusual. It may seem odd that anyone should repeatedly *wish* to demonstrate that a tendency or line of causation he or she has suggested earlier needs to be substantially reconsidered and qualified by attention to the opposite line, in the light of subsequent events or findings. An obvious reason scientists (social and otherwise) are rarely self-critical to the point of engaging in self-subversion is that they invest much self-esteem and even identity in the findings and propositions for which they have become known. In their further work, they are likely to explore, along Kuhnian "normal sci-

---

10. *Rhetoric of Reaction*, p. 149.

ence" lines, all those domains in which their original findings can be *confirmed*. In this way, much confirmatory evidence will be accumulated and resistance against self-subversion will mount.

Another reason why there is such resistance is the continuing hold on our minds of certain basic conceptions about "the way things are" in the physical world and the analogies to the social world we are apt to draw. Whether the sun turns around the earth or the earth circles around the sun, we are certain that both of these propositions cannot be true at the same time. We tend to forget that, in the social world, things are much more tangled and ambiguous. Here any connection we have established convincingly between events, as though it were a universally valid law, could be found simultaneously to hold and not to hold (or to hold in a very different form) in various subsections of human society—for the simple reason that some underlying assumptions, previously implicit and thought to be general, apply in one subsection but not in another.

Here lies also the reason why my exercises in self-subversion, while often experienced at first as traumatic, are eventually rewarding and enriching. The new dynamics I come upon in matters of dependence, linkages, exit-voice, and so on, do not in the end cancel out or refute the earlier findings: rather, they define domains of the social world where the originally postulated relationships do not hold. Far from having to hang my head in shame on account of some egregious error that needs to be recanted, I can still land on my feet and in fact come out on top as I celebrate the new complexities I have uncovered.

In closing I should therefore like to plead for the overcoming of the normal resistance to self-subversion, even wish to proclaim the virtues and attractions of indulging that activity. In the first place, I believe that what I have here called self-subversion can make a contribution to a more democratic culture in which citizens not only have the right to their individual opinions and convictions but, more important, are ready to question them in the light of new arguments and evidence. Furthermore, just as Gaston Bachelard said of Freudian repression that it is "a normal activity, a useful activity, better still, a joyful activity,"[11]

11. Gaston Bachelard, *La psychanalyse du feu* (Paris: Gallimard, 1949), p. 164.

so engaging in self-subversion can actually be a positive and enjoyable experience. When I encounter a social situation where exit stimulates voice instead of undermining it, as I had long thought, I may well pass through a moment of perplexity and concern about my exit-voice theory having been "falsified." But past this moment, I feel genuinely more alive as I now have new interrelations and complexities to explore. Wittgenstein is reported to have remarked that "he could feel really active only when he changed his philosophical position and went on to develop something new."[12] At some point of one's life, self-subversion may in fact become the principal means to self-renewal.

Coda

I recall being much moved, many years ago, by Camus and his wartime essay "The Myth of Sisyphus," and particularly by its last sentence: "Il faut imaginer Sisyphe heureux" (one must imagine Sisyphus happy). Perhaps, as a result of my reflections on the uses of self-subversion, I can now go beyond the Camus formulation and propose instead, less elegantly but more radically: one must imagine Sisyphus himself making the rock tumble down.

12. Ray Monk, *Ludwig Wittgenstein: The Duty of Genius* (New York: Penguin Books, 1990), p. 467.

II
part

On Self

6
chapter

Four Reencounters

Toward the end of 1988, I spent eleven days in Europe, four of them in Paris, where I was a member of a "jury" examining a doctoral dissertation in economics, and the rest in West Berlin, where the Free University celebrated the fortieth anniversary of its founding and, in that connection, awarded me an honorary doctor's degree. These occasions led to encounters with four people who had touched my life when I was young, and whom I had not seen for periods varying from forty-three to fifty-six years. The concentrated experience made me look back.

Jean-Pierre Cabouat
April–June 1933

Feeling threatened with arrest because of anti-Nazi political activities, I hastily leave Germany on April 2 or 3, 1933, just before turning eighteen on April 7. I travel by train, bound for Paris, via Amsterdam, the shortest route to Germany's western frontier. My father had just died of cancer, in late March. My mother, who remains behind in Berlin with my two sisters, sends me some funds, but it is obvious that I have to supplement them through earnings of my own. Moreover, until the academic year starts in October, I have nothing to do except participate

Not previously published. Written in December 1988.

in émigré politics, with which I soon become disappointed. On his fairly frequent visits to Paris, the French cultural attaché in Berlin (Henri Jourdan), with whom I had struck an acquaintance before leaving Germany, introduces me to various friends of his and recommends me as someone who can give German lessons. Thus I meet, among others, the family of Pascal and Monique Dupuy and start giving regular lessons to their two very bright boys, Michel and Jacques, ages about eleven and thirteen. They have an elegant walk-up apartment at 7, rue Médicis, overlooking the Luxembourg. This is a Protestant family with an elite Troisième République background: one of the boys' grandfathers (Steeg) has been a senator, the Governor of Morocco, and held other high positions; the other (Dupuy) was a director of the Ecole Normale Supérieure. The father is an important executive in the coal industry. I become quite friendly with the two boys, with whom I talk about politics and other matters before or after the lesson, am sometimes asked to stay for dinner (with the whole family) during which issues of national and international politics are frequently discussed with passion.

Summer 1933

The Dupuy family has invited me to spend the summer vacation with them in their Normandy summer house at St.-Aubin-sur-mer, near Dieppe. The family clan is getting together and there are visitors from branches in other French Protestant citadels, such as Geneva (the Maurettes) and Nîmes (the Cabouats). The Cabouats have a house next to the Dupuys, and there is a boy, Jean-Pierre, more or less of the same age as his cousins Michel and Jacques, and with this trio I bathe, play tennis, and attempt to speak German.

At one point during this period, I get a telegram: my sister Ursula, age twenty, has in turn had to leave Germany and has arrived in Paris. I obtain permission for her to visit. She arrives, tells about the arrests of friends and increasing repression in Nazi Germany, and after two or three days returns to Paris, where I join her at the end of the vacation.

1933–1939

In October 1933 I enter HEC (Ecole des Hautes Etudes Commerciales), but continue to give lessons to Michel and Jacques. I lose touch with them as I continue my studies at the London School of Economics in 1935–36 and then move to Trieste, after a short engagement on the Republican side in the Spanish Civil War. I have no precise recollection of having seen the Dupuys after my return to Paris in the summer of 1938, when Mussolini's anti-Jewish decrees make me leave Italy.

June 1940

I am in the French Army, in a unit composed of German and Italian volunteers. Stationed in the Sarthe during the "phony war" (September 1939–April 1940), my company joins the rest of the French Army in its headlong, southward retreat. One night we manage to convince our commanding officer to issue to each of us military passes made out in fake names of French nationals (for we risk being shot as deserters by the Germans if we fall into their hands and they learn our real identity). I become Albert Hermant, *né à Philadelphie*—as I didn't want anyone to be able to check the birth registers in a French town. Our unit dissolves, I head to Bordeaux on a bicycle, the Germans catch up with me, but in their eagerness to reach the Spanish frontier as soon as possible, they no longer take individual prisoners and simply tell stragglers to register in any prisoner camp on the road to Bordeaux. Rather than doing that, I slip into the newly established "unoccupied zone" (Vichy France) and now the question arises where to go for a military discharge. At this point I recall the Cabouat family, actually the only non-Parisian French people I can think of. So I decide to make for Nîmes. The father of Jean-Pierre, a well-known doctor in town, remembers me from St.-Aubin-sur-mer and receives me very cordially (Jean-Pierre is still in the Army). I stay a night or two at the Cabouat house, then go to a military camp for discharge. I get the discharge papers all right, in my new name, but now have to get a civilian identity card. For this purpose, not having a proper birth certificate, I need witnesses who will vouch for me. The Cabouats volunteer to do this, and I obtain the prized *carte d'identité*. (Later on, in the sixties, when all the young people passed through "identity crises" à la Erikson, I would tell them: when I was twentyish I didn't have time to have an identity crisis, I had an identity *card* crisis.)

The Cabouats are also extraordinarily helpful in other ways. They

CARTE D'IDENTITÉ

...

⑦

4.317.=

Nom : *Hermant*

Prénoms : *albert*

Profession *Interprète*

11 Fevr. 1915

Philadelphie = (U.S.A.)

Département : *Pie*

Nationalité :

Domicile : *chez Mr le Docteur Cabouat*

à Nimes, 5 rue Démians. =

TIMBRE FISCAL

13 FRANCS

SIGNALEMENT

Taille :

Cheveux :

Moustache :

Yeux :

Signes particuliers :

Photo. =

Nez { Dos .... base

{ Dimensions :

Forme du visage :

Teint :

Empreinte digitale   Le Titulaire :   Les Témoins :

Albert Hermant   *J. Cabouat*
Y. Ferran

Vu pour Légalisation   **-6 JUIL 1940**

Le

Le Commissaire de Police

My French identity card of 1940, with the signature of Mme. Cabouat
as witness

introduce me to the curator of the local Natural History Museum, who, they thought, might be able to use me as an assistant cataloguer. With this bright prospect before me—the curator said he would try—I start to study seriously a textbook on paleontology (extremely boring), but soon I hear of friends (Henry Ehrmann in particular) having made their way to Marseille with the idea of finding their way *out*. I bid goodbye to the Cabouats and leave for Marseille, where my French identity card, with the Cabouat signature on it, is of the greatest help to me (especially in my work for Varian Fry) during the next six months, that is, until I leave France for the United States in December of 1940.

1945–1988

For some reason I never manage to reconnect with Michel and Jacques Dupuy, though I retain fond memories of their youthful élan and intelligence. After the war, on a trip to Paris, I inquire after them at the rue Médicis—the Dupuy family no longer lives there. During one summer, probably in the early seventies, Sarah and I drive to Dieppe by car and I insist on continuing to St.-Aubin, but I find that all the houses close to the coastline had been destroyed by the Germans during the war and replaced by bunkers. No trace of the Dupuys or Cabouats.

1980

I meet Annie Cot, a young economist who teaches at the University of Paris-I and is writing a dissertation on the "imperialist" attempts of some neoutilitarian economists (such as Gary Becker) to account for noneconomic phenomena (marriage, politics, crime, and so on) by means of the "economic approach."

1985

On the occasion of my lectures at the Collège de France, Pierre Bourdieu introduces me to Hubert Brochier, professor of economics at University of Paris-I.

September 1988

Hubert Brochier, Annie Cot's thesis adviser, invites me to join the jury that is to examine her and her dissertation, which has grown into a huge and, it turns out, very good Thèse d'Etat. I accept and we set the date of November 28, which fits in with my Berlin trip.

Annie Cot, I learn, has in the meantime married Jean-Noël Jean-neney, a modern historian who was recently named director of the Commission for the Commemoration of the Bicentennial of the Rev-olution. Through some literature about this organization that comes my way, I learn that Jean-Pierre Cabouat is in charge of its "foreign relations"! He has made a career in the diplomatic service, and was French Ambassador to Canada before assuming his present post, which is probably his last before retirement.

Sometime in September, I call Annie Cot, telling her about my in-terest in seeing Jean-Pierre. She arranges a luncheon for November 26.

November 26, 1988

Sarah and I, Annie Cot, Jean-Noël Jeanneney, Jean-Pierre Cabouat, and Ezra Suleiman,[1] a friend of Annie's, all meet for lunch in a fine Rive Gauche restaurant. Jean-Pierre, now about sixty-seven, looks very well. My account of what happened in Nîmes in 1940 obviously inter-ests him greatly. Both his parents have died. A street in Nîmes has been named "rue du docteur Cabouat," to honor his father's services to the city and his wartime Resistance record. I had brought along for Jean-Pierre a xerox copy of my 1940 carte d'identité, and show him the Cabouat signature, which I had always taken to be that of his father. But he has one look at it and declares with considerable firmness that it is his mother's; moreover, there is another signature right under-neath, which is that of a close woman friend of his mother's. He tells me that later during the war, when he and both his parents were active in the Resistance, she made something of a specialty of false signatures and documents—so she must have got started with my carte d'identité. Jean-Pierre is very taken with the whole story and is delighted that I brought a xerox copy for him. He remembers clearly the summer of 1933 (even though he was only twelve) and our German lessons, but has a particularly strong recollection of my sister—"she was beautiful, of course, but her dramatic, sudden arrival brought home to us young-

1. Professor of Politics, Princeton University.

sters for the first time that something extraordinary and threatening was happening in Germany." He tells me a bit about the lives and the careers of Michel and Jacques, geographer and diplomat, respectively, both retired. He gives me their telephone numbers, and his own. I hope to see him soon again and plan to call Michel and Jacques next time I am in Paris.

Jürgen Kuczynski

1925–1933

René and Bertha Kuczynski are close friends of my parents, as a result of an early friendship between Bertha and my mother. René is a famous statistician and demographer (inventor of the "net reproduction rate") and also a promoter of various pacifist causes and is therefore hated by the Nationalist Right. They have quite a few daughters and one son, Jürgen. On weekends we visit them with some frequency in their beautiful villa on the outskirts of Berlin, on a lake, the Schlachtensee. Here René has built himself a big, separate study, lined with books from floor to ceiling, formidably impressive to me. I do not recall whether he taught somewhere (as he was to do after 1933 at the London School of Economics) or simply led the life of a *Privatgelehrter* (a gentleman-scholar, living on a private income). Jürgen, who is eleven years my senior, is well on his way to a similar lifestyle when I start talking to him at around age fifteen or sixteen—he already has read everything that seems to me worth reading. One day he tells me, somewhat crushingly: "One has to read a book a day—it's not really hard once you set your mind to it."

In contrast to his father, who is the eternal maverick, Jürgen is at that time already a hardline Communist. His total certainties and the age difference make it a bit difficult for a youngster such as myself to enter into discussions with him—I was then beginning to be active in the Socialist (Social-Democratic) youth movement.

1935–1936

After graduation from HEC in Paris, I spend a year at the London School of Economics, with a fellowship from the International Student

Service. I have a great deal to catch up on in terms of modern economics in the effervescent LSE atmosphere. I "hang out" primarily with, and learn quite a bit from, fellow refugees such as Hans Landsberg and George Jaszi, who are full of excited anticipation for Keynes' forthcoming *General Theory*—it is published while I am at the London School and a huge line forms immediately at the LSE bookstore. I also drop in on the demography course given by René Kuczynski and am occasionally invited to family gatherings at which I see Jürgen. He is working on a statistical proof of Marx's immiserization theory. By combining the Indian and British wages over a long period he will be able to show, so he confidently and triumphantly expects, that the *average* of these wages (a British Empire wage index) did fall, even though *both* Indian and British wages have admittedly risen in real terms—it's all a matter of differences in absolute levels and weights!

1945

I am in the American Army in Italy. After the war's end, I travel to Paris and London on leave. In London I visit my mother, who had left Germany at the last minute in the summer of 1939, and whom I had not seen for some ten years. Again I meet with Jürgen, the last time for the next forty-three years: he is firm in predicting a postwar depression in the capitalist world and tells me of his desire to stop being an émigré and to go back to a Socialist Germany: "It will be good to be able to bang on the table once again!" He indeed returns quite soon—I believe in 1946—and becomes an important member of the East German economics establishment, from then on virtually *publishing* a book a year!

1984

Wolf Lepenies, the German sociologist who has spent three years at the Institute for Advanced Study in Princeton and returned in 1984 to Berlin to direct the recently founded Berlin Institute for Advanced Study, is trying to establish contacts with scholars in East Germany. One success he has had, so he tells me in correspondence, is in discussing possible collaborative projects with Jürgen Kuczynski, who, in the course of a wide-ranging conversation, told him about the long-standing friendship between our two families. Wolf sends along a xerox copy of a page from Jürgen's autobiography, in which Jürgen reveals that in 1933 my father made it possible for his father, who was on the immediate-arrest list of the Nazis after January, to hide for a short period in my father's Berlin clinic, pending arrangements for a clandestine escape from Germany.[2] Not only did I not know anything about this episode, but probably my father never told my mother, or she would have told me about it later. As my father died of cancer a few weeks later, and was already quite sick in February, I puzzle over what may have been his "last operation." Did the convergence of general political catastrophe and impending personal doom make him assume the risks involved?

Wolf Lepenies promises to arrange a meeting with Jürgen next time I am in Berlin.

1988

I have come to Berlin in connection with the honorary degree and, on Wolf's invitation, spend a few days prior to the event at the Berlin Institute. He has already been in touch with Jürgen and arranges for me to have a luncheon with him at the Institute on Thursday, December 1. In spite of a sudden cold spell combined with snow, Jürgen, who is 84, arrives on time—his wife is not well enough to make the trip. His features are so distinctive that there is absolutely no problem in recognizing him, even though he does show his age. He carries an envelope and, after greeting me with much cordiality, says immediately, "I have something for you," and pulls out a large mounted photograph of my father. The picture was taken by the noted Berlin photographer Gerty Simon, a friend of our family, in the late twenties or early thirties. I have long had a much smaller version of the same picture, but not this full-size portrait, with strong light accentuating equally his face and his hands resting on his thighs, as though to call attention to the surgeon's essential work instruments. The picture now reminds me more than ever of the verbal portrait Flaubert drew of his own father, a physician, in *Madame Bovary*, where the highly regarded Dr. Larivière is

2. Jürgen Kuczynski, *Memoiren*, 2nd ed. (Berlin: Aufbau, 1975), p. 244.

My father, Dr. Carl Hirschmann, in Berlin, around 1930

described as having "des mains charnues, de fort belles mains et qui n'avaient jamais de gants, comme pour être plus promptes à plonger dans les misères."[3]

Jürgen explains that the picture belonged to his parents and has been in his possession since they died in London some forty years ago. This is an auspicious beginning for our meeting over lunch. But it remains the high point of the encounter.

We talk about our respective sisters, then about what economists talk about when they meet, that is, about other economists. He also tells me about his most recent books. The one on which he dwells most is an incredible bestseller: *Dialog mit meinem Urenkel* (Dialogue with My Great-Grandson), 1984, which has sold 260,000 copies. It has also changed his life, as the book has resulted in innumerable invitations to discuss its contents with various groups of citizens all over the GDR. I ask him how he explains this phenomenal success and impact. With a twinkle in his eyes, he says: because it is critical. (As I write these lines, a copy of the book has just arrived from Berlin. To my untrained eye the criticism is hardly perceptible!)

Apart from this, I have the impression that he has become overly fond of telling obviously canned anecdotes about any person that is mentioned in the course of the conversation. A rather good one sticks in my mind: Walter Rathenau[4] and Jürgen's father René were both members of some commission in the immediate post–World War I period. René defended, as usual, a rather quixotic position and, at one point, Rathenau said: "It seems to me that Dr. Kuczynski has formed a one-man party and himself occupies a position on its far-left wing!"

Upon leaving, Jürgen promises to send me his latest books. I say I will do the same. I have in mind to send him *Shifting Involvements*—a notion he could use, or might have used.

---

3. "Brawny hands—very beautiful hands, and that never knew gloves, as though to be more ready to plunge into suffering." Transl. by Eleanor Marx Aveling (New York: Modern Library), p. 365.

4. Born in 1867, prominent industrialist and intellectual, member of Democratic party after 1918, appointed minister of foreign affairs in 1922, assassinated by extremists of the Right shortly thereafter.

Inge Franck (now Ingeborg Hunzinger)

1929–30

I am fourteen or fifteen. Peter Franck is my "best friend" in the Ob-
ersekunda (10th grade) at the Französische Gymnasium. His family
lives in a comfortable apartment full of typical paintings of his *paysagiste*
grandfather Philip Franck, in the western outskirts of Berlin, near the
Heerstrasse. The father is a well-known chemist, a professor at the
Technische Hochschule, and industrial consultant, who affects broad
intellectual interests. The mother—she is Jewish, the father is not—is
a warm and outgoing person. Peter has two sisters and a much younger
brother. The older sister, Inge, is about my age (Peter is twenty months
my senior). I make frequent visits to the house, from which we stroll
to the neighboring woods, first with Peter and friends, then increasingly
with Inge alone—soon she is my first love. She is strong-willed, sturdy,
yet tender. We exchange letters, we pine—then, soon, fall out of it all.
We remain friends.

1933

I leave Germany. Peter stays and is soon arrested and sent to a concentration camp for anti-Nazi activities, gets out (presumably through intervention of his well-connected father), leaves for Switzerland, and
eventually comes to the United States. From Paris I write a letter to
Inge—I remember apologizing for not having written before and then
her prescient, astringent reply: "I believe you will always be pressed for
time."

1941

In January I arrive in the United States from France and, after a quite
brief stay in New York, move to Berkeley, California, nominally to
work, under a Rockefeller fellowship, on a research project headed by
John B. Condliffe, professor of international economics at the University, for whom I had done some research in Paris in 1938–39 and who
had recommended me for the fellowship. Actually I settle down to write
my *National Power and the Structure of Foreign Trade,* which I finish
just as I am called to join yet another army, that of the United States

(early 1943). Peter Franck is a graduate student in economics at Berkeley. Our relationship is not what it once was, and it becomes increasingly thin over the years, but we keep in some touch. His family, including his Jewish mother, survived the war in Germany, and his parents and two sisters settle in the Eastern zone of Berlin at the war's end—only his younger brother chooses the West.

1975–1987

On a few short trips to Berlin (West) I make no effort to reconnect with Inge. From the annual letters about family events that Peter's wife Dorothea (recently deceased) sends around at Christmas time, I learn that Inge has become a well-known sculptor. In 1986 I hear that she has visited my sisters Ursula and Eva in Rome, and that they liked her.

1988

Having got Inge's address from Peter, I ask the authorities at the Free University to invite her to the ceremony at which I shall receive the honorary doctor's degree. Once in Berlin I telephone her and ask her to bring along some pictures of her work. She promises to do so.

On December 3 I meet Inge briefly in the morning before the start of the ceremony, but later ask that she be seated next to me during the festive lunch at the Chalet Suisse in the middle of the Grunewald. We talk and slowly the traits of the young woman I knew reemerge: her strong and steady gaze, her sharp chin, her chubby build. She tells me how she left Germany for Italy in 1942–43, when her father told her and her sister that they had better leave the house—his connections, he said, would barely enable him to protect his wife, but probably not his daughters. So she went to Florence, where she had earlier decided to become a sculptor after seeing Michelangelo. Later she met and married a German artist by the name of Hunzinger; they have two daughters who have both managed to move West, one after having been imprisoned several months for subversion in the GDR. She and her husband went back to the East after the war, hoping to participate in the construction of an ideal socialist society. After ten years she separated from her husband and at this point seems quite disenchanted with the GDR as well.

After the long lunch, Sarah and I return with Inge to our room in the Wissenschaftskolleg (Berlin Institute for Advanced Study). There Inge shows us the photos of her sculptures she has brought along. They are quite strong, original, moving. Most are larger-than-life, allegorical figures meant for some public spaces in squares, hospitals, and the like. She tells (and shows) how she goes to some quarries in Hungary, cuts out some huge chunks of stone, begins to work on them on the spot, and eventually loads them into railroad cars to finish them at home. It is more difficult to evaluate sculpture from photographs than two-dimensional art: but clearly she has not only talent but a remarkably strong vision and sense of mission.

It is already dark when Inge calls for a taxi that will take her to an S-Bahn station on her way back to East Berlin. The whole afternoon has passed, and I feel we are friends again (which is very different from "just friends").

Alfred Blumenfeld

1928–1932

Alfred Blumenfeld joins my class in the Französische Gymnasium in the Untersekunda (9th grade), and we stay together until our graduation in March 1932. He comes from the Baltic region; his family circumstances are a bit mysterious; his father lives in Leningrad; Alfred himself is fluent in Russian and speaks German with a slight accent. In spite of his name, he is not Jewish—it appears that in the Baltic region many non-Jews have Jewish-sounding names. Alfred and I become quite friendly during the last two years, in a rather specialized way: we never talk seriously about politics or Nietzsche or capitalism or other such matters that I discuss intensely with Peter Franck and a number of others, but I am attracted to Alfred by his sense of humor and general "lightness," to use Kundera's term. For example, during our last year a number of us endlessly practice a game of which Alfred is the insti-gator *and* obvious champion, namely, how we would come to the prin-cipal's podium on the day of the Abitur-award ceremony and stumble badly in the process—the point is almost to fall, but not quite. Even though he is older than the average age of our classmates and I am quite a bit younger, the two of us have a wonderful time together making fun of our teachers, of one another, and even of contemporary politics, as when one of us, as ringleader, calls out aloud, during intermission in school, the first line of the poem "Erlkönig":[5] "Wer reitet so spät durch Nacht und Wind?"

Instead of answering "Es ist der Vater mit seinem Kind," the rest of the class (most of it anyway) chants an invented line mocking the currently surging racism: "Natürlich wieder die Juden!" (Once again the Jews, of course!)

Everybody roars with laughter. The year is 1931–32.

1988

Is this really Alfred Blumenfeld? A rather nondescript, elderly, round-faced gentleman in a dark suit, walking a wee bit insecurely, appears on December 3 in the hall where the honorary degree ceremony is to take place. I had planned to meet him in September in Bonn where he now lives in retirement from the West German Foreign Service—I spent two days visiting Köln-Bonn prior to a conference I attended at the University of Bielefeld. But he was scheduled at precisely that time to "take the waters" at some spa elsewhere in Germany, having assured me on the phone that this was most important for the somewhat shaky state of his health. He then said he would like to come to Berlin for the occasion of the degree, and I asked the Free University to send him an invitation. Here he is and we meet again after fifty-six years. He introduces his wife.

After the ceremony we move to the Chalet Suisse for lunch, where he is seated next to me. But with Inge on the other side, most of my conversation is with her. He tells me at one point that, as the oldest friend of mine present, he has been asked to say a few words at the end of the meal. He does it very simply and nicely, addressing me as "lieber Otto-Albert." I reply briefly, thanking him for resurrecting the old Otto-Albert and explaining how it came about that I switched around my two first names and how I lost an 'n' from my surname during the war upon being naturalized as a U.S. citizen in the Army. We have

5. Famous ballad by Goethe, set to music as a similarly well-known Lied by Schubert.

rather warmed up to each other and arrange to meet on the following evening at his hotel, an hour or so prior to the dinner party at the home of Dr. Velder, the current principal of the Französische Gymnasium.

Next day I sit with Alfred alone—his wife, whom I rather liked, stays discreetly away. He tells me about his life. Part of it I know, not as a result of direct communication, but because I had heard about him through common acquaintances and through my sisters in Rome, where he had been on a visit a few years back. He had studied economics in the thirties, and joined the Foreign Service after the war, and in the fifties spent quite a few years in Paris with the Marshall Plan organization (OEEC). He then returned to the Foreign Service and ended his career as German General Consul in Leningrad. Apparently he remains rather active in retirement, collaborating with the German equivalent of our Council on Foreign Relations located in Bonn.

But what about the dark years? He is anxious to tell me about them. First of all, it turned out that his father, who moved from Leningrad to Berlin in the thirties, was Jewish after all (not his mother); he had been able to get false papers to hide his origin, yet the family lived in the fear of being found out (they were not). As for Alfred, he puts his knowledge of Russian to good use: at the end of his economics studies and long before the outbreak of the war he lets himself be recruited by the German intelligence service and takes advantage of this "essential" work to escape from military obligations. "I was not a hero, I'll freely admit, but in terrible times there is also need for *débrouillards*."[6] This is clearly a formula he has used quite a few times before. I am reminded of the plea of Galileo in Brecht's play: "Woe to the country that *needs* heroes!" It is an effective excuse, but to take the argument one step further and to affirm the positive need for débrouillards is perhaps taking it too far?

6. French term for someone who knows how to slip through the net, evade controls, and generally take care of himself.

7
chapter

My Father and Weltanschauung, circa 1928

I lived in Berlin from 1915, the year of my birth, until I emigrated to France in 1933, and I wish to tell you a story from that early period. It must have happened when I was perhaps twelve or thirteen years old, so it took place some time in the late twenties. Those were relatively tranquil times, and I was not yet politicized—though it was soon to happen, under the impact of the Depression and the rise of the Nazis in the early thirties—but I began in those years to ask myself various philosophical and semi-religious questions. At the time, my relationship with my father was good and trusting, and that with my older sister Ursula was becoming very close and would remain so throughout our adolescence and youth. My father's life was fully devoted to his profession (he was a surgeon), but he always made time to talk to us. He had a questioning and skeptical mind, but lacked the defense of irony so that I recall him as a bit melancholy and occasionally even perplexed. One day we had a conversation where I must have asked him questions to which he frankly avowed he had no answers. I cannot remember at all the nature of my questions, but distinctly recall running to the other end of our apartment to report everything to my sister and to exclaim: "Weisst Du was? Vati hat keine Weltanschauung!" (You know what? Daddy has no world view!)

From a talk given in early December 1988, upon receiving a honorary degree on the occasion of the 40th anniversary of the founding of the Free University of Berlin.

Why do I remember this not particularly brilliant observation of mine so well? Is it because, perhaps for the first time, I felt that I would do better than my father: I surely would not be caught lacking a Weltanschauung by the time *I* was a grownup! Or is it rather because the moment I spoke I felt that it was *my* indignation and my statement that were ridiculous—after all, we remember best those mortifying moments in which we blunder, stumble, or make ourselves otherwise ridiculous. Finally it is possible that I remember this moment—including its spatial attributes—so clearly because it encapsulates and portends a problem that was to remain with me for the rest of my life—to the point where I am just now, over half a century later, writing an essay on whether it is good or bad to be outfitted at all times with a complete set of firm opinions. Believe it or not, I intend to present it at the next annual meeting of the American Economic Association.

Frankly, I have no idea how these ideas will be received by an audience of American economists. But I hope that this audience will have some empathy with the problem to be discussed. I am inquiring, after all, into the micro-foundations of a democratic society, into the constitution of the democratic, rather than of Adorno's authoritarian, personality. To foster the development of that kind of personality was presumably a principal objective of the founding of this university forty years ago. Normally, this sort of ultimate objective is like happiness in that it eludes a direct quest; it can only be obtained as a *by-product* of activities whose proclaimed and conscious aims are quite extraneous to that objective. But once every forty years it may be legitimate to try a direct stab.[1]

1. See Chapter 4 for the rest of this talk.

8
chapter

Studies in Paris, 1933–1935

How It Happened That I Did *Not* Study at Sciences Po

To a considerable extent today's honor must have the same significance for all three of us: it simply gives us enormous pleasure that our work and perhaps certain aspects of our lives are recognized by this major social science center of a country for which we have strong and long-standing feelings of affection. But in addition to these general emotions, I can lay claim to a personal, intimate satisfaction in terms of the particular shape of my life—and this is a story I wish to share briefly with you.

In January 1933, when Hitler came to power in Germany, I was seventeen years old. A few months earlier I had finished my secondary studies at the Lycée Français of Berlin. The knowledge of French and a good dose of francophilia I had picked up at this Lycée and during a brief trip to Paris in the late twenties made me decide on France as the land of asylum. I arrived in Paris at the beginning of April 1933. I had just begun to follow some courses in political economy at the University of Berlin and was anxious to continue my studies along those lines even though, at the time, the study of economics—as distinct from law and medicine—was widely considered a "brotlose Kunst" (breadless art).

One of my first purchases in Paris was at the Librairie Gibert on

Talk given at the Institute of Political Studies of the University of Paris in April 1989, upon receiving an honorary degree together with Henry Ehrmann and Sergio Romano.

Boulevard Saint-Michel: I acquired *Le livret de l'étudiant,* a fat volume with information on the many educational establishments of the capital. In this impressive compendium one institution immediately stood out for me as exceptionally attractive; you have guessed it, it was the then Ecole Libre des Sciences Politiques, universally known as "Sciences Po." Its curriculum had just the right balance, it seemed to me, of economics and politics, analytical and historical-philosophical topics.

During my first weeks and months in Paris, I worked hard at establishing contacts with French families and society. I had left Berlin armed with a few letters of introduction. Among them was one written by a close friend of our family, who was also a well-known pediatrician, Dr. Ulrich Friedemann. He gave me a note for a famous Paris colleague, Dr. Robert Debré. I knew that Dr. Debré was a formidable personality and waited a while before approaching him. By the time I got up my courage, probably in May/June 1933, the question of where to continue my studies was uppermost in my mind. I called him up, presented my modest credentials, and asked for an interview; to my surprise I met with instant success, and an appointment was made.

I still remember the fine bourgeois villa—I believe it was a house with two or three floors, somewhere on the Left Bank—where I was received by an impressive bearded gentleman. He seemed to take a real interest in my story—at the time I did not know about his own Jewish background, which he has explored so sensitively in his fine (and nicely entitled) autobiography, *L'honneur de vivre* (1974). Eventually I brought the conversation to the question of my education, mentioning my special interest in Sciences Po. There he interposed, "I am not too familiar with the various options you might have, but it so happens that my son Michel has recently entered Sciences Po and he should be able to give you the right kind of advice. He is at home, I believe, and I'll ask him to talk with you."

That is how I met the young Michel Debré.[1] He too listened attentively to my story, but soon began to express doubts about Sciences Po being the right place for me, even assuming I could get in (which was by no means certain). The school, he pointed out, was meant primarily

1. Michel Debré joined de Gaulle's Free French movement during World War II and held a number of high-level positions in the postwar period, including that of prime minister from 1959 to 1962. He also was responsible for the postwar reorganization of Sciences Po.

for young Frenchmen planning careers in government, diplomacy, or public administration. There were some foreign students, but they were nationals of countries to which they would *return* to pursue public service careers. Would it not be more reasonable for me, a refugee without a country of my own, to orient myself in the direction of private economic activity? Under the circumstances Michel Debré—at twenty-one only three years older than I, but who already spoke with remarkable authority—advised me to look into the possibility of pursuing my studies at the Ecole des Hautes Etudes Commerciales (known as HEC), another "grande école" with an excellent reputation. Even though a business career was not at all what I had in mind in those days—not long before, in Berlin, I had been active in the Socialist Youth Movement and had followed with considerable interest a course in Hegel's phenomenology—I had to admit that the advice I was being given was eminently reasonable. In due course I followed it and entered HEC in the fall of that year.

Two years of intensive studies followed, and I managed to convince myself that I had made the right choice. Yet every time I came close to the rue Saint-Guillaume[2] in those years, I experienced strong feelings of regret, made even stronger by the fact that some of my best teachers at HEC—Professor Basdevant in Private International Law and Monsieur Pomméry in Money and Banking—had their permanent appointments at Sciences Po.

You will now understand why today's ceremony has a special, sweet flavor for me—sweet as only revenge can be. After fifty-six years and a number of most unlikely detours, the doors of Sciences Po have finally swung open for me—a fairy tale come true! My heartfelt thanks for this happy end.

Studies at HEC and the Importance of Economic Geography[3]

Although in the long run I did not follow young Michel Debré's advice to pursue a career in the practical and private world of business, I did enroll at HEC and spent two exhausting years there. I had a lot of

2. Location of Sciences Po in Paris.
3. From a talk given at the University of Paris IX–Nanterre, in May 1993, upon receiving an honorary degree.

courses in accounting and in something called technology, which was about various sequences of industrial operations invariably starting, I seem to recall, with *concassage* (crushing). Among the economics courses, the most interesting by far were the brilliant lectures in economic geography given by Professor Albert Demangeon, an eminent authority in that field, which was a well-established one in France. Here we learnt a great deal about the location of economic activities and its determinants, the economic importance of rivers and natural resources for industrial development, and shifts in the flow of commerce between regions (I recall a superb lecture entitled "la concurrence entre Anvers et Rotterdam"). The lively green, brown, and blue colors of the geographical maps he displayed enhanced the effectiveness of his teaching.

Later, when reflecting about the origin of my thinking on economic development, I realized that this early schooling in physical geographic concreteness is probably at the bottom of my later refusal to explain growth and development exclusively through macroeconomic aggregates, such as savings, investment, income, and capital-output ratios. These sorts of models seemed to me too abstract, too mechanical, and sadly lacking in the kind of drama that Professor Demangeon had been able to impart to his lectures. To be sure, I must not forget the immediate background of my *Strategy of Economic Development*. The book was written right after I had lived for almost five years in Colombia, starting early in 1952. In the many discussions I had with that country's policy makers and entrepreneurs, I learned much about the way industrial and infrastructure investment decisions were taken and how they moved up and down the Colombian territory, with its striking topography and distinct development poles, to use the language of François Perroux. Perhaps it was the interaction of the Colombian experience of the fifties with the still live Parisian memories of the thirties that made me hit on the notion of backward and forward linkages as an important force in the dynamics of the development process.

It was a generalization or theory of the "middle range," as Robert Merton has called it. In dealing with the multiple and complex problems of development we have learnt that we must fashion generalizations at all kinds of ranges and be deaf, like Ulysses, to the seductive chant of the unique paradigm.

9
chapter

Doubt and Antifascist Action
in Italy, 1936–1938

The honor that is conferred on me today moves me deeply, because it makes me think of the familial, personal, intellectual, and sentimental ties I have with Italy. The strength of these ties is in fact surprising, considering the rather short periods I actually lived here continuously: close to two years in 1936–38 in Trieste, as a refugee from Nazi Germany, and then a comparable stretch of time during the war, this time as a brand new American citizen and soldier with the U.S. Army. Later, of course, I had a strong professional connection with Italy, when I became a so-called expert on that country in Washington during the period of the Marshall Plan. But my basic Italian experience dates back to that first prewar period, and it is this episode I wish to recall briefly.

In spite of the urgings of various friends, I have not been given to the autobiographical genre—I tend to think of it as the ultimate admission to having run out of ideas. There is, however, an exception: when the autobiographical exercise serves the purpose of *recovering* an idea. This is what I want to do here.

Looking back I can now easily see that my Italian experience of 1936–38 was important for my future development in several ways. In the practical realm, I gained the minimum amount of self-confidence everyone needs to get through life at all. I had my first scientific article published (in the *Giornale degli Economisti,* on a fine point of demo-

---

Talk given at the University of Turin, in October 1987, upon receiving an honorary degree.

graphic statistics). More important, I acquired a nicely limited area of competence: the Italian economy. I had come to Italy from France and had been asked by a Paris publication to send in, on a trial basis, some reports on the Italian economic situation. At the time, the Mussolini regime began increasingly to restrict the publication of official economic statistics, so that it took some attentive reading of what did get published and of the daily financial press *(Il Sole, Ventiquattro Ore)* to figure out what was going on with industrial production, real wages, the budget, foreign trade, foreign exchange reserves, and so on. I enjoyed the detective work involved, and whatever success I could claim in outwitting the Fascist authorities. Back in Paris in mid–1938, I was able to establish myself as an expert on the Italian economy, writing quarterly reports on it for a newly founded Institute of Economic and Social Research directed by Charles Rist and Robert Marjolin. Not only had I acquired a métier of sorts; it was a great relief to realize that one could do tolerably competent work in economics without having to resolve whether Keynes, whose *General Theory* I had bought in London in the year of its publication (1936) and then taken along to Italy for study, had all the right answers.

Actually, this experience fitted well with another of a more fundamental nature, which came to me through the example of my brother-in-law and friend, Eugenio Colorni. He lived in Trieste at this time, and we saw each other almost daily. (Colorni was imprisoned in 1938 and killed in 1944.) He and some of his friends were strongly committed anti-Fascists. Yet they were not rigidly tied to any ideology and were far from professing to have all the answers to the economic, social, and political issues of the time. Moreover, they did not seem to be particularly unhappy or bothered by this situation. By 1937, at age twenty-two, I had myself lost some of my earlier certainties, but, with my German upbringing, I still sensed it as a real defect not to have a full-fledged Weltanschauung. Colorni, who was six years older than I, seemed on the contrary to cultivate and relish an intellectual style that took nothing for granted except his doubts. At the same time, he and his friends held fast to one certainty: they were firmly committed to opposing the Fascist regime.

What was fascinating to me was that there was an intimate connection between the intellectual posture emphasizing a lack of firm ideological commitment and the commitment to perilous political action. It was precisely the questioning and exploratory style with which Colorni and his friends were approaching philosophical, psychological, and social issues that impelled them to action in situations where freedom of thought was suppressed, or where they felt that injustice was obvious and stupidity intolerable. It was almost as though they set out to prove Hamlet wrong: they were intent on showing that doubt could *motivate* action instead of undermining and enervating it. Moreover, engagement in highly risky action was seen by them not at all as a price to be paid for the freedom of inquiry they were practicing; it was its natural, spontaneous, almost joyful counterpart.

Their attitude has always seemed admirable to me as a view of political action and as a way of conjoining the private and the public life. If I had time, I would argue that we all can still learn from it. For this sort of combination of participation in public affairs with intellectual openness seems to me the ideal micro-foundation of a democratic politics.

10
chapter

With Varian Fry in Marseilles, 1940

As I return in my mind to Varian Fry and to the Marseilles days from July to December 1940 when I worked for him, I am struck by how sharply he and those faraway events stand out in my memory. One reason is, of course, the story itself, so vividly told in this book. Written down in its essentials as soon as Fry returned from France to the United States in 1941, it retains the flavor of immediate reporting. To the readers of the book it will be obvious that there was nothing routine about being associated with Fry and his Centre Américain de Secours. The work was extraordinarily absorbing and often dangerous—and being in danger is always exciting as well as highly memorable.

Moreover, when the story is viewed in its historical context, it looks wholly *improbable*. It starts in June 1940, when the German Army overran France and thus came to rule most of the European continent, from Poland to the Pyrénées. The newly installed French government

---

Introduction to Varian Fry, *Assignment: Rescue—an Autobiography* (New York: Scholastic, 1993). The first edition of this book was published in 1968, after Fry had revised and somewhat shortened, just before his death in 1967, his original account, written upon his return from Marseilles in 1941 and entitled *Surrender on Demand* (New York: Random House, 1945). I appear in the book as Albert Hermant, my assumed French name in 1940 (see Chapter 6), or as "Beamish," a name given to me by Fry. The Scholastic edition was reprinted on the occasion of the special exhibition, "Varian Fry in Marseilles, 1940–1941," shown in 1993–1995 at the newly inaugurated United States Holocaust Memorial Museum in Washington, D.C. The museum and Scholastic asked me to write an introduction to the new edition, which is reprinted here.

under Marshal Pétain had signed an abject armistice with Hitler. Article 19 of that document committed the French government to deliver to the Germans any non-French citizen living on French soil whom the Germans happened to request. Even before the Holocaust, the Nazis, once in power, were intent on systematically capturing and murdering their most prominent and hated opponents, Jews and non-Jews. Now they had trapped large numbers of these opponents, who had earlier escaped from Germany, in France. Was it conceivable that one American citizen, newly arrived from the United States, with just a list of names in his pocket, would alone be able to keep Article 19 from being carried out with the utmost vigor and dispatch? The playing field was so uneven as to make the prospect of success seem laughable. Yet we now know that Fry and his Committee actually saved the lives of some two to three thousand people. So, on looking back, the Fry story almost brings to mind the successful fight of David against Goliath, or the Greek myth that pits crafty Ulysses against the huge Cyclops.

It must not be forgotten, of course, that we experienced serious and tragic failures (all described here): the suicide of Walter Benjamin, the extradition of Breitscheid and Hilferding[1] to Nazi Germany, where they would be murdered, and the miscarriage of early schemes to evacuate our "clients" by boat to North Africa. I remember Varian's reaction to such setbacks. He went through moments of deep despair, which belied the cool exterior he cultivated.

In general, Fry's personality is another unforgettable part of the story. While it comes through here and there in the book, he was like many authors who believe in concealing their emotions. His was a complex character, thoroughly engaging yet full of contradictions. It was endlessly fascinating to try to figure him out. I still remember that when I used to leave the Committee's offices in the evenings, with Miriam Davenport or with Hans Sahl, Fry would invariably be our immediate topic of conversation.[2] There was in him a delightful mixture of earnest resolve and of wit, of methodical, almost formal demeanor and of playfulness. His sartorial elegance (his hallmark was a striped dark suit with bow tie), together with his poker face, were tremendous assets to him

1. Prominent officials of the Social-Democratic Party during the Weimar Republic.
2. Miriam Davenport and Hans Sahl are important characters in Fry's book.

in dealing with the authorities. The whole operation, from the early days in his room at the Hotel Splendide to the setting up of a well-run regular office with its bureaucratic routine, all of this in the teeth of the French police, and increasingly, as time went on, of the Gestapo, was an act of sheer defiance—how did he get away with it for as long as he did?

I should confess here that I and the other Europeans on the Committee occasionally criticized him for being a "typical American," an "innocent abroad." But we had it all wrong. That seeming innocence turned out to be precisely his strength. Had he known from the outset the odds he was up against, he might never have achieved what he did. And in a way he *knew* about this hidden strength of his, and enjoyed the part he played; for, in addition to his other qualities, he was an accomplished actor.

For many years after the war, the staggering achievements of Varian Fry were largely unrecognized in his own country. His death in 1967 (he was only fifty-nine) went almost unnoticed, except for close friends and family. Belatedly, he is now honored for what he was: "a hero for our time."

11
chapter

Escaping over the Pyrenees, 1940–41

The European honorary degrees I have received in recent years form an interesting pattern: they retrace, with remarkable fidelity, my largely involuntary wanderings during the eight long, difficult, and adventurous years from 1933 to 1941, from my native Berlin to France, from there to Italy, back to France, and then, via Spain and Portugal, to America.

It is perhaps because of this emergent pattern that I wrote, for each of those occasions, a brief autobiographical memoir relating to the period which I had spent in the respective location. Once put together, they may yield a composite picture.

Let me briefly recall the previous occasions. From my birth in 1915 to my emigration in 1933 I lived in Berlin, and when the Freie Universität of that city bestowed an honorary degree on me some five years ago, I told a story from my childhood or early adolescence—how I found out to my intense surprise and disappointment that my father did not have what I then thought was a basic necessity for any real person: a Weltanschauung! The subsequent history of my life and thought could probably be written in terms of the progressive discovery on my part of how right my father had been.

After moving from Berlin to Paris in 1933, I had trouble making up

Talk given at the University of Coimbra (Portugal) in April 1993, upon receiving an honorary degree.

my mind how to resume my studies which I had barely started in Berlin. In particular, I hesitated between the Ecole des Sciences Politiques (Sciences Po) and the Ecole des Hautes Etudes Commerciales (HEC) and eventually chose HEC. When Sciences Po decided to give me an honorary degree in 1989, I told the story behind that choice. Through a series of improbable events, I encountered, early in 1933, the young Michel Debré, later to become Prime Minister under de Gaulle. He was then himself beginning his studies at Sciences Po, but in view of my condition as a refugee he advised me strongly to go to HEC, a school that would prepare me for the private rather than the public life. Upon receiving subsequently an honorary degree from the University of Nanterre (Paris-IX), I returned in my mind to the studies at HEC and described how they had influenced and helped me evolve a point of view of my own when, much later, I met with the problems of economic development and industrialization in Latin America.

My next stop in the thirties was Italy. I went to Trieste from Paris in 1936 and stayed for two years, continuing my studies and lending on occasion a helping hand to my Italian brother-in-law Eugenio Colorni who, besides teaching philosophy, was an active anti-Fascist. So when the University of Torino gave me a doctoral degree in 1987, I told the story of my Italian sojourn in 1936–38 and how I admired my brother-in-law and his friends because they combined political activism with a continuing *search* for truth. Unlike so many other activists, they were anything but convinced that they had all the answers, in politics or elsewhere.

And now Coimbra and Portugal, and a story about the way your country or, more broadly, the Iberian peninsula has touched my life. That story takes me back to one of the most somber periods of our somber century, the second half of 1940, after France had collapsed and Hitler's armies ruled much of Europe. During that period, after having been discharged from the French Army, fortunately under an assumed French identity, I ended up in Marseilles and became a principal assistant to Varian Fry, a remarkable young American who had just arrived from New York with the mission to help in the emigration to the United States of the most immediately endangered anti-Nazi and anti-Fascist refugees in non-occupied France: prominent writers, artists, journalists, and political activists.

My work for Varian Fry and the committee he set up in Marseilles involved a number of activities that aroused—understandably, I might add—the suspicions of the police of the Vichy regime. As a result, I decided in December 1940 that the time had come for myself to leave by one of the escape routes I had helped set up. That route went through Spain and Portugal, for individuals who had been granted transit visas by the consular authorities of these two countries. As quite a few others had done, I had obtained such transit visas on the basis of an emergency visa permitting me to immigrate into the United States. The difficulty was that the Vichy French would not issue any exit visas to foreigners living in France. It was therefore necessary to leave France illegally by walking over the Pyrenees Mountains, avoiding Cerbères, the French border town near the Spanish border, and then to proceed immediately to Port-Bou, the first town on the other side, from which one could make a *legal* entry into Spain.

I well remember leaving the French Mediterranean port of Banyuls, a few miles from Cerbères, on a crisp morning on December 20, 1940, with two other refugees. We were helped initially by a guide who took us on a path up the mountains. After one or two hours our guide said he could not accompany us any further, indicating the direction we should follow. So we wandered on and eventually a town appeared below, on the Mediterranean coast. Was this Spain or still France? We were not sure and asked a cowherd whom we met along the way. He reassured us that we were already in Spain and that the town was indeed Port-Bou, our goal. Relieved and grateful, I reached into my pocket for a *propina* (tip), but he totally rebuffed me. I still remember his proud words: "Yo cuido mis vacas" (I am guarding my cows).

This was to be symbolic of the many kindnesses I received during the next few days from the people in Spain, and Portugal. I passed rapidly through Spain which had just emerged from the long and murderous Civil War. Its many traces contrasted with the then almost exasperating neatness of Portugal. Upon arriving in Lisbon I was also struck by the relative abundance of food in comparison to Marseilles, where numerous wartime shortages had begun to appear. Otherwise I must confess that my memory of the ten days I spent in Lisbon is remarkably blank. The reason is simple: I was impatiently waiting for the next boat that was to take me to the other side of the Atlantic, to New York. There is nothing quite as blank as the memory of the time that is passed just waiting.

12
chapter

A Hidden Ambition

In 1966, when I delivered the manuscript of *Development Projects Observed* to the Brookings Institution, I felt the relief and satisfaction we experience on that kind of occasion with more than the usual intensity. The reason was that, at least in my more exalted moments, I saw this book as the final volume of a trilogy: in *The Strategy of Economic Development* (1958) I had attempted to understand some basic processes making for economic progress in the developing countries; the corresponding political processes were then explored in *Journeys Toward Progress* (1963); and, after having concentrated in these two books on the macro aspects of development, my attention shifted in the present volume to the analysis of individual development projects, those "privileged particles of the development process"[1] dealing with the construction and maintenance of highways, of electric power stations, of irrigation schemes, and similar specific investment activities.

These three books were also held together by another progression: *Strategy* was based almost entirely on my experiences in Colombia where I had lived from 1952 to 1956; to write *Journeys* I returned to Colombia but also studied other Latin American countries, particularly Brazil and Chile; with *Development Projects Observed* I extended my range from Latin America (where I visited World Bank financed pro-

---

New preface (1994) to *Development Projects Observed* (Washington: Brookings, 1967).
1. *Development Projects Observed*, p. 1.

jects in El Salvador, Ecuador, Peru, and Uruguay) to Southern Europe (Italy) and to some major countries of Asia (India, Pakistan, Thailand) and Africa (Nigeria, Ethiopia).

The three books were of course conceived consecutively. The concept—or fantasy—of a unified "trilogy" emerged in my mind primarily during the writing of the third book. Over and above the overt purpose of my work—the analysis of development and the advice on policy—I came to see it as having the latent, hidden, but overriding common intent and function: to celebrate, to "sing" the epic adventure of development—its challenge, drama, and grandeur.

The subject matter of the book lent itself particularly well to this hidden ambition. While visiting the projects and talking to their administrators and other interested parties, I collected so many fascinating stories that storytelling came at times to overshadow analysis. At the same time there was, as one might expect, a tension between the overt task and the concealed ambition of my writing, a tension that became particularly apparent in the case of the *Development Projects* book. At a certain level the ex-ante choice among investment projects and the ex-post evaluation of success or failure deal with matters that should permit straightforward technical treatment. Moreover, when I wrote this book in the middle sixties, the scientific determination of correct investment choices seemed to be within reach. In the U.S. Department of Defense, under the leadership of Robert McNamara and his "Whiz Kids," much was made of new methods of allocating available funds to various purposes. These methods were given a technocratic aura by the use of an acronym, PPBS (Planning, Programming, and Budgeting System), that soon acquired considerable prestige. In the World Bank, investment choices and decisions were similarly expected to be made more rational through various devices known as "shadow prices," "social benefit-cost analysis," and other sophisticated new techniques. In this intellectual atmosphere, it was to act as something of a spoilsport to call attention to very different, and much more problematic levels of concern about projects: to speculate, for example, about the question of road versus rail construction in the light of interethnic conflict in Nigeria (where a savage civil war, pitting Ibos against non-Ibos, broke out in 1967) or about the conceivable impact of an irrigation scheme on the pursuit of land reform in Peru.

I will admit that to give pride of place to "The Principle of the Hiding Hand," the most speculative chapter of the book, was close to a provocation. Nothing could be less "operationally useful"—a term much used at the time within the Bank—than to be told that underestimating the costs or difficulties of a project has on occasion been helpful in eliciting creative energies that otherwise might never have been forthcoming. The stories told in this first chapter of the book were of course not meant to hold any immediately applicable, "practical" lesson. Yet they did have a purpose closely connected with my hidden agenda: to endow and surround the development story with a sense of wonder and mystery that would reveal it to have much in common with the highest quests ever undertaken by humankind.

That first chapter was actually meant to function as a prologue, somewhat removed from the rest of the book. The subsequent chapters deal with more mundane aspects of construction and operation of projects, and here I do come forward, particularly in the chapters on "Uncertainties" and on "Latitudes and Disciplines," with a number of useful hints, suggestions, and propositions. Many of my generalizations about the behavior of development projects have their origin in the peculiar lenses I had formed in the course of my previous writing on development. For example, the concept of "latitude for poor performance" had played a considerable role in *Strategy*. In chapter 8 of that book, I suggested that less developed countries may have a comparative advantage in tasks—such as the running of airlines—where this latitude is narrow, rather than in tasks—such as the building and maintenance of highways—where latitude is wide. In the latter tasks, developing countries would tend to gravitate toward the poor end of the performance scale in contrast to situations where the nature of the task would oblige them to do well.

This basic idea helped to cast light on various aspects of the projects I studied. Projects whose latitude is limited by being "site-bound" or whose construction is "time-bound" were duly shown to have a number of advantages over those that do not exhibit these characteristics. Parenthetically, I may note here that time-boundedness and narrow latitude for performance in general are close relatives of the "just-in-time" technique that has become well known as a key feature of Japanese industrial production methods.

Fortunately, the book is not limited to "applying" ideas already laid out in *Strategy*. Although I did not say so—for the good reason that I did not become aware of it—I encountered in some of the projects I studied the limits of the validity and applicability of the theorem that laid down the rule "the less latitude the better." This rule had been developed primarily with regard to technology. As I put it later, "a certain type of capital-intensive, advanced technology could be more appropriate, in a country with little industrial tradition, than . . . labor-intensive technology and 'idiot-proof' machinery."[2] But in *Development Projects* I looked beyond technology, at the social and cultural environment in which development projects come to be embedded. In the process I realized that it may not always be possible to effect a radical transformation of this environment by the mere injection of some development project that requires such a transformation in order to succeed.

In chapter 4 I distinguished therefore between projects that are "trait-taking" and others that are "trait-making," in analogy to price theory where the distinction between price-taking (in competition) and price-making (in conditions of monopoly or oligopoly) had long played an important role. Trait-taking stood for situations where a project fits easily into a given social and cultural structure and does not attempt to modify it, whereas a trait-making project is more ambitious—it must change some aspect of that structure somewhere if it is going to be successful. Using this distinction I could show, for example, that highways which "run themselves" through individually owned trucks were trait-taking: they fitted far better into the existing multi-ethnic structure and rivalries of Nigeria than the would-be trait-making railroads with their centralized bureaucracy which, against all probability, was supposed to be tribe-blind and staffed along strictly meritocratic lines.

In the end, my argument amounted to denouncing attempts at trait-making under certain conditions. Some narrow-latitude tasks simply go beyond the capacity of a society as presently constituted and are therefore likely to end in failure. In other words, without realizing it at the

---

2. "A Dissenter's Confession: *The Strategy of Economic Development* Reconsidered," in Hirschman, *Rival Views of Market Society and Other Recent Essays* (New York: Viking, 1986) and paperback (Cambridge, Mass.: Harvard University Press, 1982), pp. 18–19.

time I had come up against the limits of one of my most cherished insights.

In recent years I have passed through several experiences of arguing against or qualifying earlier propositions of mine because I noted that they were less general than I originally thought. I have characterized these experiences as acts of "self-subversion"—they are assembled and discussed in Part One of this book.

When I wrote *Development Projects Observed* in the sixties, I was busily building up my edifice of propositions about development, and self-subversion was far from my mind. Nevertheless, I was troubled by the finding that trait-making was not functioning properly in Nigeria, that the railways did so poorly in spite of the fact that their latitude for performance was narrow. In looking for the reason I eventually focused on a paradox: the increasing availability of highway transportation may have deprived the railroads of the criticism (or "voice") they would have been subject to if their major customers had not had this easy alternative (or "exit") open to them. This thought turned out to have manifold implications: it was the origin of my next book, *Exit, Voice, and Loyalty* (1970), as I pointed out in that book's preface.

In this manner, this book on development projects was not only the last volume of my "trilogy" on development but became the bridge to the broader social science themes of my subsequent writings.

13
chapter

Convergences with Michel Crozier

Before evoking my encounters with Michel Crozier and his ideas I shall review some possible types of intellectual convergences. The most usual type is that of a "young mind" who becomes the faithful disciple of some "maître à penser" (thought-master). In due course, that young mind will pass through the stage of revolt, will "kill the father," and perhaps find another master—or achieve mastery in turn and succeed in establishing his own "chapelle" (chapel).

Fortunately, there are other, more interesting cases of convergence. For example, the intellectual careers of two persons may intersect as might two lines in space: a momentary point of encounter takes place. This is likely to be quite pleasant and a bit surprising and perhaps fleeting, for it is possible that the area of agreement is none too wide. The two may coauthor an article—and that is all. This happened to me once with Charles E. Lindblom.[1] The fact of signing the article jointly may give it the character of a statement of common principles, perhaps

Published originally as "L'analyse du changement: Quelques convergences avec Michel Crozier" in *L'analyse stratégique: Autour de Michel Crozier,* ed. Francis Pavé (Paris: Seuil, 1994), pp. 15–20. I wrote this essay in French for a conference honoring Michel Crozier, which took place in Cérisy (Normandy) in June 1990. For the present book I translated the essay into English and, in the process, felt free to introduce a few reformulations.
   1. "Economic Development, Research and Development, Policy-Making: Some Converging Views," *Behavioral Science,* 7 (April 1962), 211–222, republished in my collection *A Bias for Hope: Essays on Development and Latin America* (New Haven: Yale University Press, 1971), pp. 63–84.

even that of a manifesto. But at the same time the effort to reach this point may contribute to exhausting the relationship.

A very different experience occurs when one notes limited but striking convergences with someone whose basic positions are far removed from one's own. This can be rather unsettling and upsetting. Recently, for example, I did some readings in the general area of "reactionary" thought and became interested in and even fascinated by the work of Carl Schmitt, the famous arch-conservative German legal philosopher, as I realized that some of his key concepts, for example the importance of crisis as a mechanism of change, are curiously close to ideas Michel and I have both emphasized. This kind of discovery may be disagreeable—but also useful in yielding points toward reformulating and refining one's position.

Finally, there are intellectual encounters—and I believe this is the kind I have had with Michel Crozier—which correspond to the well-known notion of *Wahlverwandtschaft* ("elective affinity") dear to Goethe and Max Weber. Despite the separate concerns and different fields of research of each, one notes that the two have arrived at remarkably similar points of view. Given the usual solitude of the writer, this is a most agreeable experience. Yet it also presents some difficulties: while solitude is sometimes hard to bear, one does not wish to coincide wholly with someone else, for fear of losing one's individuality. This type of convergence can result in cross-fertilization, but there is also the danger of cross-sterilization.

However that may be, as soon as I read, early in the sixties, *The Bureaucratic Phenomenon,* I had the feeling of having discovered an intellectual brother. Since then, this experience has been periodically reconfirmed up to the present: while Michel's latest book is entitled *L'Entreprise à l'écoute* (The Firm is Listening), I write in a recent article that it is important "to value both having opinions and keeping an open mind, to mix the delights of winning an argument *with the pleasure of being a good listener*" (see Chapter 4, above).

To look a bit more closely into this matter, let me return to my first encounters with Michel. They go back, as just noted, to the sixties, probably 1965–66, when I had just moved from Columbia University in New York to Harvard in Cambridge. Previously (in 1952) I had left

Washington for Bogotá, where I had been economic adviser to the Colombian government for two years and after that spent another two and a half years in Colombia as a private economic consultant. There I plunged into the problems of Latin America and of the Third World in general. Over and above economic development, I tried to understand the processes of change in these countries. Though I started with economic problems, I soon took an interest in wider topics: basic reforms of social structure such as land reform, which were widely considered desirable, or the social determinants and political effects of inflation, or the causes of backwardness of large regions such as Italy's Mezzogiorno or Brazil's Nordeste. Later on I looked into micro-processes and investigated the social and political effects of certain investments in irrigation, electric power, and transportation. At that point I encountered the "radical" critique which was particularly vigorous in the Latin America of the sixties and seventies, when the *dependencia* doctrine became highly influential. It maintained that Latin American societies were wholly blocked by a system of domination which had to be broken. My practical experience and my research had, on the contrary, led me to believe that some movement was already under way, that the ruling classes were not wholly immobile, and that various political and social experiences could be undertaken.

At that point Michel's micro-studies of bureaucracy interested me enormously, for as he studied the reasons for blockage, he often discovered possibilities for change. What I found especially attractive was that he did not present change as something that would surely happen if and only if certain prerequisites had first been put into place. He rather talked of the possibility of change as an opportunity that one may learn to seize. I have later on attempted to elaborate on this notion; I spoke of "possibilism" or of the "passion for the possible," an expression coined by Kierkegaard. The point was to perceive the whole range of the possible, to widen its perception, and even to sacrifice in the process, if necessary, the single-minded pursuit of the probable. Michel and I share this attitude, which is far from usual in the social sciences.

A related concept is the possible *mutation* of alleged obstacles to development: they may turn out to promote change instead of hindering it. To make this point plausible I gathered a collection of "blessings in disguise." In particular, I showed how an institution or social trait can turn from negative to positive as circumstances change. Here is another convergence of my thought with Michel's: we are both skeptical of the Taylor-like search for *One Best Way*.

In my case this position took several forms. At the end of the Second World War, one of the concepts dominating the discussions around development was the "vicious circle of poverty." The implication was that the circle had to be broken everywhere at once by a large-scale effort, by massive and well-planned investments, by a "big push," and so on. I opposed this way of thinking, which had an odd similitude to the idea of the radicals of the sixties, namely, that the "system" was a (rotten) whole that must be totally destroyed. It seemed to me that there were other ways of getting these societies to move and of inventing virtuous circles or sequences that bring change underway.

I opposed even more the model requiring the presence of certain preliminary conditions which had to be put into place before any "take-off" could occur: a Protestant ethic, a group of Schumpeterian entrepreneurs, or an activist state. Rather, I put forward the concept of "inverted sequences" and argued that, in matters of development, it is often possible to "put the cart before the horse." Here I converged with another figure, the late psychologist Leon Festinger and his theory of cognitive dissonance. Festinger and his school demonstrated that it was possible to adopt a certain way of behaving (by chance, accident, or absent-mindedness) and to acquire only after the fact the basic attitudes that allegedly caused such behavior. This is precisely a mechanism often utilized in developing countries: someone establishes certain activities that require imperiously that maintenance be assured—this is the case of airlines, for example—even though everything else is poorly maintained in the country, from roads to houses to bridges. But because security of operations requires it under penalty of disaster, the maintenance of airplanes is somehow assured even though it is not part of the "culture" of the country in which the airline is based. From this point on, the habit of maintenance will perhaps become "second nature" and be transmitted to other sectors where it is less rigidly required . . .[2]

2. The concept of "second nature" is further explored in Chapter 19. See also the preceding chapter for critical comments on "trait-making."

Finally, I wish to note a more general convergence with Michel. It became manifest in the course of the Conference discussions, as he was asked about certain moral attitudes implicit in his work. He said then that modesty ranked high for him as a moral value and that this attitude, moreover, was a straightforward outcome of all of his research. I very much share these feelings. Moreover, I believe that we do in fact *practice* more modesty than our forebears and are also, I might add, quite a bit more modest in our scientific claims than many of our contemporaries, who still suffer too keenly from what economists, for once under the influence of Freud, have called "physics envy"—that is, the urge to describe the social and economic world by means of a sober and transparent system of equations. This desire goes back to the origin and history of the social sciences: they are *latecomers* and arose when the prestige of the natural sciences, above all that of Newtonian physics, was enormous. Hence there was, in the nineteenth century, a remarkable proliferation of laws in economics, from the law of supply and demand to Pareto's law of income distribution.

Given the importance of iron—symbol of industry and of power—in the nineteenth century, it was not even good enough for the early economists and sociologists to come forward with laws, they had to be "iron laws"! The imitation of Newton—in particular of his mechanics—went a step further as even "laws of motion" were discovered—this was Marx's proud claim with regard to capitalism. In this manner social change itself was subjected to imagined regularities that were soon contradicted by events.

Michel and I do not share these ambitions—we have a wholly different approach to change, and modestly respect its unpredictability and the way it tends to arise out of unique constellations. One could even propose a general formulation (nonferrous, to be sure): change can only happen as a result of surprise, otherwise it could not occur at all, for it would be suppressed by the forces that are in favor of the status quo. Our work on social change is therefore not at all oriented toward the discovery of laws of motion or of change. It rather starts from the idea that by accumulating concrete experiences of change, we will acquire the ability to recognize the *Gestalt* of impending change, the emergence of new constellations that are favorable to change.

III
part

New Forays

14
chapter

How the Keynesian Revolution Was Exported from the United States

Free Trade and Keynesianism: Parallels in Their Rise and Decline

"We are all post-Keynesians now"—to paraphrase and bring up to date a famous pronouncement (by Richard Nixon when he was President). As such, we are now able to perceive the remarkable parallelism between the fate of the Free Trade Doctrine in the nineteenth century and the rise and decline of Keynesianism in the twentieth. In 1846 free trade won its major domestic victory in Great Britain, then the dominant world power, with the abolition of the Corn Laws. The doctrine soon acquired a considerable degree of international hegemony, which was manifested in and further propelled by the Cobden-Chevalier Treaty of 1860. But it suffered reverses with the coming of the depression of the 1870s, and it was superseded by neomercantilist and imperialist policies that were not only adopted by the major continental powers and the United States, but eventually also won politically powerful converts in the original protagonist, the United Kingdom.

Keynesianism, the economic doctrine fashioned by John Maynard Keynes in *The General Theory* (1936), gained its first success in ac-

Published in Peter A. Hall, ed., *The Political Power of Economic Ideas: Keynesianism across Nations* (Princeton: Princeton University Press, 1989), pp. 347–359. The last part of this essay took occasionally the form of informal comments on the other contributions to the collective volume for which it was originally written; to that extent it has been rewritten, so as to make it stand on its own feet.

quiring major influence over the economic policy of a great power in the United States in the course of the 1938 recession. This influence was substantially strengthened during World War II. As a result of the war's outcome the United States was propelled to superpower status and proceeded to promote Keynesian-type policies, not only because of its new position in the world, but also because it acquired, through its postwar aid programs, considerable direct influence on the economic policies of other major countries. In spite of much resistance, Keynesianism acquired a good measure of intellectual hegemony—curiously, it lasted for just about as long as that of the Free Trade Doctrine in the same decades of "its" century: thirty years, from the 1940s to the 1970s. It went into decline with the oil crisis of the 1970s and the concomitant unsettling experience of "stagflation." Increasingly, the theoretical predominance Keynesianism had long exercised was contested by neomonetarist and supply-side doctrines that largely originated in the very country—the United States—that had originally been spreading the Keynesian message.

The purpose of delineating this historical parallel is not to insinuate that influential economic doctrines come and go at regular intervals, like schools of painting such as Impressionism or Abstract Expressionism, nor to ponder the *curiosum* that they achieved hegemony during the middle decades of succeeding centuries. Rather, it is to bring out the common elements of both episodes:

First, a newly arisen economic doctrine came to acquire dominant influence *within* a very special country: one that was outstandingly endowed both with military power and with the prestige of being a principal beacon of economic progress.

Second, that country then became eager to export the doctrine to others and initially achieved a measure of international hegemony for it.

Third, in spite of the seemingly invincible combination of a persuasive body of thought with its sponsorship by the most "modern" country and a leading world power, the doctrines soon met with resistance and their dominions turned out to be unexpectedly short-lived. Moreover, they came to be contested within the very countries which had originally spread them.

How the U.S. Keynesians Spread the Doctrine during the Marshall Plan

A comparative look at the spread of free trade and of Keynesianism also calls attention to an important difference between the two stories. The Free Trade Doctrine arose in England, became that country's official policy, and was "exported" from it, along with its prized manufactures, to the rest of the world. Keynesianism also arose in England, but won its most significant battle for influence over domestic policy making in the United States during the 1930s and the Second World War, and then spread primarily from that country after the war's end. It is perhaps not of overwhelming interest that the originating and the missionary country were identical in the free trade story, whereas in the case of Keynesianism two different countries assumed successively the function of "invention" and that of worldwide diffusion. The arresting features lie rather in some specific aspects of "How Keynes Was Spread from America," to vary the title of John Kenneth Galbraith's well-known article.[1]

Galbraith, Salant,[2] and others have told how Keynesian ideas came to a key university (Harvard) and to some key Washington agencies (Federal Reserve Board, Treasury, Bureau of the Budget) in the wake of the protracted Depression of the 1930s, particularly the steep and troubling 1938 recession. Seldom in history were the basic propositions of an economic theory so strikingly confirmed by events as during the 1938–1945 period in the United States. The new and heterodox Keynesian concept of underemployment equilibrium illuminated the continuing difficulties of the late 1930s that were particularly evident in the United States. Shortly thereafter, the ability of government spending to energize the economy and to drive it to full employment (with wartime controls restraining the inflationary impulses) was taken as another, more positive demonstration of the correctness of Keynesian

1. "How Keynes Came to America," in his collection *Economics, Peace and Laughter* (Boston, Mass.: Houghton Mifflin, 1971), pp. 43–49.
2. Walter Salant, "The Spread of Keynesian Doctrines and Practices in the United States," in Hall, ed., *Political Power*, pp. 27–52. Other references can be found in the notes to Salant's essay.

analysis. These striking experimental verifications of the theory—so uncharacteristic for social science propositions—might have been sufficient to cause many economists to take Keynes's ideas seriously. In addition, as has often been remarked, the rhetoric of *The General Theory* also contributed to forming a band of sectlike initiates and devotees on the one hand, as well as a group of out-and-out opponents on the other.

It is useful to dwell briefly on this point. As Salant has pointed out, Keynes showed how, in an underemployment situation, numerous commonsense intuitions about economic relationships are by no means fallacious, as had long been believed and taught by the economics profession. Contrary to Say's Law, general overproduction *can* exist; deficit spending by the government *can* activate the economy; and, horror of horrors, the "mercantilist" imposition of import duties and export subsidies *can* improve the trade balance and domestic employment. In propounding these popular and populist heresies, Keynes threatened traditional economists, not just in their beliefs, but in their hard-won status as high priests of an arcane science, which owed its prestige in good part to its claim that much of commonsense understanding of economic relationships was pitifully wrong. Here is one reason for the undying hostility of some important members of the profession to the Keynesian system.

But while rehabilitating common sense, Keynes hardly presented his own theory in commonsensical terms. Rather, his message was delivered in a book whose text was uncommonly difficult. Moreover, he frequently presented his propositions as counterintuitive rather than as confirming common sense: for example, instead of telling his readers that converging individual decisions to cut consumption can set off an economic decline (common sense), he dwelt on the equivalent but counterintuitive proposition that a spurt of individual decisions to save more will fail to increase aggregate savings. In this manner he managed to present common sense in paradox's clothing, and in fact this made his theory doubly attractive: it satisfied at the same time the intellectuals' craving for populism and their taste for difficulty and paradox.

The Keynesian system thus attracted a group of extraordinarily devoted followers. It gave them the exhilarating feeling of possessing the key to truth while being beleaguered by a coalition of ignoramuses and sinister interests. Moreover, the 1930s were a highly ideological or "creedal" period, and Keynesianism, with its reevaluation of the proper roles of the state, the world of business, and the intellectuals (the economists in particular), supplied an attractive "third way" that could compete with the various fascist and Marxist creeds of the time.

It was in the United States that these various factors converged most effectively to create an energetic and influential group of Keynesians during the years just prior to and during World War II. Then comes the peculiar "exogenous" twist of the story: the outcome of the war. With the United States suddenly propelled to military and political world leadership, its group of devoted and inspired Keynesians could now fan out to the far corners of the U.S.-controlled portion of the globe to preach their gospel to a variety of as yet unconverted natives. And this is what they did, backed up by U.S. power and prestige, first by occupying positions with the military governments established in Germany and Japan and then by providing much of the qualified manpower needed for the administration of Marshall Plan aid. Their success in implanting Keynesian policies abroad varied greatly, a matter to which I shall return shortly.

By flocking to the newly opening and highly attractive opportunities to spread the message and exert power overseas, the U.S. Keynesians, who were after all still a rather small group, left the domestic front dangerously unprotected. The retreats that were imposed on the Keynesian cause in the United States in the immediate postwar period (with the emasculation of the Full Employment Bill, for example) may in part be explained by this factor[3] On the other hand, the difficulties of maintaining their grasp on domestic policy in the more contentious and conservative climate of the Truman era may have convinced many prominent and gifted U.S. Keynesians that they would have a far easier and more profitable time applying their skills in the newly opened overseas theaters of operation. Such are the dialectics of empire, especially when it is of the instant variety.

In sum, what spread of Keynesianism occurred after World War II

3. For the domestic considerations, see Margaret Weir, "Ideas and Politics: The Acceptance of Keynesianism in Britain and the United States," Hall, ed., *Political Power*, pp. 53–86.

was due to an extraordinary constellation of circumstances: first the formation of a core group of Keynesians in the United States (a function of domestic economic problems), then the military victory of that country, and then the attempt at "colonization" of the rest of the non-Communist world with Keynesian ideas. The peculiar shape of the story is perhaps better understood by invoking a seemingly odd historical parallel. In the fifteenth century the Catholic kings of Spain completed, after centuries of fighting, the Reconquest of that country from the Muslims. In the course of this epochal event, the rulers of the kingdom became imbued with an extraordinary spirit of fervor, missionary zeal, and power. With the discovery of the New World in America (the exogenous event in this story), that ardent spirit then found a ready-made outlet and inspired both the soon-to-be-staged military conquest of the new continent and the intensive subsequent proselytizing efforts by the Spanish state and Church. One significant difference between the two stories is that, unlike the United States, Spain did not switch to spreading a new and wholly different faith some thirty years later.

But this exotic parallel only serves to underline the nonreplicable character of the story I have chosen to tell. It certainly does not yield anything like a usable model of the process through which economic ideas gain political influence. Or, if it does, it is in the nature of the advice given to a young man who wishes to know the secret of how to become rich: "Get yourself a rich grandfather." It would seem that, to achieve worldwide influence, an economic idea must first win over the elite in a single country; that this country must exert or subsequently chance to acquire a measure of world leadership; and that the country's elite be motivated and find an opportunity to spread the new economic message. My account dwells on the unique features of the spread of Keynesianism and does not lend itself to deriving any stable set of "preconditions" for the diffusion of economic ideas.[4] The story may, nevertheless, have another kind of utility: it intimates that, next time around, we may have to look for a very different combination of circumstances to explain (or promote) the acquisition of political influence by an economic idea.

4. An attempt of this sort is made by Peter Hall in his concluding chapter in *Political Power*, pp. 361–392.

Something remains to be said, from the perspective here adopted, about the highly disparate degrees of influence wielded by Keynesianism in the various countries that, immediately after World War II, were exposed to considerable U.S. influence, and along with that, to Keynesian ideas. Specific historical factors peculiar to each country explain of course much of the variance. Thus the revulsion against state interference in the economy, inherited from the Fascist and Nazi experiences in Italy and Germany, must be opposed to the openness to economic policy innovation in France, which had stagnated lamentably in the 1930s, largely under the dictates of orthodox economic management (resistance to devaluation and insistence on deflation). There remains nevertheless a puzzle: if U.S. influence meant exposure to Keynesian ideas as a result of the fanning out of U.S. Keynesians as described, why was it that in Germany and Japan, which were under U.S. military occupation and government and where U.S. power was therefore strongest, the influence of Keynesian ideas on policy-making was far weaker than in France and Italy, countries that were merely subject to U.S. advice as recipients of substantial U.S. aid? To help explain this paradox I wish to propose a hypothesis which needs to be confirmed by archival research, but which, as an active participant in those events, I sense to be correct.

At the end of World War II the U.S. Keynesians formed a cohesive, combative, and influential, yet, as already noted, also a multiply beleaguered group. It was prominent in a few government agencies in Washington and in a still quite small number of the major universities. In government, these Keynesian economists had mostly advisory rather than outright managerial positions, in line with the Washington quip that economists should be "on tap, but not on top." When the U.S. government was suddenly called upon to improvise an apparatus of military government in Germany and Japan, the top positions went to military officers and to experienced businessmen, bankers, lawyers, and other managerial types. These groups had by no means been converted to Keynesianism and tended in fact to be hostile to it to the extent they had an opinion on the matter. (In the militarily occupied countries, Germany in particular, there were frequent conflicts between the top administrators and the Keynesian advisors within the U.S. military government.) Conversely, in the other countries the top jobs available to Americans were those of economic advisers to Allied governments, and they largely went to the U.S. Keynesians, who therefore had virtually the last word on the economic policy that was being urged on the local government by the United States. Hence the U.S. Keynesians were *more* influential in those countries where the United States had *less* power and exercised it indirectly via advisers rather than directly, via outright administrators.

Further Notes on the Effect of New Economic Ideas on Policy

In the postwar period during which Keynesian ideas about appropriate contracyclical policy were widely accepted, the depth and length of the Depression of the 1930s, particularly in such countries as the United States, Germany, France, and Italy, were attributed to the stubborn and retrograde refusal of unenlightened policy makers to apply vigorous Keynesian remedies, such as deficit spending on public works. It is hardly a coincidence that the recent questioning of the Keynesian system should have witnessed the rise of an alternative explanation.

As now argued by Lord Robert Skidelsky and others, Keynesian policies would have been unavailing as a stimulus of renewed economic activity so long as public opinion in the affected countries was not broadly aware of how recovery was expected to be engineered through such policies.[5] If not only the government, but the public in general was convinced that large-scale deficit spending was a disastrous policy, capital flight and further declines in private investment might have followed upon the Keynesian remedies, thus thwarting the upward spiral in consumption and investment that was supposed to be impelled by the celebrated multiplier. Put more broadly, at any one time there is a general understanding, an unwritten social contract, about the rules which make an economy work and about the boundaries assigned to the state's economic role. The harm caused by breaching these rules

---

5. See Roger Middleton, *Towards the Managed Economy: Keynes, the Treasury and the Fiscal Policy Debate of the 1930s* (London: Methuen, 1986), pp. 172, 183; see also Skidelsky's review of Middleton's book in the *Times Literary Supplement*, June 20, 1986, p. 684.

and boundaries is likely to outweigh the benefits that are calculated to accrue from the purely mechanical effects of state action.

There is an easy reply to this kind of argument. One of the functions of government is to inform public opinion, and if the mindsets and reactions of the public in the 1930s were in fact likely to neutralize (or worse) any Keynesian stimuli, then it should have been up to the governments to instruct their publics in the elements of Keynesianism before applying the doctrine in practice. So the governments must still be considered to have been at fault. Nevertheless, their failure to educate the public in the mechanics of the Keynesian system would probably be judged less blameworthy than the sheer ignorance and reactionary stubbornness with which they were charged in the earlier interpretations.

Actually, the new interpretation or justification of non-Keynesian, orthodox policy-making in the 1930s raises a fundamental question which should be briefly spelled out here. If the success of a newly proposed economic policy depends on the understanding, on the part of the public, of how the policy is expected to work, how is it ever possible for an established economic policy, which is familiar and well understood, to be superseded by another? For it seems that the revisionist view proposes a typical vicious circle: on the one hand, we are being told that the newly proposed policy can work only provided people are already convinced that it will do so; on the other hand, it stands to reason that this conviction arises most typically among the economic operators once they have lived through a positive experience with that policy. The success of the new policy depends on reshaping attitudes; proper attitudes depend in turn on prior experience with the policy. This vicious circle formulation is actually helpful: it reveals the formidable difficulties standing in the way of the adoption of new economic (and other) ideas. That process is indeed far more problematic than is usually suspected. It is not enough for even so brilliant a mind as that of Keynes to formulate a new system of economic relationships and for his ideas, with the help of some friends and students, to gain a foothold in the government. Rather, the vicious circle just described must be broken, and this can be achieved only if the normally occurring reactions of dismay and disbelief that would make Keynesian policies inoperative are suspended by some exogenous happening—in the event, the 1938 recession and, above all, the Second World War played this crucial role of first suspending traditional expectations and then, as Keynesian policies proved successful, of reshaping them.

The process as sketched here has something in common with cognitive dissonance theory in social psychology, which deals precisely with the difficult relation between acquiring new attitudes (say, of racial tolerance) and acting in accordance with such attitudes. Here again, there is a problem of sequence: how can a change in behavior take place unless the appropriate attitudes have first been acquired, and yet how can these be acquired unless an action and its positive sequel have first provided the experiential basis for the attitude change? One solution proposed by the theory was precisely for actors to "back into," to "stumble" more or less accidentally on an action that will then give rise to the new attitude.

In effect, by arguing along such lines, the revisionist historians of the economic policy in the 1930s have themselves stumbled on a complex problem area. They claim that the successful pursuit of a new economic policy may require some minimal comprehension, on the part of the public, of how the policy is expected to work. This proposition certainly holds for some policies. Yet we also know of very different ways of thinking about the relation between the effectiveness of an economic policy and its understanding by the public. The relation was in fact stood on its head by recent critics of Keynesian macroeconomic policy—the proponents of the "rational expectations" hypothesis—who argue that an economic policy will become ever *less* effective the more the public "catches on" and renders the policy ineffective through anticipatory reactions.

These apparently quite contradictory views can be accommodated in two very different ways. In the first place, there may well be one set of economic policies which require some minimal understanding on the part of the public, and a very different set of policies whose effectiveness, from the point of view of the government, depends on some sort of surprise effect. Here the policy necessarily loses in effectiveness once increasing numbers of victimized citizens get "wise" to them and refuse to be "caught twice." We all know of such usually spoliative (or, to use a less loaded term, *redistributive*) policies, from inflation to the sudden imposition of exchange controls.

But there is another possible reconciliation of the two views, a reconciliation that turns out to be rather worrisome. With regard to certain economic policies, both views could conceivably be applicable, in succession. To work at all, a policy must first be at least minimally understood, but it becomes unsustainable if it is understood too well, in the sense that the operators will neutralize it by anticipating its effects. In other words, the public's understanding of the policy must be neither inadequate nor excessive, but since that understanding presumably passes from the former of these negative conditions to the latter, the viability of any policy is likely to be limited in time. Recent experience suggests that this is not an entirely unrealistic interpretation of macroeconomic policy-making in a decentralized economy.

Keynesianism and the Shape of Postwar Politics and Economics

The powerful hold Keynesian thought and doctrine had on the mind of an entire generation affected postwar politics and economics in many crucial ways. I shall give three examples.

The Reshaping of Political Alignments

In postwar Britain Keynesian doctrine played an important role in allowing the new Labour government to shift its course without losing either its soul or its face.[6] After some unsuccessful experimentation with detailed industrial planning and physical controls, Sir Stafford Cripps, as Chancellor of the Exchequer, chose to place the emphasis on Keynesian macroeconomic demand management. At the same time, the Conservative opposition had come around to endorsing the principles of Keynesian economic management, while opposing the coercive features of Labour's economic controls.[7] A postwar consensus on eco-

---

6. Margaret Weir, n. 3, pp. 68–69.

7. In his famous last article, "The Balance of Payments of the United States," *Economic Journal,* 56 (June 1946), 172–187, Keynes aligned himself largely with this understanding of his doctrine by excoriating the hankering of some of his followers for physical controls as "modernist stuff gone wrong and turned sour and silly." Here Keynes sounded very much like Lenin, who had similarly denounced certain excesses committed in his name as "infantile maladies."

nomic policy had thus emerged. Here is an excellent example of how a new economic idea can affect political history: it can supply an entirely new common ground for positions between which there existed previously no middle ground whatever. Prior to Keynes there simply was no respectable theoretical position between centralized planning and the traditional laissez-faire policies, with their denial of any governmental responsibility for economic stability and growth.

The postwar French recovery furnishes another illustration of how Keynesian ideas provided support for a new conception of the economic role of the state. The celebrated and pivotal concept of "indicative planning" is unthinkable without the Keynesian reformulation of that role.[8]

An Infusion of Civic Spirit

The United States was the theater of another important political impact of Keynesianism—one that has gone largely unnoticed.

As I have noted elsewhere, new ideas have two principal intellectual effects: the persuasion effect and the recruitment effect.[9] The persuasion effect is the obvious one of attracting followers from among the specialists already laboring in the particular discipline where the idea makes its appearance. The recruitment effect is more important and more ambiguous. As a result of the excitement generated by the new idea and the ensuing debates, intellectually able and ambitious recruits are newly attracted toward the field where the discovery has been made, where its scientific merits remain to be evaluated, and where its ramifications are yet to be worked out. This phenomenon was extremely conspicuous in the United States, with its vast university system. Moreover, Keynesianism inspired and energized even the opposition, from Milton Friedman to James Buchanan, in accordance with Burke's dictum, "our antagonist is our helper. This amicable conflict with difficulty obliges us to an intimate acquaintance with our object."

8. Pierre Rosanvallon, "The Development of Keynesianism in France," in Hall, ed., *Political Power*, pp. 171–194.

9. "A Dissenter's Confession: *The Strategy of Economic Development* Revisited," in Hirschman, *Rival Views of Market Society and Other Recent Essays* (New York: Viking, 1986), p. 34.

The political repercussions of the powerful recruitment effect of Keynesianism were notable. Large numbers of recruits were eventually drawn to Washington and spent varying periods of time there. They came to their tasks often naively and arrogantly confident that they would solve the economic and social problems of their time, but at the same time they infused into many areas of government, from Social Security to foreign aid, a spirit of energetic dedication to public service and accomplishment.

One of the major unsolved problems of democratic political theory and practice is how to maintain a minimal degree of public-spiritedness among the citizenry in general and the bureaucracy in particular, of how to prevent what Machiavelli called *corruzione,* by which he meant not corruption or graft, but the loss of public spirit, the exclusive concentration of individual effort on personal or sectional interests.[10] Given the decline of pluralist theory and the rising impact of the Prisoner's Dilemma Theorem, we are now aware that in the public arena there is no invisible hand that will mysteriously produce the public good out of the clash of various types of self-seeking. The solution of the minimal state is utopian under modern conditions. Pure exhortation in the name of morality or love of country is likely to fail. Hence we are reduced to looking around for sundry devices that can serve as occasional and temporary boosters of that precious public spirit. Via their recruitment effect, new ideas in economics and social science provide us with just such boosters. Keynesianism's most important political effect in the United States may well have been to have raised public-spiritedness in a crucial period of its recent history—the transition to superpower status.

Keynesianism Gives Rise to New Economic Ideas

It is hardly news that one of the principal consequences of an idea is to breed new ideas, most of which were not visualized by those who formulated the original one. The second-generation ideas will then in turn have political effects along the lines sketched in the preceding pages or

10. See Quentin Skinner, "The Paradoxes of Political Liberty," in *The Tanner Lectures on Human Values* (Cambridge, Mass.: Harvard University Press, 1984). Some fresh ideas on the problem are in Steven Kelman, *Making Public Policy* (New York: Basic Books, 1987).

in other ways. Now Keynesianism has been particularly blessed with a rich and diverse progeny of second-generation ideas, and a survey of the political effects of Keynesianism would be seriously incomplete if those attributable to that progeny were wholly left out of account. This is a vast subject, but it may be helpful to mention a few major lines along which an inquiry into this matter might proceed.

First of all, as already noted, Keynes's work had the gift of seriously upsetting and antagonizing a large and important segment of the economics profession. Stung by the ridicule that was poured on them by the newly enlightened coterie of Keynesians, the traditionalists reformulated the classical position more rigorously, forcefully, *and* uncompromisingly. When circumstances became favorable in the 1970s, they counterattacked, with the well-known enormous political effect.

It may be a bit farfetched to consider this revanche of the anti-Keynesians as a consequence of Keynesianism, even though it seems incontrovertible that a theory must be held accountable for the kind of reaction it provokes. But there are of course several important intellectual currents that have their origin in Keynesianism along more obvious lines. One is the economics of growth, particularly its first Harrod-Domar phase. This major development in post–World War II economics is unthinkable without the Keynesian tools of the multiplier, the marginal efficiency of capital, and the propensity to save. Hence the claim that Keynesian economics had unlocked the secrets of the growth process. Here one point might be made: the substantial change in social and political attitudes toward capitalism and market society during the postwar period is not tied to Keynesianism per se so much as to one of its intellectual progenies, the economics of growth. The economics of growth is greatly indebted to Keynes, but it was by no means fashioned by him. If Keynes is sometimes seen as the "savior of capitalism," this is a case of indirect, rather than direct, causation.

My final example of political effects stemming from one of the ideational ramifications of Keynesianism is the economics of development. Keynesian doctrine drew a sharp distinction between the economic mechanisms ruling in a fully employed economy and those applying in an economy where manpower, capital, and other resources are underemployed. This intellectual posture made it respectable to construct yet another special economics, this one applying to "underdeveloped areas."[11] While the emergence of the anticolonial struggle after World War II stimulated thinking about the conditions of economic progress in the former colonies as well as in Latin America, the conviction, among an influential group of development economists, that they had identified and understood what one of them called the "mechanics of economic development" contributed a great deal to the launching of a determined effort to get those mechanics going.[12] The effort was conceived as a task that should be undertaken jointly by the West and the countries of the so-called periphery. Its enormous difficulties and pitfalls would only reveal themselves as time unfolded. But the process, with all its political disasters, wild gyrations, and yet enormous promise, might never have been started as a joint enterprise of rich and poor nations had not the economics of development, that other progeny of Keynesianism, held out the promise, right or wrong, that it was indeed manageable.

These filial connections of Keynesian ideas with the economics of growth and development had a remarkable consequence: a body of thought that was conceived in the Depression and was designed to deal with the problems of unemployment and stagnation has come to be intimately and deservedly associated with *les trente glorieuses*—the glorious thirty post–World War II years—that is, with the most sustained and dynamic period of economic expansion in human history, both in the economically advanced and in many of the less developed countries.

11. "The Rise and Decline of Development Economics," in Hirschman, *Essays in Trespassing* (New York: Cambridge University Press, 1981), pp. 1–24.

12. Hans W. Singer, "The Mechanics of Economic Development: A Quantitative Model Approach," *Indian Economic Review* (August 1952), 1–18.

15
chapter

On the Political Economy of
Latin American Development

In revisiting Latin America to gather impressions for this essay, I soon convinced myself that the most conspicuous characteristic of the region's more recent experience is diversity, and that the most interesting stories to be told are about specific, often contrasting experiences of individual countries. So, except for the first and last sections, I shall not deal here with Latin America in overall terms. Rather, I shall present a series of loosely connected and necessarily brief exercises in comparative political economy. Not surprisingly, primary attention will be given to the four countries I visited this time: Brazil, Argentina, Chile, and Mexico. My endeavor throughout will be to gain some perspective on current or recent issues by tying them into events and discussions of earlier decades.

Les Trente Glorieuses in Latin America?

As is well known, Latin American economies were hit quite hard during the early 1980s. The sharp cyclical downturn of 1981–82 in the United

Published in *Latin American Research Review,* 22 (1987), 7–36. This essay was presented at the Annual Meetings of the Latin American Studies Association in October 1986 in Boston as the author received the Association's Kalman Silvert Award. In preparation, he visited Brazil, Argentina, Chile, and Mexico in April-May 1986, on a travel grant from the Ford Foundation. The last section, "Final Observations on Ideology and Debt," was reprinted in the *New York Review of Books* of December 18, 1986, under the title "Out of Phase Again." Having been written largely as a topical report on current problems, this essay has been slightly revised in light of subsequent data and events.

States and in the other advanced industrial countries combined with the outbreak of the international debt crisis in 1982 and a fall in raw material prices to force sharp reductions in imports, public expenditures, and private investment in all of Latin America. Incomes fell everywhere, and unemployment rose to unprecedented levels in the more industrialized countries such as Brazil, Argentina, and Mexico, none of which had provisions for unemployment compensation. Following actual drops in total output in 1982 and 1983, uneven recoveries occurred in 1984 and 1985, with the result that the continent's total output has only now (1986) regained its 1981 level. Given the continued growth in population, per capita incomes are down about 10 percent from what they were then.

This serious setback in the development of the continent has had a curious side-effect: for the first time the preceding decades were perceived as a long, almost golden age of uninterrupted, steady forward movement. Often, it seems, we can bring ourselves to acknowledge the positive features of a period only when we enter into a subsequent one, whose troubles we now wish to underline by painting a strong contrast with what came before. This tendency is probably a fairly general human trait. In France, the expression *les trente glorieuses* (the glorious thirty-year period), referring to the unprecedented spurt of growth and modernization of the postwar decades, was coined in 1979 by Jean Fourastié. The formula probably owes much of its success to the fact that the French, like other economically advanced societies, were then entering a new era of troubles and were therefore ready to proclaim that everything had been going well—until just yesterday.[1] This reluctance to celebrate or even acknowledge progress while it unfolds before our eyes, which makes the celebration coincide with the lamentation about its passing, has been particularly marked in Latin America. It must have come as a major revelation to regular readers of current reports about Latin America that that continent too had its trente glorieuses—and perhaps a few more.

Why the conspiracy of silence about the good news so long as it was still coming? For some good reasons, of course. The information about economic growth, advancing per capita incomes, strides in industriali-

1. Jean Fourastié, *Les trente glorieuses ou la révolution invisible de 1946 à 1975* (Paris: Fayard, 1979).

zation, and the rise of the middle classes was thoroughly intertwined in Latin America with contrasting trends and perceptions: a new awareness arose of social tensions and injustice; longstanding mass poverty became urbanized and therefore more visible; economic imbalances widened as between city and countryside and the advanced and backward regions; and the performance of the state in dealing with these negative side-effects of economic growth was far from satisfactory. Most important perhaps, and in marked contrast to the steady consolidation of democracy in Western Europe during this period, Latin America experienced serious political upheavals throughout this period of thirty to forty years, its midpoint being marked by a major and influential "accident"—the overthrow of democracy in Brazil by the military coup of 1964. Finally, one must mention the tactically inspired tendency to underline the negative so as to present the continent as a long-victimized claimant upon the international economic and financial system. Small wonder, then, that Latin America's trente glorieuses have not found a cheerleader.

I do not aspire to that role. But now that the progress of Latin America between 1945 and 1980 is no longer a carefully guarded secret, it is useful to record briefly its economic and social dimensions.

During those thirty-five years, the total population of Latin America multiplied from 155 million to 388 million inhabitants.[2] The average annual rate of increase over this period works out at 2.7 percent. From 1950 to 1981 the gross domestic product of the area in real terms quintupled. It rose fairly steadily throughout these thirty-one years, the average annual rate being 5.5 percent, so that per capita incomes increased at about the same rate (2.7 percent) as the population, from 420 to 960 U.S. dollars (at constant 1970 prices). While annual incomes rose in this fashion, life spans lengthened considerably—life expectancy rose from the low fifties to the middle sixties—so that lifetime incomes expanded much more than is indicated by the per capita income statistics (which are computed on a per annum basis).

2. This figure excludes the Caribbean except for the Dominican Republic and Haiti. All statistical data in the following pages are taken from ECLA's 1984 *Statistical Yearbook for Latin America*, supplemented in some cases by figures from its data bank and the *World Development Report 1986* of the World Bank.

A major change in the social structure of Latin America has been the relative decline of the rural population, in line with the historical experience of the more advanced economies. The transfer of people out of agriculture has been exceptionally rapid during these past thirty-five years. In 1950 in countries like Brazil, Mexico, and Colombia, about 60 percent of the labor force was occupied in agriculture. In 1985 this figure declined to less than 30 percent. In Brazil and some other countries the absolute number of persons in agriculture is no longer increasing. In counterpart, and as a result of massive rural-to-urban migration, Latin American cities from Lima to Caracas and from São Paulo to Mexico City have become huge, often highly polluted conurbations. A large proportion of these urban populations live in self-built, rudimentary homes with uncertain titles and inadequate, though improving, access to public utilities, particularly transportation, water, and sewers.

Nevertheless, massive urbanization has probably been the major force behind considerable advances in health and education since the fifties. The increase in life expectancy largely reflects improved survival chances for the newborn during the first years of life. Infant mortality has declined sharply and steadily. In the early fifties it stood at the distressing level of 130 per 1,000 live births in the tropical countries; in most of these countries, the figure has fallen to around 50, although in Brazil and Peru the rates are still much higher (70 and 98, respectively). Illiteracy has similarly receded. Outside the Southern Cone (where all such social indicators have long exhibited much more advanced levels), the 50 percent rate that was the rule around 1950 has fallen by more than half. School enrollment rates have risen correspondingly: primary school attendance is now close to universal, although this statistic may not be especially meaningful. Greater confidence can be placed in figures showing real movement at the secondary and higher levels. In Brazil, Colombia, and Mexico, the enrollment rate in high schools has risen from 10 percent in 1950 to 50 percent in 1985, while university enrollment in these countries has risen from 2–3 percent in the fifties to 12–15 percent in the same period. Thus the educational pyramid is apparently growing and flattening out at the same time.

To provide a more complete picture of advances in social welfare and its current state, one would have to cite many more figures, from per capita caloric consumption to the percentage of dwellings and households with basic utilities such as water and sewers, as well as data on the diffusion of consumer durables such as refrigerators, telephones, automobiles, radios, and televisions. Some of this information (on calories, water, and sewer connections) is in poor shape. Data relative to the diffusion of automobiles, telephones, and refrigerators testify to the rise of a substantial middle class. In the case of other amenities—radios and, increasingly, televisions—diffusion has become so nearly universal that, oddly, their possession is no longer a useful measure of economic status and attainment.

Instead of looking at the new possessions Latin Americans are able to acquire, it may be more meaningful to focus on what they increasingly decide to do without—namely, the traditional family with a large number of children. Outside Argentina and Uruguay (where small families have long been common), birthrates throughout Latin America stood at the steep level of around 45 per thousand in the early fifties but declined rapidly in the sixties and seventies and in the eighties stood at around 30 per thousand in all the larger tropical countries. Sample surveys show that the percentage of married women using contraception varies from 40 percent to 55 percent in these countries (compared with 70 to 80 percent in Western Europe and North America), indicating that the practice extends considerably beyond the middle class. Although comparable figures for earlier years are not available, the diffusion of birth control to so wide a sector of the population is undoubtedly quite new.

Whether or not we dare speak of *les trente glorieuses* in Latin America, the statistical evidence indicates that the region deserves credit for two major accomplishments since the fifties. First, it has accommodated an enormous increase in population while improving their average living standards and increasing their life expectancies. Second, countering the many prophecies of demographic disaster based on projections of population growth at the alarming rates of the fifties, the region has decisively launched the "demographic transition" that will permit achieving a much more moderate population growth, although at permanently higher levels of population density.

A third achievement is implicit in the data cited: no matter what has happened to relative distribution, some improvement has taken place in the position of the poorest sectors of the population—obviously, the primary beneficiaries of the decline in infant mortality and illiteracy. In addition, some of these basic advances in social welfare may no longer be rigidly tied to the ups and downs of the economy. Thus, during the recent years of recession and stagnation, infant mortality appears to have continued its downward trend in most of Latin America, and the same is probably true for illiteracy and almost certainly for the birthrate.

Several reasons can be given for expecting such advances. In the first place, even though the loss of employment and the decline in income during recessions will cause severe economic deprivation, they no longer necessarily exact such extreme penalties as infant deaths and illiteracy, once incomes reach a certain level. At such a level, moreover, a "ratchet effect" is likely to come into operation.[3] This effect is evident when we consider the decision to use birth control. In many cases it is induced by the interrelated complex of rising incomes, urbanization, greater literacy, and the spread of specific knowledge about contraception. But once acquired, this knowledge is not going to be erased, nor will the decision to use contraception be reversed by a temporary fall in income—rather, in this case, to the contrary. The diffusion of knowledge and the irreversible adoption of new cultural practices and attitudes may also be more important than the rise and fall of income for the behavior of other social indicators. Certain sanitary and dietary practices in childrearing that are important in saving infants' lives are unlikely to be discarded once they have been adopted. New knowledge and better practice in medicine and public health, including immunization, make for advances that are largely independent of economic conditions. A good recent example is the wide (and usually free) distribution in many countries of oral rehydration kits that counteract the often-fatal dehydration accompanying diarrhea in small children.

Even with regard to education, an important determinant of school attendance (and literacy) is simply the determination of parents to send their children to school. Again, this determination, once acquired for

---

3. See Chapter 19, below, for a generalization of the point made here to the relation between economic and political progress.

whatever reasons (including economic ones), is not likely to be reversed as a result of subsequent economic setbacks except in the most severe circumstances. Also, such determination will communicate itself to other parents of similar socioeconomic strata, more as a result of cultural diffusion than of economic improvement.

Public policy also plays an important part in these matters. Retrenchment in current operating costs will inevitably take place as an economic downturn leads to budget cuts. But to the extent that providing education, health, and transportation services depends on prior capital expenditures (on schools, hospitals, and other health facilities; and on roads and subways), the effect of economic reverses on the availability of such services will be delayed and perhaps dampened.

At a certain level of development, therefore, we may expect a measure of *disjunction* between economic and social indicators, with the latter doing rather better than the former during temporary economic downturns.[4] Such a disjunction was noted for the United States by sociologist Christopher Jencks in his article "The Hidden Prosperity of the 1970s."[5] According to the conventional wisdom based on economic data, things fell apart during that decade: "inflation accelerated, unemployment rose, productivity stagnated"; and real family income, which had risen by over 30 percent in both the fifties and sixties, remained virtually unchanged.[6] But Jencks shows in considerable detail that more direct and detailed measures of material well-being relating to health, housing, transportation, and food consumption "often showed marked improvement, and some showed as much improvement during the 1970s as during the supposedly more affluent 1950s and 1960s."[7]

Such findings are unexpected. Greater reliance on social indicators relating to health and education was widely advocated in the sixties because of a spreading disbelief in the current optimistic message of the economic indicators. Many suspected that the per capita income series,

4. See Chapter 19, below, for broader considerations on "disjunction."
5. Christopher Jencks, "The Hidden Prosperity of the 1970's," *The Public Interest*, 77 (Fall 1984), 37–61.
6. Jencks, n. 5, 37.
7. Jencks, n. 5, 38.

with its relentless advance, hid from view all kinds of less happy aspects of social reality, from uneven distribution and ecological depredation to spreading crime. It is therefore noteworthy that at least some of the social indicators now paint a somewhat more cheerful picture of changes in U.S. society than the economic indicators suggest.

Because of the lag in publishing social statistics, it is difficult to say at this point whether a similar story has been in the making in Latin America during the recent recession. On the one hand, national data on infant mortality and illiteracy have initially continued their downward movement in many countries. On the other hand, research in the 1980s has turned up evidence of increases in infant mortality in São Paulo and of worsening nutrition and health conditions for children in Santiago. It remains to be seen whether these findings, which relate to the areas hit most directly by industrial unemployment, will be confirmed by nationwide data.[8]

In any event, Latin America's economic and social performance over the past decades reveals a number of strong points. Why, then, is the current mood of many pronouncements about the continent's prospects so gloomy? One reason is no doubt that most countries have not yet emerged decisively from the recession. Another reason for pessimism is the large debt overhang, whose service mortgages a substantial portion of any expansion in exports achievable as recovery and growth resume. Yet the despondency of many contemporary observers seems to me to be rooted principally in the realm of ideas. The present scene, it is often said, lacks the feeling, so strong in the thirties and forties, that all kinds of daring new directions in economic and social policy invite exploration. This nostalgic glance backward is often accompanied by the mournful observation that the paths then taken, like others that opened up subsequently, have all ended in utter failure, from the "de-

8. With respect to infant mortality, a 1984 UNICEF study reports continuing drops in infant mortality in Brazil and Chile up to 1982. See Roberto Macedo, "Brazilian Children and the Economic Crisis: Evidence from the State of São Paulo"; and Alejandro Foxley and Dagmar Raczynski, "Vulnerable Groups in Recessionary Situations: The Case of Children and the Young in Chile," in *The Impact of World Recession on Children,* ed. R. Jolly and G. A. Cornia (Oxford: Pergamon, 1984), pp. 42–43 and 57–64. The deterioration of the health situation has been reported in subsequent unpublished papers by the same researchers. Macedo notes that the 1984 increase in infant mortality in São Paulo, coming after a long decline, may have been largely due to a measles epidemic.

velopmentalism" of the fifties to the monetarist experiments in the Southern Cone of the seventies. Put side by side, these two disheartening observations may actually permit a rather more cheerful conclusion: perhaps it is a good thing that not so many brave new directions are beckoning today.

Some of the younger economists and policy-makers in Latin America are in fact acting as though they agreed with this point. They are not talking nearly as much as their elders did about wholly new directions or solutions, yet they are actually coming forward with a number of original ideas and practices (which will be noted later). I shall set the stage for this brighter side by first reviewing some of the more unhappy economic policy experiences of the recent past.

Industrialization and Deindustrialization in Argentina and Chile

Latin America has always been a heterogeneous assemblage of economies and polities, but this characteristic has been more or less pronounced in various periods. The specifics of the dissimilarities have also shifted. Up to the Second World War, the principal dividing line from the point of view of economic and social development lay between the fertile, temperate countries of the Rio de la Plata region (Argentina and Uruguay, to which Chile was sometimes added) and the others, which were predominantly tropical and (to compound their misfortune, so it was widely thought) contained large numbers of persons of African, Indian, and mestizo origin. It was one of the enormous merits of Raúl Prebisch that, transcending his own privileged status as a citizen of advanced Argentina, he launched a campaign for the economic progress of all of Latin America by emphasizing a shared characteristic: its position on the periphery of the world economic system as a result of having been relegated to the role of supplier of raw materials and foodstuffs. Emancipation from this condition was supposed to be accomplished largely through industrialization, a task proposed as though it were universally manageable, requiring only capital, entrepreneurship, and promotion or protection by the state—as though climate, race, and specific natural resources did not greatly matter. This contention was proved to be right. Over the last forty years, the tropical countries as a group have substantially outperformed the temperate ones in Latin America, and because they were originally much poorer, a movement toward greater intercountry equality has thus taken place.

Nevertheless, industrialization itself has given rise to fresh inequalities and disparities. A new division, which has become more marked with the years, has emerged between the more and less populous countries. Because of the importance of the domestic market in the course of industrialization, particularly the import-substituting kind, industry was bound to develop more vigorously in the more populous than in the less populous countries. This is the primary reason why the economic weight of the two largest countries, Mexico and Brazil, has increased considerably: their share of the total national income of the continent has increased from less than two-fifths of the total (38.7 percent) in 1950 to more than three-fifths (61.3 percent) in 1981, while their share of the total population has remained about one-half of the total.

The urge to industrialize, rooted in the Depression and war experiences of the thirties and forties, seized all but the smallest and poorest Latin American countries during the fifties and sixties. But in the seventies, what had been a unifying characteristic turned strangely into a factor accentuating diversity. Earlier, to be sure, the tempo of industrialization also differed substantially among different countries. But now a real parting of the ways occurred: some countries experienced deindustrialization, while Brazil (already the most industrially advanced country of the group) entered an entirely new stage of industrial development. The contrast is sufficiently stark to warrant a closer look.

Elsewhere I have written about the dual attack that was mounted against the industrialization drive, starting in the sixties.[9] From the Latin American left, industrialization was variously criticized for being "unintegrated" or "truncated," for increasing "dependency," or for

9. "The Rise and Decline of Development Economics," in Hirschman, *Essays in Trespassing* (New York: Cambridge University Press, 1981), and "Linkages in Economic Development," in Hirschman, *Rival Views of Market Society and Other Recent Essays* (New York: Viking, 1986).

catering (through its products) primarily to the upper and middle classes. At the opposite end of the spectrum, the international neoclassical establishment castigated "inward-oriented" industrial development for causing misallocation of resources, balance-of-payments problems, and "rent-seeking." Neither criticism entirely lacked foundation, but in the ideologically charged debates of the time, no one asked whether the assorted problems of import-substituting industrialization were conceivably growing pains that might be overcome in due course by adroit, incremental policy-making, rather than being the result of sins that had to be expiated and eliminated root-and-branch through a wholesale change of course. The merit of the growing-pains hypothesis was actually demonstrated by experiences in some countries, where a gradual transition was managed from exclusive reliance on the domestic market to substantial exports of manufactures by means of various devices, such as crawling pegs for currency devaluation, progressive reduction in protection, and policies of promoting exports.[10] But the root-and-branch school won decisively in countries (Argentina and Chile) where, in the seventies, military regimes of the radical right came to power determined to extirpate a variety of miscreant behavior, from subversion to misallocation. Considering that these regimes resolved to exile, imprison, or "disappear" thousands of citizens in the name of national security, it is easily understood that they had no qualms about eliminating hundreds of industrial firms for the sake of the "law of comparative advantage"—even though hundreds of thousands of workers would lose their livelihood in the process.

In this manner, industrialization was shifted into reverse gear in Chile after 1973, where industrial employment fell from 555,000 persons in 1973 to a low of 378,000 during the depression year of 1983; since then, a modest recovery has raised this figure back to 449,000 in 1985. At that point, one of every five persons employed in industry thirteen years back had lost his or her job. In Argentina, industrial growth also

---

10. Simón Teitel and Francisco E. Thoumi, "From Import Substitution to Exports: The Manufacturing Exports Experience of Argentina and Brazil," *Economic Development and Cultural Change,* 34 (April 1986), 455–490. On Colombia as an example, see Hirschman, "The Turn to Authoritarianism in Latin America and the Search for Its Economic Determinants," in *Essays in Trespassing,* 115.

gave way to sharp decline during the military regime that ruled from 1976 to 1983. In a few years, the industrial labor force shrank by over 10 percent, from 1,525,000 workers in 1974 to 1,360,000 in 1985.

But overall figures do not tell the whole story because some industries were much more affected than others. Among those liquidated as a result of tariff cuts and similar measures were some highly protected, blatantly inefficient operations, such as certain car assemblies in Chile. The most damaging and wholly undeserved adverse impact on domestic industry, however, did not come from the reduction in tariff protection but from two related aspects of the monetarist policies pursued, particularly after 1978, in Argentina and Chile. Of the two, the more important factor was the overvaluation of the domestic currency, which was intended as an anti-inflationary device. Although it did not prove very effective at this task, it handed an artificial cost advantage to a wide range of imports. Among the industries heavily injured were not only traditional consumer goods manufactures (such as textiles and shoes) but certain technologically advanced durables (such as color television sets in Argentina) that had made a promising beginning and were developing their own design, characteristics, and networks of local suppliers and service.[11]

In addition, the monetary experiment being pursued led to high domestic interest rates, which squeezed the smaller domestic concerns while making borrowing abroad at considerably lower rates highly attractive for the larger firms. Under these conditions, the larger, well-connected industries (which were often resource-based industries like chemicals, petrochemicals, and pulp and paper) fared much better for a while than did smaller, purely domestic industrial firms. Eventually, as the exchange rate had to be drastically devalued in the early eighties and as foreign interest rates soared in turn, the cost of the foreign loans became intolerable for those who had contracted them. But like the private banks and finance companies that had often acted as intermediaries, the larger firms were not allowed to fail. Instead, the governments stepped in with guarantees and various salvage operations, with

11. For an interesting case study, see Hugo Nochteff, *Desindustrialización y retroceso tecnológico en Argentina, 1976–1982: La industria electrónica de consumo* (Buenos Aires: GEL-FLACSO, 1984).

an ironic result: governments that had widely proclaimed that their economic mission was to privatize the economy and restore free markets ended up owning or controlling the country's banking system as well as many of its larger enterprises. In Chile, this process occurred as many industrialists and bankers became disillusioned with the Pinochet regime. But at this point, they found that the cost of any dissent had risen steeply as the result of the newly acquired, overwhelming economic power of the state.

Few will deny that the deindustrialization experience in Chile and Argentina was a most unhappy chapter in Latin American economic history. As often happens with such aberrations, its perversity is almost incomprehensible in retrospect. In trying to comprehend it, holding forth on the failure of monetarist orthodoxy or on the dangers of granting dictatorial power to ideologues, be they of the free-market variety, is not quite enough. For comparative purposes, it is useful to look at the special circumstances prevailing in international finance during the middle and late seventies. During this period, huge sums of "petrodollars" were being recycled by commercial banks in the United States, Western Europe, and Japan. Suddenly there seemed to be a virtually unlimited supply of foreign exchange not only for the petroleum exporters but for the importers as well—for every country that could convince the bankers that it was bankable. The banks, with their swollen deposits, were only too willing to be convinced. In fact, they took to marketing their petrodollars with all the aggressiveness at their command.[12]

Only under these circumstances was it possible for Chile and Argentina to sustain the overvaluation of their currencies and the resulting large deficits in their balances of payments, on both current and capital accounts, over a prolonged period. In this sense, therefore, the Chilean and Argentine policy-makers were rather less autonomous than both they and their critics had believed. Rather than being sovereign shapers of their own misfortune, they should probably be viewed as having fallen pitifully into a trap set for them by the international financial system.

12. See the last section of this chapter.

Desubstitution of Imports and a Curious Convergence in Mexico

Looking at matters in this way helps in understanding another calamitous experience of the recent past—the Mexican oil boom and its aftermath. As is well known, Mexico's economic development proceeded at a remarkably steady pace during the postwar decades, more or less until the mid-seventies. Political stability, assured by a regime in which a single party predominated but was not wholly immune from criticism, was similarly impressive, as a measure of pluralism and flexibility was provided by the six-year presidential succession cycle in which each new president endeavored to correct whatever right- or left-wing leanings had been shown by his predecessor. Then came petroleum—and with it, in short order, an end to steady growth and much concern about the viability of the Mexican political system.

After a long period of stagnant and low production from old wells, large-scale deposits of petroleum were discovered in Mexico in the late sixties and early seventies. Marketing abroad on a substantial scale started in 1975, and production increased rapidly until an output of 2.3 million barrels a day was reached in 1981, making Mexico a major producer and exporter. By 1980 petroleum had become the country's dominant export (two-thirds of total exports) and a substantial contributor to the budget (taxes paid by PEMEX, the state monopoly, brought in one-quarter of total revenue).

A sudden export boom of this kind normally leads to the accumulation of considerable foreign exchange by the freshly wealthy country, which is unable in the short run to develop a demand for imports matching the rise in exports. This pattern was the experience of many oil-rich Middle Eastern countries after the 1973 rise in petroleum prices and led to the need to "recycle" their petrodollars in the first place. What was remarkable about the Mexican story from the beginning was that the country's imports never fell behind the rapidly growing petroleum exports. Initially, this trend seemed to testify to the ability of the Mexican policy-makers to push the tempo of the country's economic development so as to take full advantage of its new opportunities. But soon the growth of imports exceeded that of exports by increasingly worrisome margins. It also became clear that the process was anything but planned. Although Mexico did not experience deindustrialization, at least not during the late seventies, it went through a related process that has been termed *import desubstitution:* in contrast with the earlier development experience, imports came to account for an increasingly important portion of total domestic supply, for consumer, capital, and intermediate goods alike.[13]

This process resulted from a familiar sequence: imports soared as domestic prices rose and the government refused either to devalue or to restrict imports through administrative controls. Eventually, as the public began to perceive that the overvaluation of the currency could not last, massive capital flight also took place, as in Argentina. Once again, both excess imports and capital flight were made possible by the international banking system. Private lending was particularly generous in the case of Mexico, whose oil wealth was thought to offer solid guarantees of repayment. There is no need to detail the outcome: the debt crisis and temporary moratorium of 1982, the headlong devaluations, the painful negotiations with foreign creditors and the International Monetary Fund, the cutbacks in public spending, and the recession in an economy that found it difficult to regain its buoyancy and was hit again, three years later, by the earthquake of 1985 and the precipitous drop in oil prices in early 1986.

Comparing the Mexican story with those of Argentina and Chile raises some intriguing questions. In all three cases, the readiness of the international banks to finance balance-of-payments deficits facilitated the surprisingly similar policies that were pursued. These policies consisted in maintaining overvalued exchange rates that boosted imports, penalized exports, and led to speculative capital outflows. But the ideologies that underlay these policies could not have been more different. In Mexico during the last years of President López Portillo (1976–1982), considerable influence was held by a group of economists and officials who, with the help of neo-Keynesian advisers from Cambridge (England), prepared an ambitious plan for pushing the country's in-

13. René Villareal, *La contrarrevolución monetarista* (Mexico, D.F.: Océano, 1984), 429–434.

dustrialization.[14] Hoping to use Mexico's oil bonanza to accelerate the country's development, they advocated strong quantitative import, exchange, and investment controls so that priority would be assured for their projects. Although they were not successful in getting these policies adopted, they (and other, differently motivated actors) effectively opposed devaluation for a long time, probably because they believed that the pressures deriving from overvaluation would force a decision imposing the policy course they favored.

The doctrines and preferences of policy-makers in Chile and Argentina, whose teachers and advisers hailed from Chicago, were all set against selective administrative controls and in favor of general monetary policy instruments—the exact opposite of those of the Mexicans and their Cambridge confederates. Yet the Chilean and Argentine policy-makers also supported overvalued exchange rates, far too long. This convergence on (wrongheaded) praxis by the two opposed doctrinal camps into which economists like to array themselves is surely remarkable. One cannot quite resist the thought that in both Mexico and the Southern Cone policy-makers were fundamentally swayed by some craving to take advantage of the unprecedented borrowing opportunities opening up in the seventies and bent whatever ideologies were at hand to satisfy that appetite. According to this interpretation, the principal contribution of ideology was not the choice of policy but the stubbornness with which policy-makers of divergent persuasions persisted in their errors.

"Forced-March Industrialization" in Brazil

Fortunately, the Latin American scene is diverse enough to provide relief from the dispiriting stories reviewed up to this point. While Argentina and Chile deindustrialized and Mexico "desubstituted," Brazil vigorously consolidated and extended its leadership as the continent's major industrial power. The paradox of Latin American economic development in the period of high petroleum prices (1973–1985) indeed

14. *Plan nacional de desarrollo industrial* (Mexico, D.F.: Secretaría de Patrimonio y Fomento Industrial, 1979).

lies in the striking contrast between the serious economic setbacks suffered by newly oil-rich Mexico and the strides made by oil-poor and oil-hungry Brazil. Here are all the elements of a fine, if puzzling, moral tale: it appears that lacking petroleum is a blessing in disguise, while being abundantly supplied with it is an even more cunningly camouflaged curse. But to leave matters at that is not quite enough for social scientists who are legitimately curious about the components of the Brazilian story.

First of all, the announcement that this story was on the whole positive may surprise those who are aware of only one often-repeated statistic: Brazil, with its one-hundred-billion-dollar debt, is Latin America's biggest debtor (followed closely by Mexico). The interest payments on this debt amount are truly burdensome, absorbing about one out of every three dollars earned by current exports. But the dollar amount of the debt must be viewed in relation to the size of the country's economy, and the interest payments in relation to the turnaround in its external accounts. Since 1983 a very large export surplus has been achieved, due about equally to vigorous expansion in exports (mostly of manufactures) and deep cuts in imports, which have not interfered with a strong revival of domestic economic activity. In contrast to Argentina and Mexico, only a small part of Brazil's debt is the counterpart of domestic capital flight; borrowing served mainly to build up large-scale industrial and other projects in the seventies. Brazil did experience a sharp recession in 1981–1983, but growth was resumed in 1984 as a result of a developing export boom. In 1985 the growth rate rose to 8 percent, and employment rebounded. In the midst of these economic developments, the country made the difficult transition from twenty years of military rule to a civilian "New Republic."

In his 1985 book, *A Economia Brasileira em Marcha Forçada,* Antônio Barros de Castro offers a convincing explanation for the performance of Brazil's economy.[15] He argues that the improvement in Brazil's balance of payments and its simultaneous rapid recovery from recession cannot be explained adequately by a routine market reaction to the

15. Antônio Barros de Castro, *A economia brasileira em marcha forçada* (Rio de Janeiro: Paz e Terra, 1985). The book was coauthored with Francisco Eduardo Pires de Souza, but I am drawing here on the first chapter which was written by Castro.

"maxidevaluation" of 1983. Rather, they must be credited to a peculiarly fortunate (and fortuitous) conjunction of market and plan: the devaluation came on top of the maturing, in the late seventies and early eighties, of numerous industrial projects that had been undertaken as part of the so-called Second National Development Plan elaborated by the Geisel administration early in its term (1973–1979).[16]

This new departure in industrial policy was decided upon after the first oil shock in 1973, which had dealt Brazil a heavy blow, given its dependence on imported oil and prevalence of automobile transportation. The prudent course might have been to apply restrictive economic policies so as to rein in imports. Instead, President Geisel and his economic advisers decided to push industrial investments away from the automobile and consumer durables of the "miracle" years (1968–1973) and into the sectors that represent the ultimate stage of import-substituting industrialization and that had remained the hardest to crack for Latin America's industrializers: intermediate inputs, especially in chemical and metallurgical industries, and capital goods. Given the increase in petroleum prices, this course could be followed only by incurring large balance-of-payments deficits, that is, by borrowing. But this approach turned out to be a feasible option because of the petrodollars that became available in large amounts. The major investments were often joint ventures of the state and private capital, both domestic and foreign; and the stimulus and the credit facilities of the Banco Nacional de Desenvolvimento Econômico e Social (BNDES), with their subsidized interest rates, played an essential role. During the subsequent Figueiredo administration (1979–1985), economic policy became much more hesitant and even erratic as well as subject to pressures from the International Monetary Fund. But because the large industrial projects of the Second Plan were already under way, they were continued willy-nilly.

In the seventies both Brazil and Mexico attempted to reach for the "ultimate" stage of import-substituting industrialization. I venture the

16. Albert Fishlow seems to me to miss this thrust of Castro's argument in his otherwise valuable critical comments. See Fishlow, *A Tale of Two Presidents: The Political Economy of Brazilian Adjustment to the Oil Shocks,* Working Papers in Economics (Berkeley: University of California, 1986), pp. 49–51.

following obviously stylized formulation: the Brazilians succeeded, without any foreign advisers, in doing what the Mexican economic planners with their Cambridge advisers planned to do but were unable to accomplish, in part because they started too late in the decade and in part because their planned investments were crowded out by the vast surge of consumer goods imports caused by the overvalued peso.

The Brazilian story, as told by Antônio Castro, sounds quite straight-forward. Yet it could be formulated only in the mid-eighties, because at an earlier stage, before the military had actually relinquished political power, no progressive social scientist would have spoken so positively of them and their policies. Once again, it was possible to acknowledge the achievements of a period only after it had safely passed.[17] Actually, the Geisel administration must also be credited with the major political accomplishment of stopping institutionalized torture and fostering the political opening or *distensão* that eventually permitted a return to elec-tions and civilian rule.

At this point, it is almost impossible to avoid returning to a debate that raged in the mid-seventies about the connection between author-itarian regimes and stages of industrial development in Latin America. It was started by Guillermo O'Donnell's imaginative proposition that the "difficult" advanced stage of import-substituting industrialization (manufacturing intermediate industrial materials and capital goods) brings with it a number of political problems that undermine populist or democratic governments in Latin America. Hence the suggestion that some correspondence exists between this stage and the establish-ment of authoritarian political forms.[18] Brazil, with its advanced indus-

17. Even that acknowledgment must have been by no means easy, for it effectively amounted to breaking some sort of code. It is worth recalling that, in spite of the authoritarian character of the Brazilian military regime, many published commentaries on its economic policies came from opponents of the regime who were unfailingly critical and won plaudits for that reason. Castro addresses himself at length to certain almost ritualized critiques of import-substituting industrialization, namely, that it leads to "strangulation" through newly enhanced needs for imports or that it caters only to the needs of a narrow middle class. He explains incisively how these critiques are not applicable to the kind of industries that were given priority in the seventies. Castro also discusses earlier polemical commentaries of other Brazilian economists—such as Carlos Lessa, Maria Conceição Tavares, and Edmar Bacha—intending (as I read him) to affirm that a more differentiated appraisal of the past economic policies of the various military regimes is now in order.

18. I refer to this conjecture in Chapter 19, below.

trial structure, is obviously a critical testing group for this hypothesis, which seems a priori not implausible. As José Serra had pointed out in 1977, however, it was disconfirmed on various counts by the Brazilian data.[19] With Castro's analysis, it is now tempting to go further and explore the inverse hypothesis: is there reason to think that some organic connection existed between the industrial development policy of the Geisel government and the gradual dismantling of repressive authoritarianism that was set in motion at that time? Or was the simultaneity of the two policies totally fortuitous? I doubt very much the existence of any direct causal link in one direction or the other. But one characteristic is shared by the two tasks undertaken by that enterprising administration: both required a great deal of delicate steering (of economy and polity, respectively) as well as much confidence that, with the proper kind of such steering from above, the country was assured of a brilliant modern destiny—the old positivist faith. In this sense, the two tasks that were shouldered by the Geisel administration can be said to have shared a common wellspring.

The Brazilian Computer Industry: Breaking the Shackles of the Product Cycle

Industrialization in Latin America has long followed the path of progressive import substitution. Impelled by the backward linkage dynamic, the last stage of the process was to be the substitution of domestic production for imports in the field of intermediate inputs and capital goods. Many writers (often intent on criticizing accomplishments to date) have presented advances into this area as essential to establishing an "integrated" industrial structure—the promised land that would bring release from all kinds of ills affecting the industrialization effort, from fragmentation to dependency. The fascination with this ultimate redeeming stage may have kept analysts from noting that it is not really the *nec plus ultra* of industrialization. Rather than completing the import-substituting sequence, a newly industrializing

19. José Serra, "Three Mistaken Theses Regarding the Connection between Industrialization and Authoritarian Regimes," in *The New Authoritarianism in Latin America*, ed. David Collier (Princeton: Princeton University Press, 1979), pp. 99–164.

country may at some point make a clean break with the whole process, dispensing with the services rendered by imports in mapping and developing its own market. This process has been at work routinely in the competition among advanced industrial nations. In fact, the mark of a country reaching industrial maturity is that it will more and more frequently short-circuit the import-substituting sequence either spontaneously, as when a country achieves a position of entrepreneurial and technological leadership in some product line, or as a result of deliberate public policy. Thus a government may decide that the domestic manufacture of some new product currently produced abroad (but not yet imported in large volume) should be encouraged, and so it temporarily reserves in one way or another the country's domestic market for the local industry that is to be called into existence. Such a policy resembles, but goes one step beyond, the familiar protectionism that is meant to foster the substitution of imports by domestic production, and it may be called *import-preempting industrialization*.

Without bothering to formulate this concept, the Brazilians have stumbled onto the policy in connection with the computer industry in the decade from 1975 to 1985. After considerable preparation by technical experts and policy-makers, the first overt step was taken in June 1977, when the government refused to allow IBM and other transnational corporations to manufacture minicomputers in Brazil. The policy was solemnly reaffirmed in 1984, when a law defining a "national policy for *informática*" was approved by a large majority in the Brazilian Congress. The basic policy embodied in the law has become known as the Reserva de Mercado (or market reserve): for eight years the domestic market is to be set aside for domestic firms manufacturing certain products in the computer industry, primarily mini- and microcomputers. After a difficult start, the Brazilian industry appears to have done well, especially in the microcomputer field. As in the leading producer countries, it has experienced rapid growth and falling costs, developed endogenous innovation capacity, and become an important source of employment.

Several excellent studies are already available on this newest chapter in the industrialization of late-coming countries, primarily by political scientists and political sociologists attracted by the light it promises to shed on the policy-making process and on the character of the state.[20] I will therefore limit myself to some further broad remarks on the political economy of the phenomenon.

The Brazilian case suggests the conditions under which this sort of industrial policy is likely to recommend itself to the policy-makers of an industrializing country. In the first place, the country must be assured of a strong potential domestic market for the products of the new industry; on the supply side, the country must be fairly advanced in industrial engineering and in the capacity to clone imported prototypes. Second, it helps considerably if, as happened in Brazil, the national defense establishment can make a strong case for having a special interest in the industry's domestic development. Third, considering that the policy is likely to be applied only in a few exceptional instances, it will probably be restricted to those "epochal" industries that have a special aura of heralding a new industrial era. Finally, the case for the policy of market reserve or import preemption will seem especially compelling when, in the absence of such a policy, transnational corporations equipped to create "consumer addiction" are poised to take over the domestic market, never to be dislodged by domestic producers once established. Import prevention can be viewed as a riposte by the industrializing country to certain practices and products of industrial leaders that are likely to create impediments to later import substitution.

This point supplies one economic justification of the new policy. Its more basic defense (against the accusation of uneconomic use of resources) rests on the classic infant-industry argument. The traditional counterargument, namely that protection is usually retained long after the infant should have grown up, does not apply in the present case. The extreme form of protection that has been granted to the Brazilian

---

20. Peter B. Evans, "State, Capital, and the Transformation of Dependence: The Brazilian Computer Case," *World Development,* 14 (July 1986), 791–808; Emanuel Adler, "Ideological Guerillas and the Quest for Technological Autonomy: Brazil's Domestic Computer Industry," *International Organization,* 40 (Summer 1986), 673–705; Fábio Stefano Erber, "The Development of the 'Electronics Complex' and Government Policies in Brazil," *World Development,* 13 (March 1985), 293–310; and Simon Schwartzman, "High Technology vs. Self-Reliance; Brazil Enters the Computer Age" (working paper, Center for International Studies, Massachusetts Institute of Technology, 1985).

industry (exclusion of the foreign product) has a counterpart in the finite period of eight years during which the exclusion is scheduled to last: domestic producers have been given notice that they had better "grow up" by 1992.

One argument often raised against the Brazilian policy is that it is wasteful and stupid to want to reinvent the wheel. But this objection dissolves upon reflection. Again, the infant analogy is useful. In the course of their development, humans have to reinvent a great many things—from learning how to walk to the proper use of language—and this intensive practice in reinvention and re-creation is surely a necessary, although not sufficient, condition for the subsequent generation of genuine creativity. The problem in industrial research and development is not how to minimize reinvention but how to achieve the best possible balance between reinvention and taking advantage of the existing stock of knowledge for the purpose of accelerating both industrialization and creativity.[21]

A final point must be made about the wider significance of Brazil's decision to build up its own computer industry. Latin Americans have long justified their industrialization policies on the grounds that if they were to adhere closely to the "law of comparative advantage" with its static framework, they would remain underdeveloped forever. Responding in part to this charge and to the realities of worldwide industrialization, some of the more enlightened economists of the West (or North) visualized a new international division of labor in manufactures that took account of dynamic comparative advantage; it was embodied in what Raymond Vernon called the "product cycle."[22] In the course of this cycle new products would be invented, manufactured, and perfected first in the most advanced industrial countries, whence they would be exported to the rest of the world. Eventually, however, the technology for any given new product line settles down and the

21. For an argument along such lines, see Richard Nelson "Uncertainty, Learning, and the Economics of Parallel Research and Development Efforts," *Review of Economics and Statistics,* 43 (November 1961), 351–364.

22. "International Investment and International Trade in the Product Cycle," *Quarterly Journal of Economics,* 80 (May 1966), 190–207; see also the survey by R. D. Norton, "Industrial Policy and American Renewal," *Journal of Economic Literature,* 24 (March 1986), 1–40.

new products become standardized, at which point the industry be-comes footloose and can often be profitably started in, perhaps even be largely captured by, newly industrializing countries with their cheaper labor. According to this construct, the less-developed countries are no longer permanently relegated to the task of producing primary products for world markets. They are now entitled to industrialize but are once again assigned a somewhat lowly role, as they are supposed to follow at a respectful distance behind the advanced countries, which are the only ones to blaze new industrial trails. The significance of the Brazilian computer policy is now becoming clear: coming some thirty years after Prebisch's call against the "outdated schema of international division of labor," it can be seen as a second-generation rebellion against a new schema that would again attempt to confine the major industrializing country of Latin America, this time according to alleged rules of dy-namic, rather than static, comparative advantage.[23]

The question of whether Brazil's daring bid for participation in in-dustrial leadership can succeed is likely to remain open for some time. The difficulties of competing in the world of high technology are no doubt formidable. But aside from such obvious benefits as training in innovation, it appears that considerable advantages as well as symbolic significance can accompany breaking into an industry when it is in its early, rather than its "settled down," stage.

The "Heterodox Shock" Therapy for Fighting Inflation in Argentina and Brazil

Observers of Latin American politics have coined a useful term: they often talk about the *new spaces* that are being opened up, constructed, or occupied by political actors, occasionally even under authoritarian regimes, by means of new social movements and initiatives. The term *space* suggests a widening of the range and repertoire of politics as well

---

23. The words in quotes are from *The Economic Development of Latin America and Its Principal Problems* (New York: United Nations Economic Commission for Latin America, 1950). This document, which I have called the "ECLA manifesto," was not signed by Raúl Prebisch, then Executive Secretary of the Commission, but was widely known to have been authored by him.

as the possibility of stepping outside of existing power relations, ideologies, and institutions. This opening up of new possibilities is what
happened with the moves to bring inflation under control by means of
Argentina's Plan Austral in June 1985 and Brazil's Plan Cruzado in
March 1986.

In discussing these experiments in monetary policy, I shall give primary emphasis to political and sociological aspects. But some of the
basic economic facts need to be laid out briefly. In both Argentina and
Brazil, inflation had been running at or close to three-digit levels for
some years (since 1975 in Argentina and 1980 in Brazil, with Argentina's inflation rate generally two or three times higher). For inflation
to persist at such levels without accelerating to hyperinflation is unusual.
It indicates that both countries were equipped with elaborate mechanisms for indexing wages, salaries, exchange rates, and interest rates
that contributed mightily to making inflation both tolerable and self-
perpetuating. In both countries fiscal deficits initially played an important role in contributing to inflation, but as prices continued to soar
for a number of years, it could be argued that the deficit, or a large part
of it, was as much an effect as a cause of inflation.

In 1981 the U.S. economy went into a recession and international
interest rates rose sharply; in 1982 net international lending came to a
full stop with the Mexican moratorium. As a result, the Brazilian and
Argentine economies came under strong pressures to contract in order
to adjust their balances of payments. In the course of the ensuing recession deep import cuts were achieved, aided by some sharp devaluations. All the while, however, inflation continued unabated—indeed, it
accelerated. Under these conditions, it is easy to understand why the
customary advice of the International Monetary Fund to fight inflation
by contracting the economy even further met with enormous resistance.

In the fifties and sixties, a group of Latin American economists had
proposed a "structuralist" alternative to the "monetarist" analysis and
prescriptions of the IMF. The structuralists distinguished between
"fundamental" inflationary pressures arising from domestic social
structures (such as antiquated land tenure systems) or certain features
of the international division of labor, and the more superficial "prop-

agation" phenomena (such as the wage-price spiral). Whatever the merits of this distinction when inflation was in the lower portion of the two-digit range (as was the case in the fifties in the more inflation-prone Latin American countries), it lost plausibility once inflation accelerated to the three-digit range. At that point, it became obvious that the "propagation mechanisms" had taken off on their own and had themselves turned into the "fundamental" factors that were driving inflation. They were now dubbed "inertial inflation" and desperately needed to be addressed.

Increasingly faced by the threat of hyperinflation, Argentine and Brazilian policy-makers were in a quandary. Disliking the IMF paradigm and left without a serviceable counterparadigm of their own, they sought a new policy space. They were fortunate in being assisted by a group of economists of considerable theoretical acumen and practical imagination who, drawing on a wide variety of insights (from the sociological theory of inflation to rational expectations), had conceived of a novel formula for bringing inflation under control: the "heterodox shock" treatment of inflation. It was used first in 1985 in Argentina and was applied again at the beginning of 1986 in Brazil.[24]

The two reform plans share a number of basic features.[25] First, the old currency is replaced by a new one (one unit of the latter equals one thousand units of the former). Second, prices and wages are temporarily frozen. Third, indexation of wages, salaries, and monetary instruments is abolished. Fourth, with the return to price stability (which should improve the fiscal position on several counts) and with the help of additional austerity moves, the government will cut its borrowing from the central bank (the Argentine government pledged to give it up entirely). Fifth, prereform contracts involving payments at future dates are assumed to have made provision for expected inflation, and their

24. The term *heterodox shock* was probably coined by Francisco Lopes; his book with this title was published shortly after the Brazilian reform move. See *O choque heterodoxo; Combate à inflação e reforma monetária* (Rio de Janeiro: Campus, 1986). Other important contributors to the discussion are Pérsio Arida, Edmar Bacha, Luiz Carlos Bresser Pereira, and André Lara Resende in Brazil; and Adolfo Canitrot, Roberto Frenkel, and Daniel Heymann in Argentina.

25. A similar plan was applied in Israel in July 1985. See the article by Michael Bruno in *Inflação zero*, ed. Pérsio Arida (Rio de Janeiro: Paz e Terra, 1986).

terms are changed by applying to future payments in the new currency a conversion table *(tablita)* that establishes a series of equivalences between the new and the old currency (depending on maturity), in line with an official estimate of expected inflation under the old and new regimes.

The principal objective of these measures was to break inflationary expectations and to contain any recessionary impact by not relying exclusively on changes in the monetary aggregates. A key role was to be played by price and wage controls, the principal "heterodox" aspect of the plan, while the tablita was its major technical innovation. To a considerable extent, the success of the reform was thought to rest on a new "social contract" or "social concertation"; this, it was hoped, would replace the tug-of-war for income shares among different social groups, which had long fueled inflation. It was this tug-of-war, institutionalized through widespread indexation, that was thought to be responsible for the growing inertial component of inflation during its accelerating phase.

In both Argentina and Brazil, the reforms were successful in stopping the inflation—for a while. In Argentina prices began to rise again at some 5 percent per month in the middle of 1986 (as against 25 percent before the reform), and in Brazil the Cruzado Plan experienced a serious breakdown in November of the same year. But even the limited success that was achieved calls for some comments.

The Brazilian and Argentine reforms have several points in common. For one, both countries experienced, at about the same time, three-digit inflation that threatened to get wholly out of control. More significantly, ideas about the "heterodox shock" had been worked out in intensive, often joint discussions among a group of prominent Argentine and Brazilian economists who, having strong democratic convictions and new technical proposals to offer, were given influential policy or advisory positions in both countries when the inflation took a turn for the worse in 1985–86. A third circumstance they shared is the most interesting: both countries had only recently reinstalled civilian governments after long spells of military rule. At the time of the reforms, the new governments had held power for some eighteen months in Argentina and for almost a year in Brazil; in both countries, inflation had worsened during those periods, causing the new governments to lose prestige and appeal.

Actually, both phases experienced by the fledgling democracies of Argentina and Brazil—the worsening of inflation and the subsequent reform move—can be seen as conditioned by the politics of the post-authoritarian situation. When a civilian democratic government first comes into power after a long period of repressive military rule, it is normal for various newly active groups of the reborn civil society—particularly the long-repressed trade unions—to stake substantial claims for higher incomes. The initial impulse of those to whom the demands are addressed is to grant at least some of them, be it for the sake of social peace or out of a sense of obligation to undo past oppression and injustice. New inflationary and balance-of-payments pressures are likely to result from granting such demands. As I have pointed out elsewhere, inflation can be a useful mechanism in this situation because it permits newly emerging or reemerging social groups to flex their muscles, while it acts as a providential safety valve for accumulated social pressures.[26] This mechanism works only up to a point, however, with the tolerance for additional inflation varying from one case to another. For example, in Spain after Franco, the tolerance for accelerating inflation was probably much greater than in postauthoritarian Argentina and Brazil, where inflation had already reached triple-digit levels by the time civilian governments took over. There, accelerating inflation risked a plunge into hyperinflation, with obvious dangers for the prestige and survival of the new democratic regimes.

It does not take much imagination to visualize a simple and dismal cyclical sequence: replacement of a military regime by a civilian democratic government, renewed combativeness of social groups, granting of new demands, worsening inflation, disrepute and then crisis in the civilian regime, return of the military. Fortunately, however, the relations between the return to democratic governance and inflation are more complex, as has been shown in Argentina and Brazil. To be sure, new democratic governments, especially when they take over from detested authoritarian regimes, have to cope with a new burst of com-

---

26. See "The Social and Political Matrix of Inflation: Elaborations on the Latin American Experience," in my *Essays in Trespassing*, pp. 201–202.

bativeness of social groups. But at the same time, the new governments can call upon a special reserve of good will and trust as a result of the political liberties and human rights that they have restored or established. This considerable asset of the new Argentine and Brazilian governments was a basic factor in the initial success of the monetary reforms, for if the inflationary tug-of-war, in which the various social groups have engaged for so long, is suddenly to be replaced by cooperation and willingness to believe in the success of the new policy, some basic trust must exist in the government that is enunciating the new program. This trust is conditioned less by the program itself, however technically excellent it may be, than by the promise the government embodies and by the mission with which it has been entrusted.[27]

This special asset of trust and hope can therefore counterbalance the tendency toward stronger inflationary pressures in the wake of political change to a more open—and a more openly contentious—society. There can be no question of any mechanical balance, only of two forces working in opposite directions, at different times, and with varying strength. Also, while the pressures toward inflation are only too obvious, the ability to call forth "from the vasty deep" the spirits of trust and solidarity can never be taken for granted, as Hotspur reminds us. Indeed, in both Argentina and Brazil, the reforms were enacted with much trepidation as a last resort by governments that were fast losing their grip, and they were the first to be surprised by the initial active cooperation of the public.

Final Observations on Ideology and Debt

More than twenty years ago, I published a short article on inter-American relations entitled "Out of Phase."[28] Intellectual fashions in thinking about development, I tried to show, tended to go through

27. The ideas of the preceding paragraph took shape during a conference on Latin American inflation held in Caracas in March 1986, primarily in a discussion of René Cortázar's paper on the problems of inflation that a new democratic Chile would have to face. The papers and discussions were published in *Pensamiento Iberoamericano*, 9 (1986), the journal that sponsored the conference.

28. Hirschman, "Out of Phase," *Encounter*, special issue on Latin America (September 1965), 21–23.

changes in the United States that were matched by shifts in the opposite direction, occurring at about the same time, in the mood of Latin America, the result being an "orgy of misinterpretation and misunderstanding." I was writing about the five-year period up to 1965, without attempting to argue that this mismatch had a necessary or permanent character. But looking at the current scene and noting that my title applies more than ever, I almost wonder whether I might have stumbled onto some sort of law.

In the earlier article, I talked about contrasting switches from one set of beliefs to another. This time I am concerned with a more fundamental, if less easily defined, shift from total confidence in the existence of a fundamental solution for social and economic problems to a more questioning, pragmatic attitude—from ideological certainty to more open-ended, eclectic, skeptical inquiry. Latin Americans have long been criticized in North America for the ideological rigidity with which they allegedly approach many issues. In the field of economic policy, where discussion often proceeds along ideological lines as the consequence of a long history of antagonistic debate between laissez-faire and interventionist economists, it is probably true that many Latin Americans have tended to take ideological positions (both left and right) on such matters as planning, the market mechanism, foreign investment, inflation, the government's role in economic development, and so on.

But there are signs of substantial change in this picture, largely as a result of bitter experience. In the aftermath of the repressive authoritarian regimes that came to power in the sixties and seventies, many Latin Americans did more than rally to a politics accommodating a range of opinions, each one firmly held. They were sufficiently shaken in their certainties to wish to engage in open-ended dialogue and deliberation, ready to discover something new about their own opinions and values.[29] In Argentina, perhaps the most conflict-ridden Latin American society over the past fifty years, the idea of "social concertation," a process involving much give and take on the part of various social groups, has achieved considerable prestige. I was told that no one

29. See my "Notes on Consolidating Democracy in Latin America," in *Rival Views of Market Society,* pp. 176–182.

today would proudly bestow the name *intransigente* upon a political party, even though a minor party with that name (dating, as might be expected, from the sixties) still exists. At the same time, the spectacular miscarriage of ideology-driven economic policies (of the left and the right) has given rise to a new experimental spirit among Latin American economists, intellectuals, and policy-makers. This spirit, with its readiness to draw on a wide variety of insights, was strongly evident in the monetary reforms enacted in Argentina and Brazil.

It will now have become clear what I mean by being "out of phase." Precisely when many influential Latin Americans were in a postideological mood, mistrusting any system of thought that pretends to have all the answers to the complex problems faced by their societies, they were confronted, particularly in the area of economic policy, with relentlessly ideological positions assumed by the government of their principal trading partner, foreign investor, and creditor. This is not the first time that the United States or multinational institutions strongly influenced by the United States have convinced themselves that they possess the key to progress and development for all those wayward, hence backward, foreign countries. In the fifties, the World Bank attempted to condition its lending on countries' establishing some form of overall economic planning.[30] In the sixties, the Alliance for Progress strongly encouraged Latin American countries to institute land and fiscal reforms—the latter then meaning stiffer taxes for the rich. But never have Latin Americans been lectured and admonished as insistently as in the eighties, this time along very different lines—on the virtues of free markets, privatization, and private foreign investment, and on the perils of state guidance and intervention as well as excessive taxation, not to mention planning. Moreover, such lectures now claim a captive audience of top Latin American economic policy-makers, who must make frequent trips to Washington to renegotiate and reschedule the heavy debt burdens that most of their countries have accumulated during the seventies.

Ideological preachings of this sort are vastly counterproductive. Be-

---

30. See Hirschman, "A Dissenter's Confession: Revisiting *The Strategy of Economic Development,*" in *Pioneers in Development,* ed. G. Meier and D. Seers (New York: Oxford University Press, 1984), pp. 90–91.

sides raising concern among Latin Americas for the sovereignty and dignity of their countries, they evoke protests that the world is far too complex to be set right by mechanically applying everywhere one identical and simplistic formula. Ironically, Latin Americans have been turning against their would-be North American preceptors the conservative critique of Edmund Burke, which emphasizes "circumstances" and refuses to "give praise or blame to anything which relates to human actions, and human concerns, on a simple view of the object, as it stands stripped of every relation, in all the nakedness and solitude of metaphysical abstraction."[31] By attempting to export its free-market credo as a universal remedy, the Reagan administration was inadvertently cutting itself off from any kind of rapport with the new leadership of the emergent Latin American democracies.

The failure of meaningful dialogue or communication between the United States and Latin America is particularly evident—and dangerous—in connection with the debt problem. This is a very large subject on which almost everything has been said, yet I feel that in closing, I must make a short statement. My emphasis will be on the way in which contrasting perceptions and ideologies contribute to complicating the problem.

As Senator Bill Bradley noted in a forceful and constructive speech, the debt accumulation of the seventies, which came to an abrupt halt in 1982 and is now known as the "debt problem," has turned into a disaster.[32] But it is a man-made disaster, so presumably man can unmake it. The question is, then, what has kept debtors and creditors from dealing decisively with a problem that has festered for over four years?[33] One reason is that creditors and debtors, or North Americans and Latin Americans, have very different ideas on where the principal responsibility for the debt accumulation belongs. North Americans have gen-

---

31. Edmund Burke, *Reflections on the Revolution in France* (1790; rpt. Chicago: Regnery, 1955), p. 18. For some remarks criticizing current U.S. policy along such Burkean lines, see Alejandro Foxley, "El problema de la deuda externa visto desde América Latina," *Colección Estudios CIEPLAN*, 18 (December 1985), 59–61.

32. "A Proposal for Third World Debt Management," 29 June 1986, U.S. Senate, Office of Senator Bill Bradley.

33. Guillermo O'Donnell asks a similar question, restricted to the Latin American debtors, in his article "Why Don't Our Countries Do the Obvious?" See *CEPAL Review*, 27 (December 1985), 27–34.

erally behaved as though the responsibility were exclusively that of the borrowers. They seem to hold to what has been called the "wallflower theory of finance," according to which banks never take the initiative of offering loans but wait to be asked by the would-be borrower, who therefore must shoulder the primary responsibility for the transaction and for everything that might go wrong with it.[34] This conception is contrary to the most elementary notion of economics, which teaches that any deal involving two or more parties is ordinarily made on the basis of anticipated mutual benefit, so that there is no reason to expect one of the parties to be wholly passive. Moreover, it is well known (and has been nicely documented in a confessional article by a former American banking official[35]) that U.S. commercial banks engaged during the seventies—as they did in the twenties and as British banks did at various times during the preceding century—in vigorous "loan pushing," sometimes even using whatever diplomatic leverage they could bring to bear on "recalcitrant" countries, such as Colombia.

So the wallflower theory is not tenable. One might oppose it with an alternative metaphor according to which the Latin Americans were the ones courted by the lenders and led down the garden path—at the end of which they were administered the "Volcker shock" of steeply rising interest rates.[36] Some Latin Americans tend to see the story more or less in this light, but most would probably agree that responsibility ought to be shared. One of the difficulties in forming a debtors' cartel has been precisely that some Latin American countries fell so much more readily into the debt trap than others.

As was noted in earlier sections, the governments of Chile, Argentina, and Mexico allowed or caused their currencies to be overvalued for prolonged periods in the late seventies and early eighties, thus providing

34. William Darity, Jr., "Did the Commercial Banks Push Loans on the LDCs?" in *World Debt Crisis: International Lending on Trial,* ed. Michael Claudon, (Cambridge, Mass.: Ballinger, 1986), pp. 199–225; Robert Devlin, "The Structure and Performance of International Banking during the 1970s and Its Impact on the Crisis of Latin America," Kellogg Institute Working Paper, 90 (Notre Dame, Ind.: University of Notre Dame, 1987), and Lance Taylor, "The Theory and Practice of Developing Country Debt: An Informal Guide for the Perplexed," *UN Journal of Development Planning,* 16 (1985), 204–205.

35. S. C. Gwynne, "Adventures in the Loan Trade," *Harper's Magazine,* 267 (September 1983), 22–26.

36. Taylor, n. 34, 212.

strong incentives for overimporting and capital flight, activities that led to and were facilitated by intensive borrowing. On the other hand, at least one major Latin American country (Colombia) managed to hold down its foreign indebtedness to a moderate level simply because it maintained centralized and somewhat restrictive control over foreign borrowing, public as well as private.

Mexico is an instructive case of particularly poor joint performance by the borrower and the international banking system. Here was a country that had discovered and developed large sources of petroleum at a time of highly favorable prices for this commodity. Development-minded economists had long advised countries with a sudden export bonanza of this kind to tax the new income flows so as to prevent the resulting foreign exchange earnings from being spent entirely on imports of consumer goods.[37] Such taxes were to finance investment or simply to ensure the accumulation of foreign exchange to serve as a cushion against a reversal in fortunes. What was enacted in Mexico was the exact opposite of this advice. Not only did the country fail to accumulate a portion of the newly earned foreign exchange, but it borrowed large amounts of funds on top of the bonanza export proceeds. A good part of these funds were "dissipated" (a phrase used not so long ago, when investment planning stood in high repute) in imports of consumer goods and capital flight.

Yet the responsibility for these events belongs as much to the international banking community as to Mexican private and public decision makers. A few years ago, before the debt crisis, the banks were often congratulated for the agility and smoothness with which they channeled funds in the seventies from Middle Eastern petroleum exporters to the petroleum importers whose balances of payments were hard hit by the sudden price increases. But the cases of Mexico, Nigeria, and others demonstrate that the banks lent with even greater abandon to those petroleum exporters that were busy developing, against all rules of prudence, a capacity to absorb foreign funds over and above their swollen export receipts. The international banks appear to have been instantly charmed by those countries that, unlike many other underdeveloped

37. For example, see Ragnar Nurkse, *Problems of Capital Formation in Underdeveloped Countries* (Oxford: Blackwell, 1953), pp. 98–103.

areas, could boast of a tangible asset of such unquestioned security as petroleum in the ground. The banks' desire to make clients out of such countries was simply overwhelming, and in this manner they contributed as much as the policy-makers in the borrowing countries to transform the bonanza into a disaster.

The Latin American perception is, then, that no good reason exists for their being lectured unilaterally. They are similarly unreceptive to the message of the lectures—unqualified praise for the free market and condemnation of the state. For one thing, the authoritarian rulers of Southern Cone countries have intensively and unsuccessfully experimented during the seventies with policies inspired by free-market doctrines, and these experiments are now associated in the minds of democratic Latin Americans with both ruthless military regimes and pitiful failure.[38] Moreover, the recent painful contraction of the Latin American economies was brought about precisely by the untrammeled operation of the international free market in loanable funds in the years prior to the debt crisis of 1982. It is indeed remarkable, after almost thirty years of orderly and productive capital transfers organized under the auspices of governments and multinational institutions like the World Bank and the Inter-American Development Bank, that the suddenly unleashed energies of free enterprise in international finance have managed to produce international economic havoc in less than a decade.

Here are some specific reasons for the current *desencuentro* (failure to meet) between North and Latin Americans. But the more basic obstacle to a useful dialogue between the two parties is that strange switch: North Americans, so proud not long ago of their pragmatism, have taken an ideological turn, while Latin Americans have become skeptical of their former sets of certainties and solutions and are naturally exasperated by the neophytes from the North who pretend to teach them yet another set.

38. Foxley, n. 31.

16
chapter

Is the End of the Cold War a Disaster for the Third World?

Social scientists, historians, and political observers in general agree on one point about the Eastern European revolutions of 1989: no one foresaw them. The collapse of Communist power in Eastern Europe, the fall of the Berlin Wall and the reunification of Germany, the implosions in the Soviet Union—the end of the cold war, in short—all these developments unfolded in a remarkably short time and as a huge surprise to experts and ordinary television viewers alike. But the lesson— that the utmost modesty is in order when it comes to pronouncements about the future of human societies—does not seem to have sunk in. As soon as those astounding changes in the world's political and economic map took place, numerous voices were heard uttering self-assured opinions about the implications of those changes for this or that country or group of countries. It does not seem to have occurred to these people that if the events, which are the point of departure for their speculations, were so hard to predict, considerable caution is surely in order when it comes to appraising their impact.

Published in the *New York Review of Books* under the title "Good News Is Not Bad News" on October 11, 1990; written originally under the present title for a special issue of *Pensamiento Iberoamericano,* which published it as "Es un desastre para el Tercer Mundo el fin de la guerra fría?" 18 (1990), 175–181.

The Neglect Effect

Particularly with respect to the less developed countries of the so-called Third World—the phrase makes less sense than ever, since there is hardly any political and ideological identity left of what was the "second world," that is, the Soviet sphere—the tendency to make strong predictions remains. To the most obvious question: are these events good or bad for the Third World? the immediate answer, on the part of most observers, is that they are surely bad. This answer is dictated by a primitive zero-sum model of the social world: anything "good" must have a "bad" equivalent somewhere else. Thus we hear that the Third World will suffer from the revolutions of 1989 because a larger share of supposedly limited amounts of Western capital, entrepreneurship, and, more generally, attention will now flow to the newly opened and newly attractive countries of Central and Eastern Europe. This may be called the "neglect effect" of the European revolutions of 1989 on other regions. In Latin America, and probably elsewhere in the Third World as well, the neglect effect is much talked about today. According to many, the period of neglect that is in store for the Latin American continent will inflict further damage on economies that are said to be already burdened by the "lost decade" of the 1980s.

This verdict is surely myopic. In the first place, should the neglect effect to some extent occur, is that all bad? The question makes one think of the "wise and salutary neglect" by the imperial power which, according to Burke, made an important contribution to the economic and political development of England's American colonies in the eighteenth century. As has occasionally been pointed out, a similar argument can be applied to the relations between the United States and Latin America. During the forty-five years of the cold war, the United States has been intensely, almost obsessively, concerned that social and political policies and experiments in Latin America might cause this or that country to fall into the expansionist Soviet orbit. The consequences of this fear were displayed in a variety of places, from Guatemala in the fifties to Brazil and the Dominican Republic in the sixties and Chile in the seventies. With the end of the cold war, with the disintegration of the Soviet bloc and the disappearance of whatever appeal it had, the North American propensity to intervene should be considerably reduced and Latin America should enjoy correspondingly more room of maneuver for social experimentation.

The end of the cold war should have an even more important and similarly positive effect on domestic politics in Latin America, where politics were acted out against the background of the cold war and molded by the belief, on the part of all domestic political forces, that a socialist alternative was available, and that there was something to be gained by playing off one superpower against the other. As a result, domestic politics became polarized. Reformers became radicals, while the traditional ruling groups and owners of capital resorted readily to repression and flight of capital. Under these conditions, domestic politics came to be characterized by a tendency to intransigence and for opposing sides to become more and more extreme. The new international situation is more favorable to the processes of democratic deliberation and reform.

Finally, the end of the cold war should have a beneficial effect on the rhetoric of Latin America, on the way in which the continent presents itself both to itself and to world opinion. There are two contrasting strategies for promoting interest in a given country or region: one, directed to capitalists and entrepreneurs both domestic and foreign, consists in pointing to the exceptional opportunities that are waiting to be tapped; the other, directed primarily to foreign providers of public funds or aid, emphasizes, to the contrary, that the country is in a desperate predicament and may therefore become an increasingly dangerous neighbor to have around. Under cold war conditions there was a permanent incentive for a region like Latin America to adopt the second, alarmist strategy. By emphasizing its misery, and the failure of its development, the region was not just awakening the distinctly limited compassion of the richer countries, but was feeding their considerable worry that Latin America might defect in one way or another to the Soviet camp.

With the end of the cold war, it now becomes more attractive to be attractive, to emphasize the positive, and to discover that one is doing better than anyone had thought. An interesting hint of such a shift can be found in a recent report of the United Nations Economic Commission for Latin America and the Caribbean (ECLAC or, in Spanish, CEPAL).[1] In addition to the usual survey of large trends, the report contains a great many "exhibits," or "boxes," with fairly detailed accounts of successful ventures in higher education, modernization of agriculture, industrial restructuring, promotion of new exports, and so on. Since CEPAL has a long tradition of painting a somber picture of the continent's situation, this is a notable change and may even point to a new direction. In fact, the strategy of stressing the negative had long produced decreasing and even negative returns. The "action-arousing gloomy vision," as I once called it, had come to spread gloom rather than to incite action. Designed as a stimulant, it became a depressant for both Latin Americans and foreign observers.

In contributing to a change in the way Latin Americans present themselves, the end of the cold war could help reduce a self-inflicted handicap from which Latin Americans have suffered, making the region more attractive to investors, domestic and foreign.

There are several reasons, then, why the end of the cold war could bring benefits rather than problems to countries that did not take part in the events of 1989, and why there need not be an exact equivalence of benefits reaped by some and costs sustained by others. The edifying phrase, "more liberty anywhere means more liberty everywhere," half trite though it sounds, may actually turn out to be true.

Substituting One Disaster for Another?

The proposition that the end of the cold war will lead to a diversion of limited resources that would otherwise have accrued to the Third World does not exhaust the arguments of those who propose a pessimistic interpretation of seemingly fortunate events. The task of such Cassandras has been made simpler by the mindless celebration of the events of 1989 on the part of some self-satisfied partisans. Gloating with triumphalism, highly influential voices in the West, particularly

1. *Changing Production Patterns with Social Equity* (Santiago: UN Economic Commission for Latin America and the Caribbean, 1990).

in the United States, have proclaimed the "victory of the market," even the "end of history." It was inevitable that others would scrutinize the emerging situation for rather different portents, predicting unhappy consequences not so much for the Third World as for the countries that have succeeded in putting an end both to political oppression and to economic arrangements that had become increasingly unworkable. The argument was once again of the zero-sum type: as one set of problems would be solved, new or quite old and perhaps more intractable problems would take the place of the ones just gotten rid of. In particular, ethnic, religious, and similar communal strife would now resume its position as the dominant form of domestic conflict.

This kind of strife has indeed reemerged in the newly liberated lands of Eastern Europe and also in the USSR itself. The case for its likely extension to the Third World has been ably articulated by the Indian writer Radhakrishnan Nayar in *The Times Literary Supplement*.[2] According to Nayar, the "idea of a socialist alternative," which was current through the cold war period, brought constructive political pressures to bear: it led to "significant measures of social reform." Nayar cites land reform in India and various unspecified cases of social reform in "Nasserite Egypt," as well as in Brazil, Mexico, Peru, and the Philippines: "Once the social order as a whole is no longer challenged, social discontents, which in these countries are of a gravity unknown in the West, are likely to cease to be expressed in terms of pan-human ideals, and to take on communal traits."[3] The article ends with a chilling prediction of sharper, more frequent, and more hopeless conflict, both domestic and international, in the years to come, with the cold war period being regarded as a Golden Age of peace and prosperity. Nayar argues that the disasters of the cold war era will now be replaced by other disasters of possibly greater magnitude.

The argument may have its uses as a corrective to Western triumphalism, but it has several weaknesses. First of all, it exaggerates the usefulness of the cold war in helping to bring about social reform in

---

2. "A Vacuous Optimism," *The Times Literary Supplement,* May 18–24, 1990, pp. 526, 533.

3. Pan-human seems to me a much more expressive term than the Parsonian "universalistic."

the Third World. An interesting parallel can be drawn with the economic analyses that became common in Latin America at the time of the debt crises and the economic downturn in the early 1980s. That downturn was now contrasted with the preceding thirty-year-long period of steady and dynamic progress. But the progress had never been noted, much less dwelt on, when it was taking place—public opinion was informed about this good news only in retrospect, when it served to enhance by contrast the bad news of the current turn of events.[4]

Nayar's claim that considerable social progress took place during the cold war has a similar quality. As long as the cold war persisted, opinion on the left was in general scathing in its judgments of land, tax, and other reforms introduced to reduce various social inequities in India, Latin America, and elsewhere in the Third World. I distinctly recall an analysis of land-reform experiences in Latin America which opened with the famous phrase of Giuseppe di Lampedusa, "Everything must change here so that everything will remain the same." Only now that the cold war has ended is it revealed to us that it had a marvelously stimulating effect on real reform. Actually many of the reforms that were made, partly no doubt to counteract revolutionary pressures, were less futile than they were made out to be by their critics, particularly during the fifties and sixties. (The Chilean land reform under the Frei regime is a conspicuous example.)

Nayar, however, now overstates the beneficial effects of the cold war on social reform, for from the later sixties on, the situation shifted considerably, at least in Latin America. The conflict between the two superpowers eventually produced a situation that was destructive of social reform rather than helpful to it. Polarization and intransigence took increasingly the place of openness to reform. Left-wing resort to guerrilla warfare had its counterpart in military intervention and the extensive flight of capital. Members of the entrenched elites claimed that reform measures would begin a slide down the "slippery slope" to left-wing dictatorship; and, in truth, there was an increasing number of people among the "reformers" who meant the slope to be slippery.

---

4. This point is made at greater length in the first section of the preceding chapter.

It therefore seems to me that the passing of the cold war need not be mourned on the ground that it helped stimulate social reform in the Third World. If it had any uses of the kind—such as permitting the Third World to extract funds from the superpowers by playing one off against the other—these were long past by the time the Berlin Wall came down.

But what about the more general and more worrisome point that with the passing of the socialist alternative destructive communal conflicts will now thrive? The proposition reminds me of the old joke that prediction is difficult, especially when it is about the future. The fact is that Nayar's prophecy long ago came true. Violent religious, tribal, and other communal conflicts have been with us for several decades now, in a great number of countries, from Sri Lanka to Ireland, and from Nigeria to the Punjab, to mention just some of the more conspicuous ones, without waiting for the end of the cold war. In no way has the availability of the socialist alternative kept these numerous, long, and cruel conflicts at bay.

One might even wonder whether the cold war and the ensuing worldwide antagonism between its contestants has not actually contributed to the frequency and intensity of ethnic, religious, and similar communal violence, as the participants in these conflicts were often able to obtain support, or promises of support, from one or both of the superpowers. It is therefore impossible to tell whether the end of the cold war will lead to more or to less communal strife than would have continued to occur in a cold-war-as-usual world. The same reasoning is applicable, incidentally, to international terrorism.

Finally, the demise of "actually existing socialism"—that wretched Brezhnevian mixture of political oppression and economic deterioration—need not spell the end of the long aspiration toward a more just and compassionate social order. In the first place, the end of the cold war may have the opposite effect from the one suggested by Nayar in at least one major country—the United States. Here the cold war has long had the effect of muting class conflict, since no important interest group was willing to use arguments or take positions that might suggest it was influenced by Marxism-Leninism. As a result, and in contrast to the thirties, any domestic conflict in this country was widely seen and explained in terms of race and ethnicity, rather than class. Now, with the passing of cold war taboos, there are already some signs that it is possible once again to speak about the rich and the poor as conceivably having divergent interests.[5]

No doubt the disasters that have befallen a great historical experiment which was supposed to end the "exploitation of man by man" will cast a shadow on future programs and movements that aim at combining equity with democracy and economic progress. Nevertheless, in the West as in the East and the South, the search for a just society is rooted in ancient and powerful religious and philosophical teachings. To some extent, these teachings are already incorporated in the constantly evolving institutions—known as the welfare state—of modern societies. Furthermore, the intellectual traditions just noted continue to exhibit considerable vitality: they have been vigorously renewed in recent decades through the writings of philosophers and economists such as John Rawls, Amartya Sen, and many others. The quest for "panhuman" ideals is far from being forsaken.

5. I am indebted for this point to a discussion with Gary Gerstle.

17
chapter

Industrialization and Its Manifold Discontents: West, East, and South

The title of this paper obviously takes off from Freud's classic essay, "Das Unbehagen in der Kultur" or "Civilization and Its Discontents" (1929). But at the same time my title was chosen to express a basic difference. Freud actually chose the singular "Das Unbehagen" for his title, and that was no accident; for in analyzing the psychological impact of increasing wealth and "Kultur," he intended to identify a *unitary*, robust phenomenon or one basic cause of discontent. He duly revealed it as the increasing demands and restraints which the superego necessarily imposes upon the ego as "culture" expands. This Freudian intent or nuance is unfortunately lost in the English translation: under the title "Civilization and Its Discontents" the essay did become extremely well known in the Anglo-Saxon world, but with the plural "discontents" Freud's monistic claim was watered down to a vague pluralism. Now that kind of wishy-washy pluralism is precisely what I want to proclaim in these pages. I am interested here in the multiplicity and variety of resistances, criticisms, and anxieties that have been aroused by industrialization at different points in time and in different countries.

In this spirit, my essay takes as its starting point two contrasting

Published in *World Development,* 20 (September 1992), 1225–1232 (copyright © by Elsevier Science Ltd; reprinted by permission). This essay was written in German while the author was a Fellow at the Wissenschaftskolleg (Institute for Advanced Study) in Berlin during the academic year 1990–91; it was also published in *Geschichte und Gesellschaft,* 18, (1992), 221–230.

observations. One results from a look at the industrial establishment in Eastern Europe after the collapse of Communism, the other from my long-standing interest in Latin American economic development.

In Eastern Europe, industrialization as it has been promoted there in the postwar period is today subject to severe criticism. Above all there is the shortage of consumer goods; the priority long given to heavy industry is now seen as wholly misguided. As is known, that priority fed on itself as the production of steel led perennially to more need for steel, and this was also the case for the other privileged sectors, such as heavy chemicals and machinery. Moreover, these industries were particularly polluting and their infrastructure and maintenance were often neglected; also, whether dating from the prewar or postwar periods, they were unable to keep up with technical progress in the West.

To a person conversant with Latin American development it is striking that the principal critique of industrialization in the East, that is, the priority given to heavy industry and the neglect of consumer goods, is the exact opposite, a mirror image in fact, of a critique of industrialization that is or has been widespread in Latin America. There, industrialization started with the production of consumer goods and often confined itself to, or at least remained largely focused on, such goods. Hence the reproach that industry failed to make proper progress in the direction of machinery and semi-finished industrial goods. This allegedly "incomplete" industrialization is largely responsible for the critical attitude of Latin American economists and intellectuals toward the industrial development of their countries.

I shall have more to say about these contrasting critiques later. But at this point I should like to point out that critiques of industrialization have existed from the very beginning of modern industry in the eighteenth century. It will be easier to evaluate the just mentioned current critiques (and to view them with a bit of irony) once we become aware of the earlier ones.

What one should attempt here is to create a counterpart to the famous and brilliant essay of Alexander Gerschenkron of some forty years ago on "Economic Backwardness in Historical Perspective" (Gerschenkron, 1952, pp. 3–29, and 1962, pp. 5–30). In this essay Gerschenkron compared the policies of various European countries

(France, Germany, Russia) where industrial development had remained behind that of England toward the end of the eighteenth and at the beginning of the nineteenth century.

The knowledge about the English advance and the relative backwardness of one's own country led in these various nations to a series of reactions, from the manner and style of industrialization to the way it was financed and to the diverse ideologies which favored or preached it. So one can say that Gerschenkron's principal theme was the Unbehagen or discontent with *under*industrialization. As with Freud, this was for Gerschenkron a fairly unitary phenomenon (even though I do recall distinctly that Gerschenkron, who lived for many years in Vienna, did not have much use for Freud). The counterpoint to Gerschenkron's work would then be to deal comparatively and historically with the discontents that come *with* industrialization.

It is to be expected that this topic should be more ample than Gerschenkron's. In the first place, Gerschenkron's scheme excluded by definition England, which is historically the leading industrial country. Second, and more important, it is only human to be more broadly and more multiply dissatisfied with something one already *has* than with something one lacks. I shall therefore have to confine myself to just a few varieties of the many discontents with industrialization. Fortunately it so happens that I have repeatedly dealt with this phenomenon in previous books and articles; the concept of discontent over industrialization now makes it possible to tie these various writings together.

Let me start with England. Strong criticism of industry and of industrial goods arose here practically alongside the very rise of manufacturing. We are all familiar with the vehement critique of industry and capitalism that was raised in the first half of the nineteenth century—from Coleridge, Carlyle, and Ruskin on the conservative-romantic side to Friedrich Engels's pamphlet on the situation of the working class in England and Marx and Engels's *Communist Manifesto*. But there is a much earlier critique centered less on the conditions under which industrial goods were produced than on their consumption—curiously enough, that critique comes from a person who is known primarily for having celebrated "opulence" and the *Wealth of Nations,* that is, from Adam Smith.

I have written about the ambivalent attitude of Adam Smith toward material wealth in my book *Shifting Involvements* (Hirschman, 1982, pp. 48–50). There I cited several passages, primarily in the *Theory of Moral Sentiments,* but also in the *Wealth of Nations,* where Smith speaks repeatedly of the products of industry as "trinkets and baubles" and where he declares new inventions and innovations—his favorite examples are toothpicks and "a machine to cut the nails"—as contemptible, frivolous, and even useless. In Smith's opinion, these contraptions are "fitter to be the play-things of children than the serious pursuits of men." This contemptuous attitude toward industrial consumer goods which then became newly available led Smith to an early formulation of his most famous metaphor: the Invisible Hand. It is an invisible hand, he explained, that drives men to work and to earn money, and in a way it deceives them, since the "trinkets and baubles" which are bought with those earnings are nothing but "trifling conveniencies."

A characteristic passage from the *Theory of Moral Sentiments* actually has a seventeenth-century, Hobbesian ring:

> Power and riches appear then to be . . . enormous and operose machines contrived to produce a few trifling conveniencies to the body. . . . [T]hough they may save [the owner] from some smaller inconveniencies, [they] can protect him from none of the severer inclemencies of the season. They keep off the summer shower, not the winter storm, but leave him always as much, and sometimes more, exposed than before to anxiety, to fear, and to sorrow: to diseases, to danger, and to death.   (Smith, 1976, p. 183)

In France there were similar currents. Rousseau often used a term that is an almost exact equivalent of Smith's trinkets and baubles: "colifichet." The term, which designates frivolous and virtually useless objects—often bought by or for women—can be found in almost all of his political works, always with a derogatory meaning (Hirschman, 1982, pp. 50–51).

At one point Rousseau even made a distinction between two kinds of luxuries or *luxe,* the *luxe des colifichets,* that is, luxury of objects, on the one hand, and the luxury of keeping many retainers, on the other. In his last large-scale political treatise, the *Considerations on the Government of Poland,* he advised the Poles to opt for the luxury of retainers rather than for the *colifichets,* which he regarded as peculiarly corrupting. A similar distinction was made by François Quesnay, the eminent Physiocrat, and by other members of this school or sect, between the luxury of objects, which they called the *luxe de décoration,* and the lavish spending on food, designated, strangely to our ears, as *luxe de subsistance.* Again, definite preference was expressed for spending on an abundant table over the purchase of more durable objects, for reasons no doubt related to the physiocratic doctrine on which I shall comment shortly.

The contempt for worldly goods shows up also during the French Revolution, as when Robespierre, a great admirer of Rousseau, coined the expression "chétives marchandises" (miserable, pitiful, sickly merchandise) in a famous speech. Using this term, he criticized the looting of certain city stores by the Parisian crowd in 1793. Robespierre thought that the revolutionary energies of the people should be preserved for nobler deeds than the stealing of sugar and coffee. This reminds one now of the attitude of certain intellectuals in the former German Democratic Republic during the fall of 1989: they thought it was highly disappointing and contemptible that the Berliners from the Eastern part of the city should be yearning not only for liberty, but also for bananas and VCRs.

Among French eighteenth-century voices, the Physiocrats must be specially singled out as critics of emerging industry. One of their best known propositions was that agriculture is the sole source of wealth, in contrast to commerce, handicraft, and industry. Many sophisticated explanations have been proposed for this odd thesis, but to my mind they never satisfactorily answered the naive question: how is it conceivable that Quesnay and Turgot, penetrating and ingenious as they were in so many ways, came up with something quite so wrong-headed, not to say absurd? A possible explanation appears as one sees their views in conjunction with the just reported critiques of manufactured objects by Adam Smith and Rousseau. At the time, the products of the industrial and artisan trades were perhaps seen as inferior because they were subject to continuous variation dictated by the whim of fashion—specially during the second half of the eighteenth century with its extravagant rococo style. Those objects failed to satisfy basic human needs through the production of ever identical goods, a function so reliably performed by agricultural activities and their output.

In spite of his well-known interest in industrial crafts, even Diderot criticized the world of objects in such terms. In a passage in which he speculates about the effect of expanding trade with the new colonies on the European mind and temper, he wrote: "The variety and multiplicity of objects which industry has presented to our minds and senses have diminished the emotions of men and have weakened the energy of our sentiments. Our characters have become blunted."[1]

So the principal reproach to new goods was perhaps industry's propensity for continuous innovation, which was sensed as essentially frivolous. It is important to realize that the concept of innovation received only much later the positive connotation it has today. In spite of its belief in progress, the eighteenth century remained in this regard under the influence of the value judgments of the more pessimistic seventeenth century. Let me recall here Pascal's exclamation: "L'homme— quelle nouveauté!" which was meant as anything but a compliment.[2]

Perhaps we should place the eighteenth-century voices which I have rapidly recalled here against the general background of the considerable *ambivalence* toward material wealth that marked the previous century. In the seventeenth century Dutch and Flemish painters perfected two genres that seem antithetical to us: on the one hand, there were the magnificent still lifes of fruits, flowers, musical instruments, and other objects that celebrate life, the senses, and wealth, and on the other, sometimes the identical painters would excel in the *vanitas* paintings that also portray valuable earthly possessions, but include a skull, an hourglass, and similar reminders of perishability, fragility, and human mortality. As far as I am aware the relation between these two genres has not aroused the curiosity it surely deserves.

I must, however, move on to the nineteenth century and consider a new set of complaints and accusations against industry. For industrial

1. This passage is in a section Diderot contributed to Raynal, 1781, vol. 10, p. 11. It was brought to my attention by Anthony Pagden.

2. As is clear from the context; the full quote from Pascal's *Pensées* (p. 1206) is: "Quelle chimère est-ce donc que l'homme! Quelle nouveauté, quel monstre, quel chaos, quel sujet de contradiction, quel prodige!" (What a chimera is man! What a novelty, what a monster, what a chaos, what a subject of contradiction, what a marvel!).

England a comprehensive, if a bit monotonous, description of this broad intellectual current in literature, history, and politics has been compiled by the American historian Martin Wiener, *English Culture and the Decline of the Industrial Spirit, 1850–1980* (1981). After a brief period of enthusiasm for the new industry, Wiener argues, most influential English intellectuals subscribed instead to the "gentlemanly ideal." Some critics have contested this thesis and thereby also questioned the main point of the book, namely, that the retardation of industry in England relative to Germany and the United States in the late nineteenth and early twentieth century can be explained by these intellectual currents (see, for example, Collini, 1981, p. 1426).

In any event, the English critiques were directed against industry in general and not against any particular pattern of industrialization, as was to be the case later on in other industrializing countries. In general, the discontents of industrialization led in England to a lament over irreparable damage to the quality of life ("The World We Have Lost" being a famous and representative title). There was no feeling of an immediate, specific danger against which one could and should act—rather, one was faced with unfortunate happenings which could not be helped.

In Germany the situation was very different. Here the various discontents were primarily formulated with the intention of requesting the state to undertake specific remedial action.[3]

Two principal concerns were voiced. First of all, there was the fear, arising before the turn of the century, that Germany, with its rapid industrialization, might "lose" its agriculture and its ability to feed itself, just as had already happened in England in the course of the 1870s with the importation of cheap grain from overseas. Now England could afford such a development, said the German observers, for it had a huge empire as well as a mighty fleet. But for Germany a similar shrinking of domestic agricultural production would be a real catastrophe. A bit later this fear was complemented by another. It was becoming clear that not only Germany but many other countries were setting out on the road to industrialization. This development was fa-

---

3. The basis for the following paragraphs is in Hirschman, 1945 [1980], pp. 146–151, and Hirschman, 1952, pp. 270–283.

cilitated by the unimpeded export of machinery from the older industrial countries. Worldwide industrialization, so some writers prognosticated, would soon bring a decline in the exports of industrial goods. Hence it was foolhardy for an industrializing country to put all its eggs into the industrial basket. At the time, people found it hard to believe that trade could consist of anything but an exchange of manufactured goods against agricultural staples or minerals. The enormous potential of intertrade of industrial goods was as yet beyond the imagination of most observers.

These two fears were, of course, criticized as unjustified by liberal, laissez-faire thinkers of the time. The titles of their writings mock quite aptly the two anxieties I have mentioned. Thus a 1901 essay by Lujo Brentano is entitled *Das Schrecken des überwiegenden Industriestaates* (The Terrors of the State where Industry is Predominant) and that by Heinrich Dietzel bears an even more alarming title: *Is Exporting Means of Production Equivalent to Economic Suicide?* (1907).

Nevertheless, these anxieties were real. Some forty years ago I dealt with them in lines that still seem pertinent:

> German writers took a certain delight in showing that the industrial countries were digging their own grave through the export of machinery and industrial techniques. This propensity for discovering apocalyptic historical vistas has been a general trait of German historical and sociological writing since the nineteenth century. It can, for example, also be found in the familiar Marxist analysis which showed how capitalism was preparing its own destruction through the creation of a proletariat and how competition was destined for extinction because of the way in which the competitive struggle led to monopoly. These numerous prophecies of doom do not teach us so much about the real nature of industrialism, capitalism, and competition as about the state of mind of their intellectual authors, ill at ease in the industrial age, and therefore inordinately fertile in finding proofs for its inevitable dissolution. (Hirschman, 1952, p. 281)

The German discontents with industrialization, as distinct from the English variety, had an important impact on politics. They were in part responsible for a series of fateful actions of the Wilhelmine Reich, from colonial expansion, primarily in Africa, to naval construction, to the protection of agriculture and the famous alliance of "steel and rye," that is, the compact between heavy industry and the Junkers. All of these policies contributed to the outbreak of World War I. The prophecies of doom turned out to be self-fulfilling, if in a form rather different from the original scripts.

Let us now turn to the more recent discontents with industrialization in Eastern Europe and Latin America, which have been mentioned at the beginning of this essay. These discontents have their common origin in complaints that the model of industrialization that had been followed was "lopsided" or "biased" in relation to the Western model, which is seen as "balanced." I am talking about the Soviet and the prevailing Latin American models: their onesidedness was very different; in fact, as already noted, it was diametrically opposite. I shall deal with each in turn.

In the age of Stalin, heavy industry jointly with machinery and armament construction stood in the center of forced-march industrialization in the USSR. This policy was preceded in the 1920s by a long and now well known debate among various Soviet economists about the "correct" investment and industrial policy (Erlich, 1960, and Lewin, 1974).

Of greater interest today is the question why the Stalinist pattern was continued for so many decades after the end of World War II, and why it was also imposed on all the countries that came to be dominated by the Soviet Union. Odd as it may seem from today's perspective, the reason lies perhaps in the saying "nothing succeeds like success." The fact is that after the end of the war, the emphasis on heavy industry was widely sensed as justified by the events—the Soviet victory was taken as proof for the correctness of Stalin's industrialization policy. Moreover, from the point of view of the Soviet Union, the political structure of the world had not changed fundamentally—the "capitalist" countries still faced the "socialist" ones and it was essential to be prepared for another conflict. Thus the Stalinist model was everywhere taken over and carried further.

An important factor in this policy was the belief that heavy industry and machinery was somehow superior to all other forms of industry. This belief has a long history which is bound up with the stubborn efforts of distinguish "productive" from "nonproductive" activities.[4]

---

4. For an excellent historical survey, see Boss, 1990.

One of the most influential was Marx's discussion of the "reproduction of the social capital" in the second volume of *Das Kapital*. There he made his famous distinction between *Abteilung* (Department) I, which he defined as the means of production "which are in a form such that they can or must serve productive consumption," and Department II, defined as the "means of consumption which are in a form in which they will serve the individual consumption of workers or capitalists" (Marx and Engels, 1977, vol. 24, p. 394). Marx used this difference mostly to visualize the difference between "simple" and "enlarged" reproduction of capital, but his choice of words was such that he proclaimed—perhaps involuntarily—the superiority of Department I. Thus he repeatedly contrasted "monetary capital," of the capitalists with "productive capital" which serves to acquire the means of production of Department I.

This value judgment or prejudice was later to be strengthened by Germany's economic upsurge, which was, until World War I, largely based on the performance of heavy and machinery industry. In the 1930s the prestige of those sectors was further enhanced by the studies of the German economist Walther Hoffmann (1931), who showed that these branches tended to develop most vigorously in the leading industrial countries. Finally, World War II revealed once again the decisive significance of steel and machine tools (the "machines that make machines") for the war potential of the belligerents (Knorr, 1956).

It is therefore not so difficult to understand that after the war Stalinist industrial policy and the emphasis on heavy industry were strongly promoted all over the expanded Soviet Empire, but the question remains why this was never basically changed later on. To be sure, attempts were made from time to time to improve the supply of consumer goods, but it proved impossible to effect a basic change in the traditional model. It is this immobility that needs to be explained. Here some economists and social scientists from the East European countries have come forward with excellent suggestions. The Hungarian economist Janos Kornai has shown in his *Economics of Shortage* (1980) how central planning leads to what he calls "investment hunger" and therefore to a constant favoring of investment goods. This is so because central planning, as practiced in the so-called real socialist countries, takes place under the aegis of the "soft budget constraint," by now a well-known concept. Its essence consists in the fact that in a centrally planned economy no firm is ever exposed to the risk of failure.

A further explanation has been suggested by the Polish sociologist Lena Kolarska (1980). She noted that in the countries of the Soviet zone it was permissible to criticize—in the newspapers and other media—the quality of *consumer* goods. Though this criticism was meant as a way of blowing off steam, it could lead to disciplinary sanctions against those who were responsible. But firms producing machinery and semi-finished goods were not exposed to that sort of public criticism—small wonder that the better managers were not particularly motivated to busy themselves with consumer goods.

There were several reasons, then, why it was difficult to shift priorities away from the "heavy" sectors. This became evident when the central authorities, worried by increasing discontent, made real attempts to turn things around. The well-known "sorcerer's apprentice" syndrome applied: "I cannot get rid of the spirit I called up from the deep."

A good example is a curious policy that was promoted in the German Democratic Republic in the 1980s, when the economy of that country had already entered a declining phase. Here the "Kombinate" (groupings of firms of similar type) turning out producer goods were ordered in the early or mid-1980s to organize the production of consumer goods up to the value of 5 percent of their aggregate output (Schreiber, 1990, p. 903). But the results of this measure were soon subjected to considerable criticism: the quality of the new consumer goods left a great deal to be desired and the Kombinate suffered additional losses.[5]

Too much importance should not be attributed to this episode, but it does have its ironic aspects. Without actually saying so, the latter-day Marxist rulers of the German Democratic Republic were intent on subverting the basic distinction Marx had established between Abteilung I and Abteilung II and did their hurried best to mix up the consecrated categories of the master.

---

5. See Schreiber, 1990, and the following diary entry of Jürgen Kuczynski, 1990, p. 98: "There are numerous instances of total failure in such attempts to go against nature. Expensive and wholly ineffective."

The story reminds me of the poem "The West Coasts" by Christian Morgenstern, which starts out as follows:

> The West Coasts assembled one day
> And declared they were not West Coasts
> Neither East Coasts nor West Coasts,
> —"Not as far as they knew!"
> They intended to have their freedom back
> And shake off forever the yoke of the name.[6]

The discontents with industrialization in the Soviet zone of influence thus took strange and unexpected forms. Because of the repressive nature of the political regime, the unhappiness over the neglect of the consumer could not find a direct expression. Nevertheless, it eventually managed to manifest itself, if only in the form of this pathetic and ineffective administrative interference with the output of heavy industry.

Now to Latin America, where we find complaints over a sectoral bias that is the exact inverse of the pattern encountered in Eastern Europe. The relative lagging of heavy industry and machinery construction behind the manufacture of consumer goods in Latin America has been widely interpreted as willful neglect and even as a pattern reminiscent of the "Colonial Pact," which prohibited the colony to produce its own manufactures. This neglect of, or bias against, the most sophisticated industrial sectors has been extensively described, underlined, and often exaggerated—the way critiques by Latin American authors regarding the character, development, and culture of their own countries have often been overdrawn.

At this point it should be noted that the specific form industrialization took in Latin America was the outcome of market forces—that is, anything but the result of deliberate economic planning by government. As I have described it elsewhere, industrialization in Latin America started quite spontaneously with the domestic production of the last bits of value added of desirable consumer goods, and then

---

6. The German text in Morgenstern, 1930, p. 42, reads: Die Westküsten traten eines Tages zusammen / Und erklärten, sie seien keine Westküsten, / Weder Ostküsten noch Westküsten /—"dass sie nicht wüssten!" / Sie wollten wieder ihre Freiheit haben / Und für immer das Joch des Namens abschütteln . . .

progressed slowly through backward linkages to semi-processed goods and machinery. As was only normal, the latter categories of goods were initially imported from the established industrial countries (Hirschman, 1958, chapters 6 and 7, and 1971, pp. 85–123). Again, because of prevailing market forces rather than because of deliberate policy, it was often difficult to undertake domestic production in these categories, in part because it was against the short-run interests of the new industrialists to produce machinery and intermediate goods within the country. On the whole, largely because of these obstacles to all-around industrialization, the coming of industry to Latin American countries was not sensed in most countries (with the possible exception of Brazil) as a fundamental change or "modernization" in their economies and societies. The result was considerable unhappiness of many intellectuals of these countries with the Latin American type of industrialization and with their own bourgeoisie, which, in a characteristic book title, was castigated as *Lumpenburguesía* (Frank, 1971).

The industrialization itself was widely criticized as "inferior," "unintegrated," "incomplete," "mutilated," "truncated," "fragile," and so on.[7] The idea arose naturally that only a strong intervention on the part of the state would be able to remedy the fragmentary character of the industrial establishment. To be sure, because of the importance of and the resistances against the backward linkage investments, the role of the state in Latin America's industrialization, especially in the states with large domestic markets such as Brazil and Mexico, was bound to be more crucial than it was in the older industrial countries of Europe and North America, where industrialization began much earlier and where the construction of machinery and the production of consumer goods therefore took place virtually at the same time. But this does not mean that industrialization in Latin America was totally misguided and deserves that contempt with which it has been met on the part of many Latin American economists and commentators of the most diverse political orientations.

---

7. A typical title is Fernando Fajnzylber's *La industrialización trunca de America Latina* (The Truncated Industrialization of Latin America) even though this book contains valuable data and analyses. A good survey of the Argentine literature in this area is Korol and Sábato, 1990. See also my comments in Chapters 2 and 3 above on the dangers of "getting stuck."

I believe that this attitude has historical and cultural roots—similar to those I have earlier invoked for the German anxieties over industrialization at the turn of the century. In the case of Argentina, for example, the political scientist Juan Carlos Torre has suggested that the contempt for what local industry there is expresses a hidden nostalgia for the good old days of the "belle époque," at which time Argentina's role in the world economy—to supply England and other industrial countries with livestock products and other unchanging agricultural materials—was felt as both brilliant and nature-given.[8] In other cases, the critical attitude toward industrialization can be traced to half-nationalist and half-Marxist images of what a "true" or "complete" or "integrated" industrialization should look like.

Not long ago I wrote an article about various conceivable favorable consequences for Latin America and the Third World of the events of 1989 in Eastern Europe.[9] I can now add to my list the possibility that Latin American economists and intellectuals will learn something from the bitter experiences of East Europeans with *their* distorted pattern of industrialization. As a result, their attitude toward the industrialization of their own countries might become less negative than hitherto. Similarly, East Europeans should perhaps become acquainted with the Latin American critiques, for in this manner they might realize that *their* industrialization was not wholly misguided. A historical perspective and mutual perception of the mirror-image character of the two critiques might thus mitigate the widespread and dispiriting feeling on both sides that "we have done everything wrong."

This is the end of my brief and highly selective review of the many discontents with industrialization. The sole, not very interesting generalization which I venture at this point is that some of these discontents are surely useful—I have not even mentioned the many warranted ecological concerns of today—for they can lead to needed corrective policies. But others were and are based on treacherous fantasies which can cause considerable damage.

One might ask then: how is it possible to tell the one kind of discontent from the other? At this point I could take refuge in a well-

8. In conversation.
9. See the preceding chapter.

known maneuver designed to hide the writer's ignorance. It consists in the plea that the question exceeds the scope of his essay. I prefer to say it more plainly, in the words of an old French song: "Ce n'est pas dit dans ma chanson."

References

Boss, Helen. *Theories of Surplus and Transfer: Parasites and Producers in Economic Thought.* Boston, Mass.: Unwin Hyman, 1990.

Brentano, Lujo. *Die Schrecken des überwiegenden Industriestaates.* Berlin: L. Simion, 1901.

Collini, Stefan. "Counterrevolutionary Gentry," *Times Literary Supplement,* December 4, 1981.

Dietzel, Heinrich. "Bedeutet Export von Produktionsmitteln volkswirtschaftlichen Selbstmord?", in *Volkswirtschaftliche Zeitfragen.* Berlin No. 227/228, 1907.

Erlich, Alexander. *The Soviet Industrialization Debate, 1924–1928.* Cambridge, Mass.: Harvard University Press, 1960.

Fajnzylber, Fernando. *La industrialización trunca de América Latina.* Mexico, D.F.: Centro de Economía Transnacional, 1983.

Frank, André Gunder. *Lumpenburguesía, lumpendesarrollo.* Mexico, D.F.: Era, 1971.

Gerschenkron, Alexander. *Economic Backwardness in Historical Perspective.* Cambridge, Mass.: Harvard University Press, 1962.

Gerschenkron, Alexander. "Economic Backwardness in Historical Perspective," in Hoselitz, Bert, ed., *The Progress of Underdeveloped Areas.* Chicago: Chicago University Press, 1952.

Hirschman, Albert O. *Shifting Involvements: Private Interest and Public Action.* Princeton: Princeton University Press, 1982.

———— "The Political Economy of Import-Substituting Industrialization in Latin America," in Hirschman, *A Bias for Hope: Essays on Development and Latin America.* New Haven: Yale University Press, 1971.

———— *The Strategy of Economic Development.* New Haven: Yale University Press, 1958.

———— "Effects of Industrialization on the Markets of Industrial Countries," in Hoselitz, Bert, ed., *The Progress of Underdeveloped Areas.* Chicago: University of Chicago Press, 1952.

———— *National Power and the Structure of Foreign Trade.* Berkeley: University of California Press, 1945 (1980).

Hoffmann, Walther. *Stadien und Typen der Industrialisierung.* Jena: G. Fischer, 1931.

Knorr, Klaus. *The War Potential of Nations.* Princeton: Princeton University Press, 1956.

Kolarska, Lena. "The Functioning of 'Voice' in the Polish Economy," *Polish Sociological Bulletin,* no. 1 (1980).

Kornai, Janos. *Economics of Shortage,* 2 vols. Amsterdam: North Holland, 1980.

Korol, Juan Carlos, and Sábato, Hilda. "Incomplete Industrialization: An Argentine Obsession," *Latin American Research Review,* 25 (1990).

Kuczynski, Jürgen. *Schwierige Jahre: Tagebuchblätter, 1987–1989.* Berlin: Tacheles, 1990.

Lewin, Moshe. *Political Undercurrents in Soviet Economic Debates.* Princeton: Princeton University Press, 1974.

Marx, Karl, and Engels, Friedrich. *Werke.* Berlin: Nega, 1977.

Morgenstern, Christian. *Galgenlieder.* Berlin: Bruno Cassirer, 1930.

Pascal, Blaise. *Pensées,* in *Oeuvres Complètes.* Paris: Pléiade, 1980.

Raynal, Guillaume Thomas François. *Histoire philosophique et politique des établissemens et du commerce des Européens dans les deux Indes,* 10 vols. Geneva, 1781.

Schreiber, Gerhard. "Konsumgüterproduktion in produktionsmittelherstellenden Kombinaten—ja oder nein?," *Wirtschaftswissenschaft,* 38 (June 1990), p. 903.

Smith, Adam. *The Theory of Moral Sentiments,* D. D. Raphael and A. L. Macfie, eds. Oxford: Clarendon, 1976.

Wiener, Martin J. *English Culture and the Decline of the Industrial Spirit, 1850–1980.* Cambridge: Cambridge University Press, 1981.

18
chapter

Does the Market Keep Us Out of Mischief or Out of Happiness?

Eighteen years in the making and over 600 thickly annotated pages long, Robert Lane's monumental book is a unique and admirable achievement. In the brief appraisal that follows I shall first attempt a summary of what I see as the main thrust and message of the book and then offer some critical remarks.

Sprawling as it is, *The Market Experience* is actually held together by a nicely unitary theme. Setting out to examine how the institution of the market contributes not so much to the "wealth of nations" or to the gross national product, in monetary terms, as to the sum total of human happiness and personal development, Lane surveys the enormous sociological and psychological literature that deals with cognition, self-esteem, friendship, work and work satisfaction, reward systems, and finally with happiness itself in an intrepid search for the market's effect on these much more elusive personal experiences and relations.

The first remark that is in order here is that Lane is commendably fair-minded and nuanced in this comprehensive appraisal. From Carlyle and Marx to Marcuse and Fred Hirsch, the market has long been harshly criticized for the way it (or money) subverts all human rela-

This essay was written as a review article of Robert E. Lane, *The Market Experience* (Cambridge: Cambridge University Press, 1991), p. 630. It was published in *Contemporary Sociology*, 26 (November 1992), 741–744.

tionships and even undermines the ethical foundations of society; in many of these well-trodden areas Lane comes up with a less negative or less one-sided verdict. The market is in fact given rather high grades for its effect on self-esteem, which is shown to be more enhanced by economic achievement (in the market) than by traditional ascription in tradition-bound, hierarchical societies (p. 203). The evenhandedness of Lane's findings is particularly striking when he discusses the alleged "commodification" of human relations in market economies, a phenomenon that is largely discounted (p. 219). Neither does he find that markets systematically degrade work through "deskilling"—a more recent critique.

Nevertheless, Lane's final verdict on the market is quite severe, to the point where he advocates, toward the end of the book, a new "axial turning of the wheel" away from the primacy of the market as we know it. How does he reach this conclusion? According to Lane, the market performs poorly in a number of areas that have been neglected in the discussions. To my mind, the original contributions of the book are to be found largely in the fascinating, if complex, chapters on the hidden costs of rewards (chaps. 18–21) and on the misinterpretation of happiness and satisfaction in a market society (chap. 27).

Interest in the hidden costs of reward goes back to the theory of cognitive dissonance; these costs arise because intrinsic enjoyment of work, particularly creative work, decreases when it is directly remunerated. Here Lane brings together an impressive amount of evidence from research in social psychology that has shown how a whole "world of satisfaction and motivation . . . lies outside the boundaries of exchange" (p. 382). The market, it seems, is not capable of tapping some very precious creative energies which will come forward only when they are *not* elicited by monetary rewards. Although Lane qualifies this judgment in chapter 19 ("The Limits of Hidden Costs in the Market"), the inability of the market to come to grips with the "intrinsic"— something as important as intrinsic work satisfaction is not given its due in the accounting practiced by the market—is for him a major reason for "market failure."

Another important shortcoming of the market is its power to create the illusion that monetary success holds the key to happiness. As a result of converging data on the determinants of happiness in the advanced market economies, Lane is convinced that the nonmonetary dimensions of happiness—family life and friends, feelings of direction and control over one's life, self-esteem, and so on—far outweigh the "mere" material dimensions. The trouble which Lane identifies is, in a sense, reminiscent of Freud's notion of sublimation. For Freud, people whose sexual drives are repressed by society will on occasion create works of art "in compensation"; for Lane, people who are not doing well in crucial nonmonetary areas of human relations are tempted to compensate for these failings through strenuous efforts in the market. They labor under the illusion that by doing well in the market they will achieve the happiness that has eluded them. Thus the market acts as a permanent temptation that diverts people from making a genuine effort to take hold of their lives where it really counts. In this sense the availability of the market acts as a dangerous saboteur of *real* happiness.

I have some critical comments to make on this intriguing thesis but must first complete my admittedly skimpy summary. In a concluding chapter, Lane calls for an "axial change or rotation" in values and socioeconomic regime, from the "economistic axis" to one that would focus on "satisfaction with life-as-a-whole," from a "consumer economy" to a "producer economy," or toward a "wellbeing-developmental axis" (p. 594). In attempting to sketch how we might get from here to there, Lane is modest and decidedly nonutopian. As I already noted, he has little use for what he calls the "humanist critique" of the market, put forward by those who have previously lamented the human injuries inflicted by the unreconstructed market. These critics, he claims, suffer from an excessive confidence in government and from an inadequate appreciation of the market's ability to develop both affluence and certain valuable human traits, such as self-esteem. Lane is also totally dismissive of the traditional proposals of the Left for more-or-less radical changes in the regime of private property.

Taking nevertheless an unacknowledged leaf out of Marx, the final pages of the book then scrutinize the present-day reality for any emerging features that might favor or foreshadow the proposed axial rotation (p. 603). Lane is encouraged by the wide support which, according to survey research, is already given to such values as personal control, self-attribution, and self-esteem and by the rise of a "post-materialist value culture" in the United States and Western Europe, as portrayed by Ronald Inglehart in his *Silent Revolution* (1972). In a book replete with footnotes, it would be churlish to criticize the absence of a specific reference; yet, in his pursuit of various straws in the wind, Lane might have also taken comfort from the findings of Michael Piore and Charles Sabel on the emergence of a new culture of work in the "post-Fordist" age, which they describe in their important book *The Second Industrial Divide* (1984).

It looks as though Lane relies wholly on a spontaneous change in values to produce the desired transformation. As far as I can tell, he does not come forward with a single institutional suggestion or proposal.

Lane's strongest and most stimulating proposition is the critique of the market on the grounds that money's "glittering attractiveness . . . invites compensatory choice more than most" (p. 554); "It is easy in a market society to find a substitute in the market for something lying outside the market" (p. 555). Thus are people "distracted" from genuinely authentic, or "ego-syntonic," choices. I have two comments on this trenchant critique.

First, Lane's point is really a variation on an ancient theme. It echoes a famous observation of Adam Smith in the *Theory of Moral Sentiments* that the bustle of the market is due to deception, a "deception which arouses and keeps in continued motion the industry of mankind" (Smith 1976, p. 183). Smith argues forcefully that people are mistaken about their real (Lane's ego-syntonic) interests in going after all the "trinkets and baubles" or "trifling conveniencies" the market offers. He disagrees with Lane only in asserting that a superior end is nevertheless served by the ongoing charade—for in this manner the rich are occupied with chasing after useless trifles while sharing inadvertently the "necessaries of life" with the poor! This is in fact Smith's early concept of the Invisible Hand, a metaphor he appealed to for the precise purpose of explaining the benign, if highly ironic, mechanism he had laid bare (p. 184, see also preceding chapter).

Second, it may be more interesting to *contrast* Lane's point about the seductive distractions offered by the market with a well-known observation of Keynes. Toward the end of his *General Theory,* Keynes said, memorably, "Dangerous human proclivities can be canalized into comparatively harmless channels by the existence of opportunity for moneymaking and private wealth, which, if they cannot be satisfied in this way, may find their outlet in cruelty, the reckless pursuit of personal power and authority, and other forms of self-aggrandizement" (Keynes, p. 374). As I noted in my book *The Passions and the Interests,* Keynes echoed here eighteenth-century ideas on *doux commerce* and moneymaking as "innocent" pastimes and outlets for men's restless energies—energies that otherwise were likely to be deployed in ruthless and disastrous struggles for power (Hirschman 1977, p. 134).

Once Lane and Keynes are contrasted in this manner, it appears that our attitude toward moneymaking must depend on what we conjecture it *replaces:* according to Keynes (and his eighteenth-century predecessors) moneymaking substitutes for destructive power-seeking, whereas for Lane, it keeps people from engaging in all kinds of constructive pursuits, from the consolidation of friendships to the search for beauty and truth. For Keynes, the market keeps us out of mischief, whereas for Lane the market seduces us or, at best, sidetracks us: it keeps us from engaging in more worthwhile activities. It is of course possible that Keynes and Lane were or are both right, each for his own period of world history. This would mean that in the age of Keynes most people would have been bent on power-seeking in the absence of the diversions offered by the market, whereas fifty years later, the selfsame market diverts people from fulfilling themselves. But here I must confess to considerable doubt that the history of human nature in this century could conceivably be as progressive as that. Even in our enlightened era, the activities that are displaced by moneymaking, if any, are likely to consist only in part of those ego-syntonic ones which Lane likes to stress.

In any event, with these contrasting conjectures about what it is that market activities replace or displace—not to speak of the relation of these displacement ideas to Freud's sublimation theory—the story becomes quite complex and begins to resemble the famous Minsk-Pinsk joke, which goes like this. Two competing traveling salesmen meet in the central Moscow railway station. Salesman A: "Where are you going?" Salesman B: "To Minsk." Salesman A: "Look, you are telling me that you are going to Minsk to make me think that you are going to Pinsk. But I know you really *are* going to Minsk. So why are you lying to me?" Analogously, one almost wonders whether it might not be advisable to go along with the naive economist and to assume that people are in the market as a matter of "revealed preference" and to leave matters at that.

My second comment deals with a strange omission in Lane's book. Comprehensive as it is in addressing the effects of the market on numerous facets of individual life experience, there is not a word in it on the *political* effect of the market. It almost looks as though Lane felt this were the "turf" of his Yale colleagues Robert Dahl and C. E. Lindblom, who have indeed written a great deal on this very topic. Yet here the history of our century surely suggests strongly that it very much belongs in Lane's book; for what becomes of human happiness and development (Lane's two overarching criteria and objectives) without political liberty?

If there is some causal connection between market society and political liberty—be it purely permissive or facilitative in the sense that, as Milton Friedman put it, market society is a necessary but not a sufficient condition for the emergence of political liberty—then we have an extremely weighty argument in favor of the market. And we could then say that all arguments that fault the market on one or another count of human happiness could be considered irrelevant, frivolous, or of a lower order of significance. Lane probably thought he had good reasons for not dealing with this issue. If I understand him correctly, the axial rotation he advocates stops well short of changes in the constitution of our economic, social, and political order that would threaten the political systems of the West. But he might have reassured us on this count.

My third point is about the strange fate reserved for books on burning issues in our fast-moving world. When Lane labored on *The Market Experience* fifteen or ten or even three years ago, he could not have imagined that, by the time his book, with its quite temperate but nevertheless unequivocal indictment of the market, would appear, a miraculously transformed Second World would be looking forward to precisely that experience as providential salvation, or at least as the only available alternative to the economic disruption and malfunctioning into which it had fallen. It is tempting to ironize on this score, but in my opinion that would be a mistake, as well as a cheap shot. The fact that the Soviet-type economies have succumbed to their assorted ills obviously does not mean that those of the First World are exempt from any problems and dysfunctions. It is more intelligent to continue to scrutinize these problems than to sport triumphalist airs.

Nevertheless, with the wisdom of hindsight, it seems to me that Lane's book is a bit more vulnerable to criticism and irony than it need be. The bulk of the book was obviously written when the two superpowers and their economic systems were facing each other, and it was only natural to think of each system as a well-defined, fairly unitary whole: the Market or the Plan. I do not say that only under the conditions of the Cold War would social scientists resort to such binary oppositions, but these conditions certainly made it particularly tempting to reify the Market and the Market Experience.

Today the intellectual atmosphere is rapidly changing. The disintegration of "really existing socialism" is already having an interesting effect on the analysis of market systems; suddenly it is easier to perceive the many and deep differences between them. In France a book by Michel Albert with the title *Capitalisme contre capitalisme* is having considerable success; at the same time, a group of English and German sociologists are teaming up to investigate the "varieties of capitalism," contrasting the German-Japanese to the U.S.-English variety. It is indeed obvious that in reality there is not just one market experience; surely there is a number of quite different such experiences, if only because the institutions of the market are necessarily embedded, as Granovetter has reminded us, in very different national and local institutions, traditions, and values.

Thus Lane's book is just the beginning—a most valuable one—of our knowledge about market experiences. We must now inquire to what extent his findings are applicable in different environments, in "really existing" market systems.

References

Albert, Michel. *Capitalisme contre capitalisme*. Paris: Le Seuil, 1991.

Hirschman, Albert O. *The Passions and the Interests: Political Arguments for Capitalism before Its Triumph* Princeton: Princeton University Press, 1977.

Inglehart, Ronald. *The Silent Revolution: Changing Values and Political Styles among Western Publics*. Princeton: Princeton University Press, 1977.

Keynes, John Maynard. *The General Theory of Employment Interest and Money*. London: Macmillan, 1936.

Piore, Michael, and Charles Sabel. *The Second Industrial Divide: Possibilities for Prosperity*. New York: Basic, 1984.

Smith, Adam. *The Theory of Moral Sentiments*. Oxford: Clarendon Press, 1976.

19
chapter

The On-and-Off Connection between Political and Economic Progress

In somewhat old fashioned but straightforward terms, my subject is the relation between economic and political progress. This relation has often been visualized in a very few alternative, functional forms such as the following:

1. "All good things go together"—economic progress begets political progress as well as vice versa: the two go harmoniously hand in hand.

2. Next, there is the opposite pessimistic view that "everything has a cost" or "there is no such thing as a free lunch"—meaning in the present context that economic progress necessarily exacts a cost in the political domain or vice versa: political advances are bound to jeopardize economic progress.

3. A third, intermediate, case might be labeled "per aspera ad astra": during a first period, economic progress goes it alone while political progress must be held back or even reversed, sacrificed for the sake of the growing economy; during a second period, a reward is reaped for the temporary sacrifice as political

This essay was written for the 151st Annual Meeting of the American Economic Association (Boston, January 1994), as a contribution to a session on "The Role of Democracy in Securing Just and Prosperous Societies." It was published in *American Economic Review—Papers and Proceedings*, 84 (May 1994), 343–348.

progress catches up. The opposite process, with economic progress being sacrificed temporarily for the sake of political advance, has been less frequently articulated, but also has a realistic ring. Here the two variables evolve in a slightly more complex pattern, as in Simon Kuznets's (1955) proposition about the curvilinear relation between economic growth and inequality, or as in my own models of unbalanced growth and of "sailing against the wind" (Hirschman, 1992, pp. 26–33).

From Economics to Politics: The Ratchet Effect and Related Metaphors

In attempting to establish the true nature of the connection between political and economic progress, these various patterns have been found to prevail in some countries for some periods, but it is now fairly clear that none can claim to be predominant. This is convincingly shown in a recent article by Adam Przeworski and Fernando Limongi (1993) on the subject. Their careful and comprehensive review of the literature is in the end thoroughly and discouragingly inconclusive. Under the circumstances, there is an almost cruelly mocking ring to the article's last sentence: "Clearly, the impact of political regimes on growth is wide open for reflection and research."

One reaction to this difficulty in establishing a solid connection between economic and political progress is to revert to the idea that economics and politics are two wholly separate domains. As Stephan Haggard and Robert Kaufman (1992) noted, political scientists analyzed the recent wave of democratization in Latin America and Asia largely in such autonomous terms. This may well reflect disappointment over certain once popular but by now discarded analyses of political events in the 1960s and 1970s, which represented a last-ditch effort to understand those events—in particular, the turn to authoritarianism during that period—in terms of "underlying" economic forces.

However, this reversion to proclaiming the autonomy of politics and economics may be an overreaction. The two domains do exhibit many linkages that are quite intimate at one point, only to evaporate later. The trouble is that researchers have been unwilling—or that the model builders have been unable—to think in terms of *on-and-off connections,* or of *couplings and uncouplings,* or of *alternations between interdependence and autonomy.* I would like to review here some already available ways of thinking in such terms. For this purpose it pays to scrutinize ordinary language as well as the world of myth. As on-and-off connections have been experienced time and again, myth, language, and occasionally social thought have come up with a series of stories and expressions that gesture effectively toward what is to be understood.

Let me first recall a metaphor from hand tools that entered the language of economics over 40 years ago. I refer to the "ratchet effect."[1] James Duesenberry (1949) created this term to describe the behavior of consumption in relation to income during the business cycle: consumption is a rising function of income as long as income increases but will resist following income on the downward path; in a recession people will dig into their savings to maintain their accustomed standard of living, at least for a time. Here is precisely the idea of uncoupling (or unyoking or unhinging), that is, of a functional relationship which ceases to operate at some point.

Some time ago I came upon a similar situation in a growth context. During the 1980s, when indexes of economic performance leveled off or declined in some Latin American countries under the impact of the debt crisis, important social indicators such as infant mortality, illiteracy, and the extent of birth control continued showing improvement.[2] Such improvements had occurred earlier in response to rising incomes, but they had apparently assumed "a life of their own." At some point they were no longer narrowly tied to the "vagaries" of income. To the extent that these social advances were due to learning processes they became irreversible and started diffusion processes of their own. Such processes are essential to understanding growth and development.

That a behavior which is originally resisted and acquired only under the influence of extrinsic (positive or negative) incentives can become irreversible is also well rendered by the expression that the behavior eventually becomes "second-nature." A good deal of learning consists

1. A ratchet is a hinged catch that permits motion in one direction only.
2. See the first section of Chapter 15, above.

in fact in this mysterious process through which a *behavior originally acquired under duress* (because it goes against "first-nature") *becomes second-nature*. It has not been widely realized that this process—the replacement of extrinsic incentives toward a certain behavior by intrinsic ones—is the exact opposite of the "crowding out" of intrinsic motivation as a result of the introduction of extrinsic (usually monetary) rewards.[3] The becoming-second-nature process appears to have aroused less interest than the crowding-out one, perhaps because it is auspicious, rather than worrisome and dismal.

Returning from ordinary language to social science, the term "disjunction" has been used by Daniel Bell (1976) to describe how the cultural and artistic life of modern societies no longer reflects the evolution of society and economy in general. The term was meant to convey dissent from those sociological thinkers, from Karl Marx to Emile Durkheim and Talcott Parsons, who cultivated a vision of society as an integrated whole. In the Marxian scheme, for example, culture, the "superstructure," is supposed to correspond somehow to economy and society (the "infrastructure"). So, from the point of view of that scheme, when culture takes on a "life of its own," it seems fair enough to speak of disjunction: something that was supposed to be controlled by something else acquires autonomy. Curiously, despite his solid non-Marxist convictions, Bell saw this autonomy as something vaguely abnormal and threatening.

This negative interpretation comes to the fore in a fairy tale or myth that reflects once again the notion of uncoupling. It is the story of the sorcerer's apprentice who, unlike the master, turns out to be unable to control and reverse the forces he has unleashed. Social processes of the sorcerer's apprentice type are not hard to find. In the United States, for example, the Prohibition Statute of 1919–20 gave rise to the emergence of Big Crime syndicates, which organized illegal networks of production and distribution of alcoholic beverages. But the repeal of Prohibition in the 1930s did not cause Big Crime to disappear (Thomas Schelling, 1984, p. 178).

In similar ways, the processes previously described as the "ratchet

3. As famously described by Richard Titmuss, 1970, extensively surveyed by Robert Lane, 1991, and recently reanalyzed by Bruno Frey, 1992.

effect" and "taking on a life of its own" have potential for both good and evil. Only when a behavior is said to become "second-nature" is it normally assumed that one is in the presence of genuine learning. Even this process can sometimes be given a negative interpretation by presenting it as the outcome of "brainwashing."

Some important connections between economic and political progress or decline are best described in terms of the concepts just surveyed, particularly when the initial causation runs from economics to politics, as in the following two well-known examples.

The vigorous development of the Spanish economy during the three postwar decades contributed in various ways to undermining the authoritarian regime established after the end of the Civil War by Francisco Franco. After the death of the long-time dictator in 1975, a fairly smooth transition to democracy got under way. But just then the international oil crisis temporarily halted economic expansion and caused large-scale unemployment to appear. Fortunately, the new democratic institutions were able to acquire a "life of their own" and became "second-nature" to Spanish society (Juan Linz and Alfred Stepan, 1989, pp. 43–46).

The opposite case is tragically illustrated by the history of Germany in the earlier part of this century. Here it was the rise of Adolf Hitler that was powerfully assisted by economic forces—the Great Depression and the ensuing mass unemployment. Then, once in power in one of the world's most technically and culturally advanced countries, the Nazi regime went on its madly "autonomous" course to suppress democracy, unleash war, and commit genocide.

From Political to Economic Progress: Toward a Repertoire of History's Tricks

In exploring connections between economics and politics, social scientists have ordinarily given preferential attention to sequences where economic events clearly influence and shape the realm of politics. As just illustrated, politics then has a way of taking over; it becomes unhinged from economics in line with the "on-and-off" scheme. Examples for the opposite sequence, where politics would be the prime mover, do not spring to mind as readily, but it may be helpful to proceed by analogy with the Spanish and German cases. This involves examining sequences of events starting with some important advance toward democracy and then looking at the economic consequences. Here a basic difference appears between economic and political change: the latter is more likely to be discontinuous than the former. Advances toward democracy have typically occurred not as a result of some gradual "democratic upswing," but because an oppressive regime has been overthrown or because a voting-reform law broadening the franchise has been adopted.

It is because such democratic advances typically happen as one-time events that much of the analysis of the economic consequences of political change ends up as exercises in comparative statics. One compares the economic performance of democratic and nondemocratic countries and hopes to be able to conclude that the former do better in the economic realm as well. An early example of this way of disposing of the problem is Adam Smith's well-known dictum: "Little else is required to carry a state to the highest degree of opulence from the lowest barbarism than peace, easy taxes, and a tolerable administration of justice" (Dugald Stewart, 1858, p. 68).

Two remarks are in order. Such a construction assumes that all that is needed for economic growth to happen is some set of political prerequisites such as peace and secure property rights. With that set in place, it is the economy that is expected to acquire "a life of its own," with no need for further interaction between economic and political forces. But such interaction obviously exists on a continuing basis and needs to be understood. Secondly, the usefulness of the propositions about the political prerequisites of economic growth is doubtful. The exhortation to countries lacking "democracy" or "peace" to get their act together and procure such blessings is not notably helpful. If a country is unable to end its civil war or to stop the killing, is it likely to do so to achieve a better rate of growth?

I do not wish to be wholly negative. Comparative statics does have its uses. An example is Amartya Sen's (1983, 1994) point that a country like India with a reasonably free press, able and willing to denounce intolerable conditions and abuses, has a better chance to avoid famines than an authoritarian country like China. If nothing else, such a finding packs a considerable hortatory punch.

Yet the main task of political economy remains to provide a better understanding of the *ongoing* interactions between politics and economics. Not to attempt the construction of building blocks here is in fact an evasion of a real opportunity, in view of the very characteristics of a pluralist market society. As this society creates new wealth, it also generates problems of emerging inequality and regional or sectoral decline that are often unjust or felt as such. Hence there arise, in the political domain, demands for reform and political action. In turn, these reforms and actions have economic consequences.

Political economists have not come forward with many generalizations or conjectures in this field, perhaps for good reasons. What indeed can one say about the likely consequences of democratic and social advances for economic growth? Without detailed knowledge about the nature of the advance and the surrounding historical circumstances it would seem foolish to hazard an answer. A democratic advance can either inaugurate or put an end to an era of political instability, and thus it can lead to either economic decline or growth.

Fortunately, the historical record raises doubts about such total indeterminacy, at least for the countries with the most advanced economies in Western Europe and North America. These countries are also those that have enacted, discontinuously, a series of political and social reforms over the last two centuries. Does it then follow that these democratic advances have had on the whole a stabilizing effect and have improved the investment climate so that economic growth could gather strength?

This is a rather surprising conjecture, in part because it directly contradicts Alexis de Tocqueville's famous proposition that, in France, attempts at reform prior to 1789 and in the earliest phase of the Revolution had fatally destabilizing effects on the ancien régime. This was surely a remarkable insight for the events Tocqueville undertook to analyze. But, just *because* the French Revolution had aroused widespread expectations that its history of progressive radicalization is apt to repeat itself, subsequent reforms often played a different, self-limiting and stabilizing role. I now wish to advance one possible explanation, building on what I call the "jeopardy thesis" in my (1991) book, *The Rhetoric of Reaction*. By that term I understand the argument that a proposed reform will endanger previous accomplishments, an argument that played a central role in the history of opposition to reform in the nineteenth century.

After the French Revolution, democratic and social advances were fought tooth and nail by the now alerted and highly articulate reactionary forces: every advance was denounced as though it were in fact synonymous with revolution and would mean the annulment of previous advances toward "liberty." But then, after a reform came to be adopted in spite of that strenuous opposition, it often turned out, to much surprise, that the reform, that ominous "leap in the dark," *could be lived with*. The result was enormous relief among the owners of capital, political stabilization, and a period of sustained economic growth and prosperity.

This interpretation yields a political business cycle that would be determined by each wave of reform. Concern and alarm over reform proposals and over the agitation linked to them brings a decline in investment activity, which then rebounds once the reform has been passed and is being assimilated. The more persuasive the warnings about the disastrous consequences of reform, the more vigorous will be the actual upswing after the reform is passed and the warnings are disproved.

This sequence is suggested by the story of how the hotly contested Reform Laws of 1832 and 1867 in England had a peaceful and prosperous aftermath. It should be interesting to examine whether this somewhat paradoxical pattern can be found to hold for similar episodes in other countries. But economists familiar with rational-expectation models should not be overly surprised if prophecies of destabilization à la Tocqueville turn out to be self-refuting, rather than self-fulfilling.

Of course, I would never want to rely on the mechanism I have sketched. It would be folly to encourage reactionaries to make outrageous claims about the evil consequences of a proposed reform, with the cunning thought of eliciting feelings of relief, and hence economic upswing, once reform is adopted and proved not to be all that disastrous. Even if this conjunction of events has been found to occur here and there in the past, one cannot have any confidence that it will do so again. Samuel Johnson once issued a fine warning against the intellectual pride that would lead one to act on the basis of such putative insights. In his philosophical novel *Rasselas,* he wrote: "Man cannot so far know the connexion of causes and events, as that he may venture to do wrong in order to do right" (1958, p. 576).

What, then, is the point of my story? It is to affirm once again that political and economic progress are not tied together in any easy, straightforward, functional way. There are the various on-and-off connections of the first part of this chapter. Then there are stories, intricate and often nonrepeatable, like the one I have just told, that look more like tricks history has up its sleeve than like social-scientific regularities, not to speak of laws. To make an inventory, to survey history's repertoire of such tricks, seems to me an appropriately modest way of trying to make progress with this difficult topic.

References

Bell, Daniel. *The Cultural Contradictions of Capitalism.* New York: Basic Books, 1976.

Duesenberry, James. *Income, Saving and the Theory of Consumer Behavior.* Cambridge, Mass.: Harvard University Press, 1952.

Frey, Bruno S. "Tertium Datur: Pricing, Regulating and Intrinsic Motivation," *Kyklos,* 45 (1992), pp. 161–184.

Haggard, Stephan, and Kaufman, Robert R. "Economic Adjustment and the Prospects for Democracy," in Haggard and Kaufman, eds., *The Politics of Economic Adjustment,* pp. 319–50. Princeton: Princeton University Press, 1992.

Hirschman, Albert O. *The Rhetoric of Reaction: Perversity, Futility, Jeopardy.* Cambridge, Mass.: Harvard University Press, 1991.

———— "A Dissenter's Confession: *The Strategy of Economic Development* Revisited," in Hirschman, *Rival Views of Market Society and Other Recent Essays,* pp. 3–34. Cambridge, Mass.: Harvard University Press, 1992.

Johnson, Samuel. *Rasselas, Poems and Selected Prose,* B. H. Bronson, ed. New York: Holt, Rinehart and Winston, 1958.

Kuznets, Simon. "Economic Growth and Income Inequality," *American Economic Review,* 45 (March 1955), pp. 1–28.

Lane, Robert E. *The Market Experience.* Cambridge: Cambridge University Press, 1991.

Linz, Juan, and Stepan, Alfred. "Political Crafting of Democratic Consolidation or

Destruction: European and South American Comparisons," in R. A. Pastor, ed., *Democracy in the Americas,* pp. 41–60. New York: Holmes & Meier, 1989.

Przeworski, Adam, and Limongi, Fernando. "Political Regimes and Economic Growth," *Journal of Economic Perspectives,* 7 (Summer 1993), pp. 51–69.

Schelling, Thomas C. *Choice and Consequence.* Cambridge, Mass.: Harvard University Press, 1984.

Sen, Amartya. "Development: Which Way Now?" *Economic Journal,* 93 (December 1983), pp. 745–762.

———— "Freedom and Needs," *New Republic,* 10–17 January 1994, pp. 31–38.

Stewart, Dugald. "Account of the Life and Writings of Adam Smith," in *Collected Works,* vol. X. Edinburgh: Constable, 1858.

Titmuss, Richard M. *The Gift Relationship.* London: Allen and Unwin, 1970.

20
chapter

Social Conflicts as Pillars of Democratic Market Societies

The question "How much community spirit *(Gemeinsinn)* does liberal society require?" reminded me of a well-known tale of Tolstoy's with a similar sounding title, "How Much Land Does a Man Require?" This is the story, you may remember, of a peasant called Pakhom who becomes obsessed by the passion for acquiring more and more land. At one point he subjects himself to an excessive exertion that is supposed to bring him riches but actually leads to physical exhaustion and death. By then, of course, Pakhom needs only the small piece of land where his body is being put to rest—"three Russian ells." Even though these words, coming at the very end of the story, look like the answer Tolstoy gives to the question he asks in the title, he obviously did not mean to say that this is all the land that peasants truly require. His real point is that this is the amount of land we may well end up with if we fall prey to the accumulating passion.

Published in *Political Theory,* 22 (May 1994), 203–218 (copyright © by Sage Publications, Inc.; reprinted by permission). This article was originally written as basic document for the 100th session of the "Bergedorfer Gesprächskreis" (discussion circle of Bergedorf), which took place on November 13–14, 1993, in Dresden. These sessions have been organized and held periodically by the Körber Foundation of Hamburg. For the Dresden discussion the organizers proposed the theme "Wieviel Gemeinsinn braucht die liberale Gesellschaft?" (How much community spirit does liberal society require?) As will be obvious from my introduction, I start out with this question very much on my mind and also return to it at the end. The bulk of the essay, however, deals with problems which, though related, are better epitomized by the title given here.

From *Gemeinschaftsschwärmerei* to *Verfassungspatriotismus*

Pakhom and his passion for land may teach a lesson about how much community spirit a society requires: there may be danger that a group of people will become intoxicated with the idea of, or with the passion or *Schwärmerei* (enthusiasm) for, community spirit (Gemeinschaft). Recent German history provides the most emphatic warning in this regard. During the Weimar period there was much concern in Germany about the lack of certain characteristics a community was supposed to exhibit: a sense of direction and mission, a feeling of togetherness and warmth—a community spirit, in short. The rise of the Nazi movement owed much to its promise to provide all of these alleged needs in abundance by creating a new, popular compact, the *Volksgemeinschaft*. The catastrophe that followed gave a long-lasting bad name to the very terms of community and community spirit, in the Federal Republic at any rate. From 1945 on, the Germans' communal feelings were to be limited to the consciousness—with perhaps, little by little, a bit of pride—that their country was now firmly built on a liberal constitution guaranteeing basic human and civil rights—hence the term *Verfassungspatriotismus*, or patriotism grounded on the Constitution. Originally suggested by Dolf Sternberger and later endorsed by Jürgen Habermas, this concept became popular: it conveyed a new and minimalist kind of patriotism, far removed from earlier varieties. It was as though Pakhom, the peasant of Tolstoy's tale, had come back to life, had learned from his misadventures, and had decided to settle from now on for a radically downscaled plot of land.

The Communitarian Critique of Liberalism in the United States and Its Reception in Germany

The events of 1989–90 led to some new reflections as reunification gave rise to serious economic, cultural, and moral problems. The existence of these problems and particularly their unexpected persistence were often attributed to some deficiency in common spirit or purpose. Argumentation along such lines was facilitated at that point by the close contact between German and American intellectual circles. The need for greater community spirit could be invoked in terms borrowed from the debate that had developed in the United States in the 1970s and 1980s, largely in reaction to John Rawls's *Theory of Justice* (1970), and which became known as the "communitarian critique of liberalism."[1] Significantly, earlier German contributions to the debate were hardly mentioned. That contribution starts, of course, with the classic monograph *Gemeinschaft und Gesellschaft* (Community and Society) by Ferdinand Tönnies, who, as early as 1887, had engagingly portrayed—and, to be sure, vastly overdrawn—the contrast between atomistic society and cohesive community. That book certainly contributed to an intellectual climate marked by a widespread yearning for *Gemeinschaft* (and corresponding scorn for "mere" *Gesellschaft*). Nevertheless, there were countercurrents, such as the subtle, if rather opaque, critique of the Gemeinschaft creed in Helmuth Plessner's *Grenzen der Gemeinschaft* (Limits of Community).[2] But in recent German volumes devoted to the discussion of community spirit—now called pointedly *Kommunitarismus* rather than *Gemeinsinn, Gemeinschaftslehre,* or some such earlier German term—there is hardly any mention of Tönnies or Plessner; instead, one learns a great deal about the thoughts of Michael Sandel, Alasdair MacIntyre, Robert Bellah, Charles Taylor, and Michael Walzer.[3] Obviously, it was found attractive, in reviving the discussion on the need for greater community and community spirit, to "launder" the concept, as it were, by importing the contemporary debate that had just run its course in the United States.

This does not mean that the American communitarians made a triumphant entry into Germany. In the new circumstances a feeling did arise that Verfassungspatriotismus was no longer quite enough, that it was too minimal a conception of the ties and mutual obligations that

1. This is the title of an article by Michael Walzer, *Political Theory,* 18 (February 1990), 6–23, which strikes me as an incisive critique of the critique.
2. (Bonn: Friedrich Cohen, 1924). Wolf Lepenies underlines the current interest of this book in *Folgen einer unerhörten Begebenheit* (Berlin: Siedler, 1992), pp. 67–70. A useful summary and comment on Plessner's book are Joachim Fischer's "Plessner und die politische Philosophie der zwanziger Jahre," in Volker Gerhardt et al., eds., *Politisches Denken, Jahrbuch 1992* (Stuttgart: J. B. Metzler, 1993), pp. 53–76.
3. See, for example, Christel Zahlmann, ed., *Kommunitarismus in der Diskussion* (Berlin: Rotbuch, 1992); Axel Honneth, ed., *Kommunitarismus: Eine Debatte über die moralischen Grundlagen moderner Gesellschaften* (Frankfurt: Campus, 1993).

were now required among the citizens of the suddenly reunited country. Hence there was much interest in the American communitarian voices. But at the same time and for the solid historical reasons already noted, the resistance against having the reunited Germany propped up by some Bellah-style "civil religion" remained considerable.

Some time ago, while reflecting on the impact of the views on economic development I put forward in the 1950s, I proposed a distinction between two effects of new ideas. The first, direct and obvious—often the only one to be considered—is the "persuasion effect": the new theory is adopted more or less widely by the people who already are working in the field. The second effect of a new theory is that the field itself "comes alive with discussion and controversy and [thereby] attracts some of the more intelligent, energetic, and dedicated members of a generation."[4] This "recruitment effect" renders the influence of new ideas far more unpredictable than would be the case if only the persuasion effect were operative: new thinkers may be drawn into the discussion but may end up generating ideas that are quite different from those that originally "seduced" them into the field. It is conceivable that the recruitment effect could swamp the persuasion effect.

Something of this sort appears to have happened in Germany. A recent collective volume assembling in German translation some of the major American articles of the communitarian debate carries an introduction by Axel Honneth that is rather critical of the communitarian position.[5] Another collective volume with comments by German authors on the American debate contains many more critical than favorable articles on the communitarians.[6] Finally, it is in the logic of the recruitment effect that a discussion which was stimulated by some new position should lead to ideas that represent an original alternative to that position. This indeed happened: one participant in the debate, Helmut Dubiel, of the Frankfurt Institut für Sozialforschung, put for-

4. Albert O. Hirschman, "A Dissenter's Confession: *The Strategy of Economic Development Revisited*" in Hirschman, *Rival Views of Market Society and Other Recent Essays* (1986, rpt. Cambridge, Mass.: Harvard University Press, 1992), p. 34.

5. Honneth, n. 3, pp. 7–17.

6. Zahlmann, n. 3; see in particular article by Wolfgang Fach.

ward a *new minimalist* position on the need for community spirit, which seems to me of considerable interest.

The Gauchet-Dubiel Thesis:
Conflict as the Builder of Community

Dubiel radically repudiates the possibility as well as desirability of building up any kind of consensus on the "good life" based on commonly accepted substantive ethical values or standards. But he accepts and affirms the need for a degree of social integration that goes beyond Verfassungspatriotismus, that is, the universal acceptance of the constitutional norms. This integration of modern society will come about quite simply, unbeknownst to its citizens, as a result of their experience of passing through and somehow managing or tending *(hegen)* a variety of *conflicts.*[7] Generally, to be sure, conflicts have been viewed as dangerous, corrosive, and potentially destructive of the social order and therefore precisely in need of being contained and resolved by some standby reserve supply of community spirit. But Dubiel argues that social conflicts themselves produce the valuable ties that hold modern democratic societies together and lend them the strength and cohesion they need.

Dubiel is fully aware that he proposes a paradox and readily acknowledges his indebtedness to contemporary French theorists of democracy and primarily to Marcel Gauchet, who put forward similar ideas in the late 1970s and early 1980s. In a remarkable article ostensibly written as a comment on Tocqueville, Gauchet undertook to show how conflict is an "essential factor of socialization" in democracies and how it is an "eminently efficient producer of integration and cohesion." He too is aware of the paradox he is thus putting forward, for he speaks of the process as the "democratic miracle."[8] The miracle happens in the

7. Helmut Dubiel, "Konsens oder Konflikt" (manuscript, 1991); "Das ethische Minimum," *Süddeutsche Zeitung,* March 27–28, 1993; and "Zivilreligion in der Massendemokratie," *Soziale Welt,* 41 (1990), 125–143.

8. Marcel Gauchet, "Tocqueville, l'Amérique et nous," *Libre,* 7 (1980), 116–17. This and related articles by Gauchet and other French authors were brought together in German translation in Ulrich Rödel, ed., *Autonome Gesellschaft und Libertäre Demokratie* (Frankfurt: Suhrkamp, 1990).

course of the democratic process, as individuals and social groups go through the motions of out-and-out confrontation and end up building in this odd manner a cohesive democratic order.

Social scientists such as Dubiel and Gauchet, who analyze the democratic process in this manner, are obviously quite proud of having come upon what is (and probably must remain) largely hidden from the participants. In reading these authors with a great deal of admiration, I can perhaps be forgiven if I in turn call attention to a matter *they* have apparently overlooked: their paradoxical and miraculous process has much in common with Adam Smith's invisible hand, where the individual pursuing "only his own gain" also achieves a positive overall outcome that is "no part of his intention."[9]

Gauchet wrote his article at a time when many French intellectuals, shaken by Solzhenitsyn's account of the Gulag, broke definitively with various neo-Marxist doctrines that had long been influential in postwar France. Gauchet's sophisticated argument became an important stage in the itinerary of a generation that was ready to appreciate anew the attractions of democracy. The class conflicts that Marxists had long considered as constituting the "contradictions" that would lead to the breakup or breakdown of capitalism were suddenly declared to constitute the true pillars of society!

Some ten years later, the same point provided a way out of the quite different ideological problems people faced in Germany after reunification: Verfassungspatriotismus was no longer considered adequate, and distaste for some synthetic "community spirit" as a prerequisite for national coherence continued. Dubiel thus welcomed the thought that such a spirit was already being adequately produced through the process of "tending" the various domestic conflicts that arise naturally in the course of events.

Social Thought about the Contribution of Conflict to Cohesion

The idea that conflict can play a constructive role in social relationships has a long history. An early and spectacular contribution comes from

9. Adam Smith, *Wealth of Nations* (New York: Modern Library, 1937), p. 423.

Heraclitus: "war is the father of everything."[10] It is continued by Machiavelli and his chapter in the *Discourses* entitled "How the Disunion between the Plebs and the Senate Made [the Roman] Republic Free and Powerful."[11] Yet the dangers posed and the damage caused by conflict and crisis have been most of the time so obvious and overwhelming that the major effort of social thinkers has gone into the search for order, peace, harmony, and equilibrium, that is, for the *absence* of feared, abhorred conflict. Thus at any given period the idea that conflict, or some degree of conflict, can play a constructive role in social relations strikes the persons who happen to think of it as a nonconformist, paradoxical, and wholly original insight. As a result, they typically *do not bother to look for forerunners* and the idea is *reinvented* with considerable regularity.

Gauchet and Dubiel confirm this proposition. They do not even mention the numerous kindred social scientists in *our* century who have written extensively about the positive function of conflict. The earliest and most famous among them is Georg Simmel, whose *Soziologie,* published in 1908, contains a long chapter on *Streit,* which is better translated by "conflict" than by the literal "quarrel."[12] Simmel's contribution was rapidly forgotten and to some extent buried by the overwhelmingly destructive impact of the conflicts through which the world passed during the period 1914–1945. But Simmel's ideas on conflict were reawakened by an English translation that appeared in the United States in 1955 and by Lewis Coser's *The Functions of Social Conflict* (1956), which was presented as an extended commentary on key paragraphs taken from Simmel. In his important *Class and Class*

10. Writing over two hundred years before Heraclitus, Hesiod made a distinction between two kinds of strife. One "fosters evil, war, and battle, being cruel"; the other is "far kinder to men . . . [it] stirs up even the shiftless to toil . . . and neighbor vies with neighbor as he hurries after wealth. This strife is wholesome for man" (*Works and Days*, 11–26). With this distinction, which he makes at the outset of his poem, Hesiod corrected his own previous statement in *Theogony* (225) where he characterizes *Eris* (strife) as purely destructive: "Toil . . . and Famine . . . Sorrows, Battles, Murders, Quarrels, Lying Words, Disputes, Lawlessness and Ruin." I owe this remarkable point in intellectual history to André Laks.

11. Chapter 4 of Book I.

12. As noted by Kurt H. Wolff, who translated Simmel's text into English. See Georg Simmel, *Conflict and the Web of Group-Affiliations,* trans. and with an introduction by K. H. Wolff (Glencoe, Ill: Free Press, 1955), p. 11.

Conflict in Industrial Society (1957), Ralf Dahrendorf largely endorsed Coser's propositions on the positive functions of conflict. At about the same time, the South African anthropologist Max Gluckman published *Custom and Conflict in Africa* (1955), in which he dwelt on the essential role played by conflict in ritual. My own books of that period, *The Strategy of Economic Development* (1958) and *Journeys Toward Progress* (1963), emphasized the positive role of imbalance in economic development and of crisis in the achievement of social and economic reform in Latin America. At about that time, Michel Crozier published his influential *The Bureaucratic Phenomenon* (1963), which also assigned to crisis a key role in the promotion of progressive change in organizations.

Even closer to the spirit of Dubiel are some political scientists who rejected, also in the 1960s, the notion that democracy can be successfully instituted in a country only if some preconditions, such as the existence of a consensus about democratic values, are properly fulfilled (or if some obstacles are lifted). This idea may be the counterpart in political theory of the concept of institutional and cultural prerequisites (or of obstacles) to economic development that was then fairly popular among students of that problem. Here the concepts of prerequisite or obstacle were sharply criticized by Alexander Gerschenkron and myself as an evasion of the needed praxis of economic development.[13] The political version of the prerequisite idea was in turn rejected by a political scientist in terms strikingly similar to those used by Dubiel when he doubts the need for some prior community spirit:

> It is often thought that for [politics] to function, there must be already in existence some shared idea of a "common good," some "consensus" or *consensus juris*. But this common good is itself the process of practical reconciliation of the interests of the various . . . aggregates, or groups which compose a state; it is not some external and intangible spiritual adhesive . . . These are misleading and pretentious explanations of how a community holds together . . . *Diverse groups hold together because they*

13. Alexander Gerschenkron, "Reflections on the Concept of 'Prerequisites' of Modern Industrialization," in *Economic Backwardness in Historical Perspective* (Cambridge, Mass.: Harvard University Press, 1962), pp. 31–51; Albert O. Hirschman, "Obstacles to Development: A Classification and a Quasi-Vanishing Act," in Hirschman, *A Bias for Hope: Essays on Development and Latin America* (New Haven: Yale University Press, 1971), pp. 312–327.

practice politics—not because they agree about "fundamentals," or some such concept too vague, too personal, or too divine ever to do the job of politics for it. The moral consensus of a free state is not something mysteriously prior to or above politics: it is the activity (the civilizing activity) of politics itself. (p. 24, my emphasis)

This passage comes from *In Defence of Politics* (1962) by the English political scientist Bernard Crick. It was approvingly cited and applied to the problems faced by countries searching for democratic development by Dankwart Rustow in an article that has remained a standard reference in the political science literature on developing countries.[14] Rustow strongly argued that democracy has generally come into existence not because people wanted this form of government or because they had achieved a wide consensus on "basic values," but because various groups had been at each other's throat for a long time and finally came to recognize their mutual inability to gain dominance and the need for some accommodation.

Conflict as Glue and as Solvent

The literature on the positive effects of conflict and crisis turns out to be quite rich. But I must criticize it, including my own contributions, in one respect. It tends to be so conscious of staging a perilous attack on orthodoxy that it often limits itself to accomplishing that daring feat and does not proceed to a careful examination of the conditions that permit the paradox of conflict and crisis to generate progress.

Clearly, Dubiel does not affirm that *any* kind of social conflict will produce the sort of useful residue that will make for integration. The very verb *hegen* (to tend) he uses in conjunction with conflict evokes the sort of controlled promotion of natural growth that is practiced in botanical gardens or nurseries and also implies that some types of conflict neither behave nor can be managed so properly.

Is it possible to distinguish between two varieties of social conflict, those that leave behind a positive residue of integration and those that tear society apart? An attempt to make such a distinction was made at

14. "Transitions to Democracy: Toward a Dynamic Model," *Comparative Politics*, 2 (April 1970), 337–364.

one point by Soviet analysts who, in the 1950s, could not help noticing that their own society and economy were undergoing considerable difficulties as industrial expansion was being pushed forward by successive five-year plans. With bottlenecks, excess capacities, and other problems appearing at various points, in spite of the smooth expansion path obviously intended by the planners, the Soviet analysts hit on a marvelous semantic invention meant to put their minds to rest. First, they followed the Marxist convention according to which any more or less conspicuous and recurring difficulties experienced in an economic regime are automatically categorized as "contradictions" of that regime. The Marxist scheme then suggested to them a basic distinction: the contradictions that are experienced in capitalist countries and that can only be resolved by revolution are bound to be far more serious than those occurring in countries where capitalism has already been overthrown and where revolution is therefore pointless and inconceivable. Given these certainties, the contradictions experienced by the capitalist countries were labeled, logically enough, "antagonistic," whereas those affecting the socialist world were declared to be of the far milder "nonantagonistic" variety.[15] It turned out, of course, that the societies said to be afflicted by antagonistic contradictions have weathered them fairly well and have outlived those regimes that were allegedly experiencing just nonantagonistic ones! (Here, one is reminded of a passage in Koestler's *Darkness at Noon* where the long-time prisoner in a Soviet jail, an old partisan of the Tsar, has a far better prospect of survival than the novel's hero, an Old Bolshevik, who had been recently arrested for "deviations from the party line.")

15. V. Kozlovskii, *Antagonisticheskie i neantagonisticheskie protivorechiia* (Antagonistic and Nonantagonistic Contradictions) (Moscow: Moskovskii Rabochii, 1954). These concepts probably go back to Stalin's *Economic Problems of Socialism in the USSR* (Moscow: Foreign Languages Publishing House, 1952), pp. 24–27, where Stalin speaks of "essential" and "nonessential distinctions" between town and country, between mental and physical labor, and so on, with only the nonessential ones still to be found in the Soviet Union. Later the distinction between "antagonistic" and "nonantagonistic" contradictions was given considerable prominence by Mao Tse-Tung in a 1957 speech. See "On the Correct Handling of Contradictions among the People," in *Selected Readings from the Works of Mao Tse-Tung* (Peking: Foreign Languages Press, 1967), pp. 350–387, in particular pp. 351 and 359. For some of the above references I am grateful to Björn Wittrock, Bo Gustafsson, and Luca Meldolesi.

The story lends itself to pouring heavy, if rather cheap, irony on the Communist ideologues, but a serious conclusion can be drawn from it: in order to decide whether the difficulties or conflicts a society faces are destructive and lethal, or whether we can manage and "tend" them, we seem to need the *wisdom of hindsight*—to want to make this determination firmly in advance would be to commit instead the *folly of foresight* (the folly of pretending to foresight).

Hence a problem arises with regard to Gauchet and Dubiel's attractive idea that conflicts will provide society with the "social capital" (to use Robert Putnam's term) it needs to be kept together.[16] What if, in addition to producing this capital or social glue, conflict also acts as a solvent which dissolves social ties or as dynamite which blows them apart? To view conflict in this apprehensive way is, after all, closer to the conventional wisdom, which should not be entirely discounted. The problem can also be formulated as follows: how does Gauchet-Dubiel's idea relate to Whitehead's penetrating observation that "the major advances in civilization are processes which all but wreck the societies in which they occur"?

Could Whitehead and Gauchet-Dubiel both be right? This interpretation becomes possible if we view Whitehead's somewhat delphic phrase in an optimistic light: his "all but" qualification could be taken to point to a view of the world in which narrow escapes from threatening disaster are always happening: conflicts *almost* wreck societies but never quite do so and therefore actually strengthen them because of the salutary experience of passing through crisis and struggle. In the end, crisis is likely to strengthen societies *the more* the greater the crisis. This is close to Hölderlin's beautiful lines: "Wo aber Gefahr ist, wächst / Das Rettende auch" (But where there is danger/Salvation also grows) and to Nietzsche's kindred, if more brutal, maxim, "Was mich nicht umbringt, macht mich stärker" (That which does not destroy me makes me stronger).

Unfortunately, this century has conclusively taught us that we cannot rely on narrow escapes any more than on miracles. Despite the beauty of Hölderlin's lines, there simply is no providential proportionality be-

16. Robert D. Putnam, *Making Democracy Work: Civic Traditions in Modern Italy* (Princeton: Princeton University Press, 1993), pp. 167–185.

tween the dangers caused by conflict and the chances of overcoming them. Hence there is no alternative to an independent evaluation of these dangers and chances, hopefully to be undertaken in a less doctrinaire spirit than the one that presided over the distinction between antagonistic and nonantagonistic contradictions.

Conflicts Typical of Pluralist Market Societies . . . and the Others

To make some progress with the evaluation of conflict, it is necessary to step down from the exalted level of generality of Hölderlin, Nietzsche, and Whitehead. The question whether conflicts act predominantly as glue or as solvent cannot be decided in general; it must be brought down to earth through a closer look at the interaction between a specific kind of society and its typical conflicts.

When Gauchet and Dubiel affirmed that conflicts enhance social cohesion, they did refer specifically to the democratic market societies of the West. But the systemic reasons for this happy outcome were rather left in the dark. In the following, I hope to make the argument more persuasive by drawing on the political economy of pluralist market society; in the end, I shall also point to situations where the effect of conflict on the social system is likely to be more complex and less auspicious.

In my book *The Passions and the Interests,* I wrote about the favorable political effects that eighteenth-century observers like Montesquieu and Sir James Steuart expected to arise from the expansion of market society: greater control of the passions in general and more predictability of the actions of the sovereign and restraints on *grands coups d'autorité* in particular, thanks to increased stability and *douceur* in the management of human affairs. After presenting these hopes and expectations, which had been largely forgotten, I was obliged to point out, on the basis of the evidence accumulated in the course of the two subsequent centuries, that those eighteenth-century visions were engaging, ingenious, and . . . wrong.

Can we do better today in visualizing the interaction between economics and politics? We can try. Perhaps we should pin our hopes not so much on the *douceur* invoked by Montesquieu but on a seemingly negative factor, the frequency and ubiquity of *conflict!*

Conflict is indeed a characteristic of pluralist market society that has come to the fore with remarkable persistence. It is the natural counterpart of technical progress and of the ensuing creation of new wealth, for which market society is rightly famous. Conflicts arise from newly emerging inequalities and sectoral or regional declines—the counterpart precisely of various dynamic developments elsewhere in the economy. In societies with freedom of speech and association, concerns about those matters tend to mobilize the people who are immediately affected as well as citizens who are sensitive to more or less widely shared feelings about social justice. These two groups make demands for corrective action and reform, demands that are based *both on self-interest and on genuine concern for the public good,* or, to use a distinction due to Jon Elster, on *both bargaining and arguing.*[17] The secret of the vitality of pluralist market society and of its ability to renew itself may lie in this conjunction and in the successive eruption of problems and crises. The society thus produces a *steady diet of conflicts* that need to be addressed and that the society learns to manage. Correspondingly, the basic reason for the deterioration and loss of vitality of the Communist-dominated societies may reside in the success these societies had in suppressing overt social conflict.

As long as the Communist systems were in approximate working order, it could never be suggested that the strength of market society may lie in its propensity and vulnerability to conflict: the Communists proclaimed that the conflicts were signs of the imminent or eventual collapse of capitalism, and the partisans of market society were too defensive about the system to dwell on a characteristic that is normally viewed as damaging.

Significantly, one type of conflict escaped from this defensive stance prevailing in the West: the famous "cross-cutting cleavages" that result from the many affiliations that citizens normally entertain not only to a social class but to race, gender, religion, and so forth.[18] During the

17. Available so far only in Italian: *Argomentare e negoziare* (Milan: Anabasi, 1993).

18. See, for example, Seymour Martin Lipset, *Political Man* (New York: Anchor, 1963), pp. 76–79 and passim.

cold war, a great deal was made by Western social science of multiple allegiances, for it was plausible that their presence would *reduce* the intensity of conflict that would be characteristic of a society where people are arrayed along a single axis, such as the capital-labor dimension privileged by the Marxists.

But cross-cutting cleavages are just one type of conflict resulting from the multiplicity and ubiquity of conflict prevailing in democratic market societies. By singling out and celebrating this variety, Western social scientists implicitly accepted the notion that conflict is normally destructive and kept themselves from fully appreciating the extent and characteristics of conflict in their societies.

For one thing, a pluralist market society spawning a never-ending series of social conflicts in fairly rapid succession differs from other types of socio-political arrangements in one important respect: it cannot pretend to establish any permanent order and harmony; all it can aspire to accomplish is to "muddle through" from one conflict to the next.[19] The muddling-through mode of problem solving is facilitated not only by the quantity and variety of conflicts likely to erupt in market society but also by their quality. Many conflicts of market society are over the distribution of the social product among different classes, sectors, or regions. Highly varied though they are, they tend to be divisible; they are conflicts over getting more or less, in contrast to conflicts of the either-or, nondivisible category that are characteristic of societies split along rival ethnic, linguistic, or religious lines.[20] Nondivisible conflicts have recently also become more prominent in the older democracies and particularly in the United States, as a result of the importance assumed by such issues as abortion and by problems arising out of multiculturalism.

The distinction between the two categories is not always clear-cut, as nondivisible issues have ordinarily some components that are negotiable. Conversely, conflicts that look as if they were over who gets more

19. See C. E. Lindblom's classic article, "The Science of Muddling Through," *Public Administration Review*, 19 (1959), 79–88.

20. An early discussion of this difference is in W. Arthur Lewis, *Politics in West Africa* (Toronto: Oxford University Press, 1965), chap. 3. The most important contributions to it are found in the writings of Arend Lijphart, Kenneth McRae, Val Lorwin, and David D. Laitin.

and who less often have a nondivisible component or source. In Latin America, for example, striking workers have often proclaimed that they are fighting not just for higher wages but primarily for *respeto* (respect), which they felt was being withheld from them by the upper class because of its distinct racial or ethnic background. In Europe some historians have similarly attributed the chasm between the upper and lower classes in the nineteenth century to residual ethnic hatreds between the Saxons and their Norman conquerors in England, between Gauls and Franks in France, or between Slavs and Teutons in much of Germany.[21] It is nevertheless useful to abstract from these complications for the moment and to contrast the two types of conflict—the more-or-less and the either-or—as if they existed in pure form.

As is well known, conflicts of the more-or-less type are intrinsically easier to settle than conflicts of the either-or variety: even when the parties are initially far apart, they can theoretically "split the difference" or "meet halfway" ("half a loaf is better than none"), whereas these kinds of compromise solutions are often less available when the sectors making up a society and coming into conflict are divided by matters of religion, language, race, or gender. In the light of this distinction, it is today difficult to understand how Marxism was so long so successful in presenting social conflict, impressively dressed up as *Klassenkampf* or class struggle, as the principal, ultimate, and most irreconcilable type of conflict of modern society, when it is in fact the conflict that lends itself most readily to the arts of compromise.

The distinction between more-or-less and either-or types of conflict reinforces the previous point about the prevalence of the muddling-through mode of conflict-solving in market societies. Take first the either-or type of conflict. Ways have, of course, been found to overcome it, either through the outright elimination of one contending group or through a toleration agreement to "live and let live." These

---

21. This is an important theme in a course Michel Foucault gave in 1976 at the Collège de France. Notes taken at this course have been published so far only in an Italian translation, *Difendere la Società: Dalla guerra delle razze al razzismo di stato*, ed. and trans. by Mauro Bertani and Alessandro Fontana (Florence: GEF, 1990). See also Rudy Leonelli, "Gli eruditi delle battaglie: Note su Foucault e Marx," *Altre Ragioni*, 2 (1993), 139–150, for comments on these Foucault lectures and specific references to the historical literature on which Foucault based his assertion. My sincere thanks to Giovanna Procacci for this information.

are very different solutions, but in both cases the impression tends to arise that the problem has been solved *once and for all.* Often, this turns out to be an illusion, of course, but the idea of the existence of, or of the possible return to, some just, good, or well-ordered society from which conflict has been banished remains intact. The contrast with the more-or-less conflict typical of market society is considerable: whatever compromise is reached in the distribution of the social product between various classes, sectors, and regions, it is here clear to all concerned that agreements are temporary, are tied to the particular circumstances in which they were made, and can be reopened at the next opportunity.

To summarize, the conflicts typical of pluralist market society have the following characteristics:

1. They occur with considerable frequency and take on a great variety of shapes.

2. They are predominantly of the divisible type and therefore lend themselves to compromise and to the art of bargaining.

3. As a result of these two features, the compromises reached never give rise to the idea or illusion that they represent definitive solutions.

A society that has substantial practice over a prolonged period in dealing with conflicts of this type is indeed likely to have the positive experience described by Gauchet and Dubiel. All the support that such a society needs is that which derives from its cumulative experience of muddling through its numerous conflicts: these conflicts are or become its supporting pillars. The period that corresponds most closely to this pattern is probably the "glorious" thirty-year period of all-round vigorous growth in Western market societies that followed the conclusion of the Second World War.

Unfortunately, there *are* other types of conflicts, and our problem today seems to be that this category is everywhere on the increase, from abortion to fights over ethnicity and fundamentalism. When Benjamin Constant was faced with the restless Napoleon, he cried out, full of nostalgia, "Que Dieu nous rende nos rois fainéants!" (May God give us back our do-nothing kings!). Similarly today, as we experience the surge or resurgence of conflicts around nondivisible issues, we almost feel like exclaiming, "May God give us back the class struggle!"

This reflection actually helps to push the discussion forward by calling attention to matters of timing and sequencing. The class struggle or the social question may have loomed so formidable in the nineteenth century in part because of the residual ethnic cleavages mentioned earlier, but even more because those conflicts were perceived as being similar to the wars of religion that were fresh in historical memory. This historically conditioned misdiagnosis probably contributed to the conviction that the conflict between capital and labor required radical solutions: either Socialism-Communism, which would eliminate one of the two sides to the conflict, or Corporatism-Fascism, which would make sure that the two sides are permanently yoked together. Only after World War II did it become generally accepted that the social conflicts typical of the industrialized countries were amenable to gradual mitigation and ever shifting compromise.

Just as this experience had been assimilated, very different types of conflict appear to be resurging. Having behind us a lengthy experience of dealing with negotiable conflicts we are now likely to experience an optical illusion contrary to the one that prevailed in the nineteenth century: we cannot quite bring ourselves to believe that the participants feel as strongly as they do about the issues involved. Extremely serious mistakes can once again be committed in consequence. Two examples that come to mind are the underestimate of the mutual hatreds that came to the fore in Yugoslavia after the breakup of that country, and the underestimate of economic and cultural distances between East and West Germany after forty years of separation.

But the long practice in bargaining and in searching for compromise solutions that is characteristic of the more recent experience with conflict management in the West should not have only negative consequences for our ability to "tend" the new conflicts. However formidable and irreconcilable they may look at first sight, they could, for example, have negotiable parts or aspects that will be easier to tease out when they are approached with a spirit that is well trained in the art of bargaining and experimentation.

Two final remarks. I said before that the discussion about the constructive or destructive effects of conflicts must be brought down to earth
by focusing on the different types of conflict that arise characteristically
in whatever specific society is being investigated. The concept of muddling through and the distinction between divisible and nondivisible
conflicts were meant to serve this purpose. But these notions are meant
only as a first approximation to "earth" and should not be seen as a
definitive or unique key or paradigm. After all, we should learn something from the sad fate of the earlier attempt at discriminating between
constructive and destructive conflicts, the one that relied on the distinction between antagonistic and nonantagonistic contradictions! I
suspect, for example, that the category of either-or or nondivisible conflicts is essentially a convenient label for a vast array of new and unfamiliar problems having quite different degrees of manageability. These
conflicts can only be properly mapped out as we experience them.

Second, I must briefly return to our main theme, the need for community spirit. I have agreed in part with Dubiel's new minimalism—
the community spirit that is normally needed in a democratic market
society tends to be spontaneously generated through the experience of
tending the conflicts that are typical of that society. But what about the
atypical conflicts and problems that seem to be on the increase today?
Does community spirit truly come into its own here? I have my doubts.
To invoke the need for community spirit in these situations is essentially
an admission that concrete ways of dealing with the respective problems
have not yet been discovered—community spirit is called upon as some
deus ex machina. What is actually required to make progress with the
novel problems a society encounters on its road is political entrepreneurship, imagination, patience here, impatience there, and other varieties of *virtù* and *fortuna*. I cannot see much point (and do see some
danger) in lumping all of this together by an appeal to Gemeinsinn.

Acknowledgments

I wish to thank a number of people and institutions for encouragement, useful advice, and support.

My greatest appreciation goes to Wolf Lepenies and to the Wissenschaftskolleg (Institute for Advanced Study) which he directs in Berlin. Shortly after the Berlin Wall fell in 1989, he invited me to spend the following year (1990–91) in the newly reunited city. I accepted; while I had spent my first eighteen years in Berlin, this was the first time I returned for a longer stay, at age seventy-five. The story of the recent collapse of the German Democratic Republic induced me to write a paper that eventually became the first chapter of this book. That chapter was completed only in 1992, when I visited at the Kolleg for two more months and was able to conduct interviews about the 1989 events in Leipzig and Dresden. During another Berlin stay, in 1994, I prepared this book for publication and wrote the Introduction.

The other essays were largely written at the Institute for Advanced Study in Princeton, which makes the life of an emeritus professor even more agreeable than it is before one reaches this stage. At the Institute, my colleague Joan Scott was particularly kind in insisting that I bring together the autobiographical fragments I had come to write for special occasions in recent years. Her encouragement made me watch out for additional opportunities to pursue this genre.

Rebecca Scott provided me with extensive and remarkably helpful comments on several essays, and Harry Frankfurt gave me some excellent advice on the title essay.

At Harvard University Press, Aida Donald was again most hospitable to the new book project while Elizabeth Suttell and Anita Safran prepared and copyedited the manuscript with admirable skill.

Rose Marie Malarkey word-processed most of these essays. Anyone who has ever received a handwritten note of mine knows that she deserves a special note of thanks.

Index